IARIA

ICN 2020

The Nineteenth International Conference on Networks

February 23 - 27, 2020

Lisbon, Portugal

ICN 2020 Editors

Eugen Borcoci, University "Politehnica" of Bucharest (UPB), Romania
Carlo Vitucci, Ericsson, Sweden

Printed from e-media with permission by:

Curran Associates, Inc.
57 Morehouse Lane
Red Hook, NY 12571

Some format issues inherent in the e-media version may also appear in this print version.

International Academy, Research, and Industry Association (IARIA)
412 Derby Way
Wilmington, DE 19810

Phone: (408) 893-6407
Fax: (408) 527-6351

petre@iaria.org

Additional copies of this publication are available from:

Curran Associates, Inc.
57 Morehouse Lane
Red Hook, NY 12571 USA
Phone: 845-758-0400
Fax: 845-758-2633
Email: curran@proceedings.com
Web: www.proceedings.com

Table of Contents

Design and Implementation of Password less Single Sign On Authentication Mechanism 81
Fatima Hussain, Rasheed Hussain, Damir Samatov, Andrey Bogatyrev, and Salah Sharieh

ICN 2020

Forward

The Nineteenth International Conference on Networks (ICN 2020), held between February 23-27, 2020 in Lisbon, Portugal, continued a series of events organized by and for academic, research and industrial partners.

We solicited both academic, research, and industrial contributions. We welcomed technical papers presenting research and practical results, position papers addressing the pros and cons of specific proposals, such as those being discussed in the standard fora or in industry consortia, survey papers addressing the key problems and solutions on any of the above topics short papers on work in progress, and panel proposals.

The conference had the following tracks:

- Communication
- Networking
- Advances in Software Defined Networking and Network Functions Virtualization
- Next generation networks (NGN) and network management
- Computation and networking
- Topics on Internet Censorship and Surveillance

We take here the opportunity to warmly thank all the members of the ICN 2020 technical program committee, as well as all the reviewers. The creation of such a high quality conference program would not have been possible without their involvement. We also kindly thank all the authors who dedicated much of their time and effort to contribute to ICN 2020. We truly believe that, thanks to all these efforts, the final conference program consisted of top quality contributions.

We also thank the members of the ICN 2020 organizing committee for their help in handling the logistics and for their work that made this professional meeting a success.

We hope that ICN 2020 was a successful international forum for the exchange of ideas and results between academia and industry and to promote further progress in the field of networks. We also hope that Lisbon, Portugal provided a pleasant environment during the conference and everyone saved some time to enjoy the historic charm of the city.

ICN 2020 Chairs

ICN Steering Committee

Pascal Lorenz, University of Haute Alsace, France
Yenumula B. Reddy, Grambling State University, USA
Eric Renault, Institut Mines-Télécom - Télécom SudParis, France
Sherali Zeadally, University of Kentucky, USA

ICN Industry/Research Advisory Committee

Marc Cheboldaeff, Deloitte Consulting GmbH, Germany
Megumi Shibuya, The University of Electro-Communications, Japan
Arslan Brömme, Vattenfall GmbH, Berlin, Germany
Cristian Anghel, Politehnica University of Bucharest, Romania / Pentalog, France

ICN 2020

Committee

ICN Steering Committee

Pascal Lorenz, University of Haute Alsace, France
Yenumula B. Reddy, Grambling State University, USA
Eric Renault, Institut Mines-Télécom - Télécom SudParis, France
Sherali Zeadally, University of Kentucky, USA

ICN Industry/Research Advisory Committee

Marc Cheboldaeff, Deloitte Consulting GmbH, Germany
Megumi Shibuya, The University of Electro-Communications, Japan
Arslan Brömme, Vattenfall GmbH, Berlin, Germany
Cristian Anghel, Politehnica University of Bucharest, Romania / Pentalog, France

ICN 2020 Technical Program Committee

Khelil Abdelmajid, Landshut University of Applied Sciences, Germany
Alireza Abdollahpouri, University of Kurdistan, Sanandaj, Iran
Abdelmuttlib Ibrahim Abdalla Ahmed, University of Malaya, Malaysia
Ahmedin Mohammed Ahmed, FDRE Ministry of Innovation and Technology (MInT), Ethiopia
Francisco Airton Silva, Federal University of Piauí, Brazil
Sami Marzook Alesawi, King Abdulaziz University | Faculty of Computing and Information Technology at Rabigh, Saudi Arabia
Madyan Alsenwi, Kyung Hee University - Global Campus, South Korea
Reem Alshahrani, Kent State University, USA
Cristian Anghel, Politehnica University of Bucharest, Romania / Pentalog, France
Imran Shafique Ansari, University of Glasgow, Scotland, UK
Suayb S. Arslan, MEF University, Turkey
Mohammed A. Aseeri, King Abdulaziz City of Science and Technology (KACST), Kingdom of Saudi Arabia
Michael Atighetchi, BBN Technologies, USA
Jocelyn Aubert, Luxembourg Institute of Science and Technology (LIST), Luxembourg
Marco Aurélio Spohn, Federal University of Fronteira Sul, Brazil
Alvaro Barradas, University of Algarve, Portugal
Luis Bernardo, NOVA University of Lisbon, Portugal
Robert Bestak, Czech Technical University in Prague, Czech Republic
Lucas Bondan, Research and Development Center in Information and Communication Technology (CTIC) of the Brazilian National Research and Educational Network (RNP), Brazil
Eugen Borcoci, University Politehnica of Bucharest, Romania
Fernando Boronat Seguí, Universitat Politecnica de Valencia-Campus de Gandia, Spain
Radoslav Bortel, Czech Technical University in Prague, Czech Republic
Christos Bouras, University of Patras, Greece
An Braeken, Vrije Universiteit Brussels, Belgium

Copyright Information

Proposal of a Quadrature SSB Modulation Scheme for Wireless Communication Systems

Hiroaki Waraya and Masahiro Muraguchi
Department of Electrical Engineering, Tokyo University of Science
6-3-1 Niijuku, Katsushika-ku, Tokyo, 125-0051, Japan
E-mail: 4319583@ed.tus.ac.jp, murag@ee.kagu.tus.ac.jp

***Abstract*—Recent wireless communication systems strongly require modulation scheme with higher spectral efficiency. In this paper, we propose a new modulation scheme, i.e., the Quadrature Single Side Band (Q-SSB) modulation scheme, which orthogonally multiplexes two SSB signals and it has twice spectral efficiency. Under Additive White Gaussian Noise (AWGN) channel environment, the Bit Error Rate (BER) performance of the Quadrature Phase-Shift Keying (QPSK) based Q-SSB signal, i.e., two independent Amplitude-Shift Keying SSB (ASK-SSB) signals, is superior by 3.5dB in Carrier-to-Noise Ratio (CNR) in comparison to the same data rate and the same occupied bandwidth of 16 Quadrature Amplitude Modulation (16QAM) signal. A key idea of our Q-SSB modulation scheme is to introduce a power-domain multiplexing type of Non-Orthogonal Multiple Access (NOMA) technique for removing the Hilbert transform terms from in-phase and quadrature components in the receiver side.**

Keywords-SSB; Hilbert; Quadrature; NOMA; Multiplexing.

I. INTRODUCTION

Recently, the demand of wireless communication system has been increasing with the spread of smartphones, digital terrestrial broadcastings, and wireless Local Area Network (LANs). Frequency resources are depleted in the Ultra High Frequency (UHF) and Super High Frequency (SHF) bands used by many wireless systems, so the high-priority issue for next wireless systems is a revolutionary modulation scheme with higher spectral efficiency. Here, to improve spectral efficiency, we propose the combination of the SSB scheme and the quadrature modulation scheme.

The Single Side Band (SSB) system sends data at half of the occupied bandwidth compared with the Double Side Band (DSB) system. The SSB signal can be made by combination of Hilbert transformation and quadrature multiplexing, which causes in-phase addition of one sideband and cancellation of the opposite sideband. The SSB system, however, is only effective scalar modulation, such as an Amplitude-Shit Keying (ASK) modulation.

On the other hand, the quadrature modulation, which is a typical DSB modulation, employs the two carrier waves of the same frequency which are out of phase with each other by 90°. The transmitted signal is created by quadrature multiplexing the two carrier waves. The SSB modulation has a single data rate and a single sideband and the quadrature modulation has a double data rate and double sidebands. As a result, the both have same spectral efficiency. Here, if we incorporate the SSB modulation with the quadrature modulation, twice spectral efficiency will be expected.

Unfortunately, since both modulations use the same signal processing of quadrature multiplexing, it is not independent each other. Thus, a lossless demodulation cannot be performed analytically. The in-phase component includes I-data and the Hilbert transform of Q-data, and the quadrature component includes Q-data and the Hilbert transform of I-data in the receiver side. Those Hilbert transform terms cannot be removed analytically if this goes on. In fact, several recent researchers have investigated the SSB modulation. For example, the research in [1]-[3] successfully transmitted SSB signal using the turbo equalization technology in the receiver side. We present our proposed system that can solve the problem about Hilbert transform terms in the transmission side.

A key idea of our Q-SSB modulation scheme is to introduce a power-domain multiplexing type of Non-Orthogonal Multiple Access (NOMA) technique for removing the Hilbert transform terms from in-phase and quadrature components in the receiver side [4]. Thus, on the receiver side, IQ-data can be demodulated by estimating the amplitude of data [5].

In this paper, we confirmed Bit Error Rate (BER) performances in both of the Q-SSB NOMA signal, and the multiplexed Q-SSB NOMA signals. We also confirmed that under Additive White Gaussian Noise (AWGN) channel environment the BER performance of the Quadrature Phase-Shift Keying (QPSK) based Q-SSB NOMA signal is superior by 3.5dB in Carrier-to-Noise Ratio (CNR) in comparison to the same data rate and the same occupied bandwidth of 16QAM signal.

The remainder of this paper is organized into sections as follows: Section 2 explains a method of DSB modulation, and Section 3 explains how SSB modulation is performed. Section 4 presents our proposed system that uses Q-SSB NOMA modulation, and explains how to multiplex two data in the proposed system. Section 5 presents the performance evaluation and simulation results of the proposed scheme. Finally, we conclude the paper in Section 6.

II. DSB MODULATION

Amplitude Modulation (AM) is a technique that multiplies carrier wave into the information signal, and change the amplitude of the transmission signal in proportion to the size of the information signal. A transmission signal S(t) in a general AM method can be represented as

$$S(t) = A[1 + k \cdot m(t)] \cdot cos(2\pi f_c t + \varphi), \quad (1)$$

where A is the signal amplitude, k is the modulation index $(0 \leq k \leq 1)$, f_c is the carrier frequency, and φ is the phase of the carrier. A general envelope waveform of AM method has m(t) waveform centered around $\pm A$ amplitude.

Next, consider the transmission spectrum of AM method. Note that multiplication on the time axis is the convolution on the frequency axis, and the Fourier transform of (1) is represented as

$$\begin{aligned} S(f) &= [\delta(f) + M(f)] \otimes \frac{1}{2}[\delta(f - f_c) + \delta(f + f_c)] \\ &= \frac{1}{2}[\delta(f - f_c) + M(f - f_c)] \\ &\quad + \frac{1}{2}[\delta(f + f_c) + M(f + f_c)]. \end{aligned} \quad (2)$$

Here, to simplify (2), $A = 1, k = 1$, and $\varphi = 0$. Thus, by multiplying the carrier wave, the baseband signal is shifted to the carrier wave band. A spectrum diagram showing this state is shown in Figure 1.

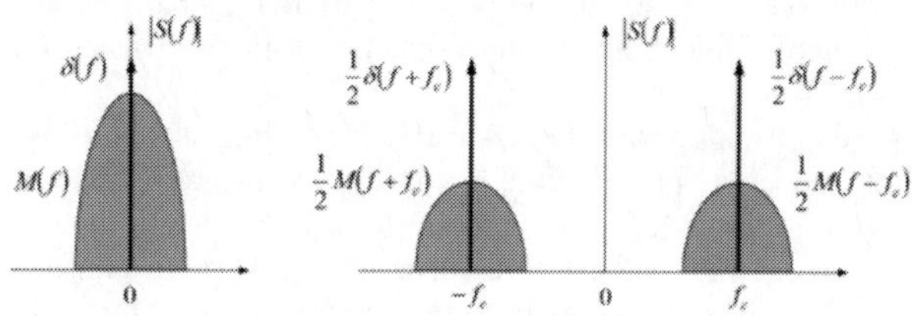

Figure 1. Spectrum diagram of AM method

As an example, consider the case of $m(t) = cos\, 2\pi f_m t$. If $\varphi = 0$ is set, (1) is rewritten as

$$\begin{aligned} S(t) &= A(1 + 2\pi f_m t) \cdot cos\, 2\pi f_c t \\ &= A\, cos\, 2\pi f_c t + \frac{A}{2} cos\, 2\pi(f_c - f_m)t \\ &\quad + \frac{A}{2} cos\, 2\pi(f_c + f_m)t. \end{aligned} \quad (3)$$

In (3), the first term represents a carrier wave component. The second and third terms are components of the information signal m(t).

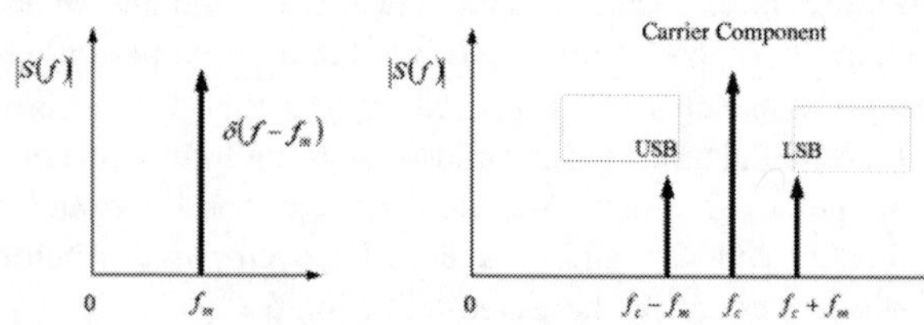

Figure 2. Spectrum of DSB modulation

The lower frequency component than the carrier wave in the second term is called Lower Side Band (LSB), and the higher frequency component than the carrier wave in the third term is called Upper Side Band (USB). As shown from Figure 2, a spectrum is generated at a location separated by $\pm f_m$ from the carrier frequency f_c. In this way, a method of moving an information signal to a carrier band and performing communication using LSB and USB is called Double Side Band (DSB) modulation method.

III. SSB MODULATION

We present how SSB modulation is performed, by explaining about the characteristic of SSB modulation and Hilbert transformation.

A. The characteristic of SSB modulation

In the previous section, we described that the DSB system performs communication using both the left and right sidebands centered on the carrier frequency. However, as can be seen from (3), since the LSB and USB contain the same information, all information transmission is possible by using only one of the LSB and USB. In this way, a method for performing communication using only one sideband is called Single Side Band (SSB) modulation method.

Figure 3 shows the SSB transmission spectrum by LSB. Here, the negative frequency region is also shown as an arithmetic expression, but only the positive frequency region appears as a real signal. Compared to the DSB method the greatest feature of the SSB method is that the frequency occupation band is halved [6].

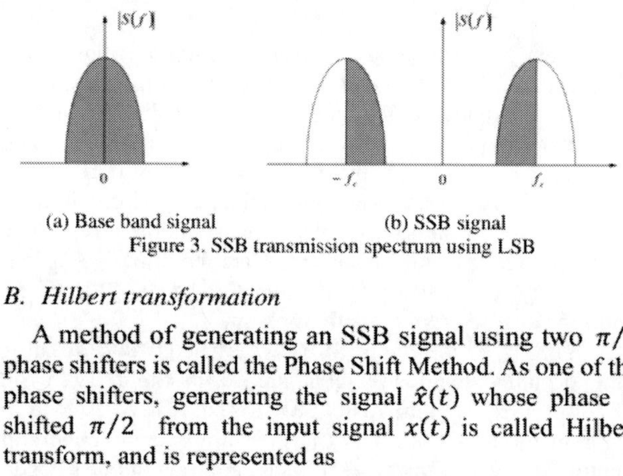

(a) Base band signal (b) SSB signal

Figure 3. SSB transmission spectrum using LSB

B. Hilbert transformation

A method of generating an SSB signal using two $\pi/2$ phase shifters is called the Phase Shift Method. As one of the phase shifters, generating the signal $\hat{x}(t)$ whose phase is shifted $\pi/2$ from the input signal $x(t)$ is called Hilbert transform, and is represented as

$$\hat{x}(t) = H[x(t)] = \frac{1}{\pi}\int_{-\infty}^{\infty} \frac{x(\tau)}{t - \tau} d\tau. \quad (4)$$

Here, the frequency characteristic of Hilbert transformation $H(\omega)$ is represented as

$$\hbar(t) \Leftrightarrow H(\omega) = \begin{cases} -j = exp(-j\pi/2)\,(\omega > 0) \\ +j = exp(+j\pi/2)\,(\omega < 0). \end{cases} \quad (5)$$

The Hilbert transformation delays $\pi/2$ at positive frequencies, and advances $\pi/2$ at negative frequencies. Also, the amplitude characteristic is constant regardless of the frequency. Figure 4 shows the conversion characteristics [7].

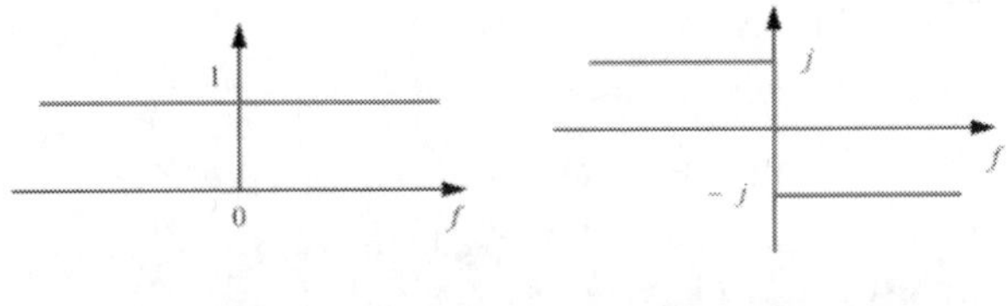

(a) Amplitude characteristic (b) Phase characteristic
Figure 4. Hilbert transformation characteristics

The following explains about the repeatability of Hilbert transformation. First, (6) is obtained by expressing (5) of the Hilbert transformation in the form of Fourier transform and combining them into one equation. That is represented as

$$\hat{X}(\omega) = -j\, sgn(\omega) \cdot X(\omega), \tag{6}$$

where the $sgn(\omega)$ is a sign function. The value of this function is 1 at positive frequency and is -1 at negative frequency. Therefore, when the Hilbert transform is performed again on the signal that has been conducted Hilbert transformation, the equation is represented as

$$\begin{aligned}\hat{\hat{X}}(\omega) &= \{-j\, sgn(\omega)\} \times \{-j\, sgn(\omega) \cdot X(\omega)\} \\ &= -X(\omega),\end{aligned} \tag{7}$$

and the signal inverting the original signal is output. Thus, the Hilbert transformation has repeatability. Moreover, it is a linear transform, and the equation is represented as

$$\begin{aligned}H[m(t) \pm n(t)] &= H[m(t)] \pm H[n(t)] \\ &= \hat{m}(t) \pm \hat{n}(t).\end{aligned} \tag{8}$$

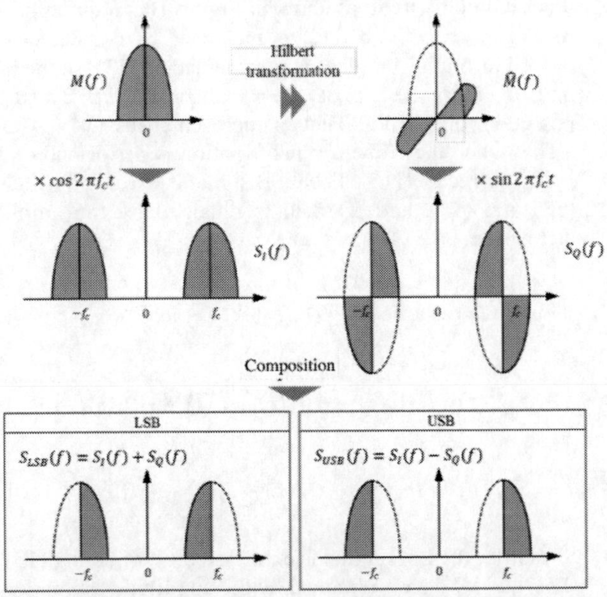

Figure 5. Generation method of SSB modulation signal

Figure 5 shows the spectrum transition in the SSB signal generation circuit. In Figure 5, $S_{USB}(t)$ *and* $S_{LSB}(t)$ of transmitted signal at this time is represented as

$$S(t) = m(t) \cdot cos\, 2\pi f_c t \pm \hat{m}(t) \cdot sin\, 2\pi f_c t, \tag{9}$$

where $m(t)$ is the modulation signal and $\hat{m}(t)$ is the Hilbert transformation of $m(t)$. In (9), when the second term is added, SSB modulation by LSB is performed. And when the second term is subtracted, SSB modulation by USB is performed. As shown from (9), the modulation signal can be restored by multiplying $cos\, 2\pi f_c t$ on the receiver side, and can demodulate SSB modulation signal [8].

IV. Proposed Method

In this section, we present our proposed system that uses Q-SSB NOMA modulation, and explain how to multiplex two data in the proposed system.

A. *The method of Q-SSB NOMA modulation*

The conventional Q-SSB modulation scheme considered the transmission method in which the phases of I-data and Q-data differ by 90° as shown in Figure 6. The transmission signal of the conventional method is expressed as

$$\begin{aligned}S_u(t) = \{I_u(t) + \widehat{Q_u}(t)\}\, cos\, 2\pi f_c t \\ + \{-\widehat{I_u}(t) + Q_u(t)\}\, sin\, 2\pi f_c t.\end{aligned} \tag{10}$$

From (10), it is possible to extract I-data by multiplying $cos\, 2\pi f_c t$, and to extract Q-data by multiplying $sin\, 2\pi f_c t$. However, the BER performance is extremely deteriorated because the extra Hilbert component cannot be removed analytically.

Therefore, as shown in Figure 6, we introduce the method like NOMA that adds two data with different amplitudes on the same frequency. Here, our proposed system is different from the real NOMA method. We use the term of NOMA to help understand that two data have different amplitudes on the same frequency. The demodulation method on the receiving side uses the original method using amplitude estimation. The transmission signal of our proposed method in the case of USB is expressed as

$$\begin{aligned}S_u(t) = \left\{I_u(t) + \frac{1}{2} Q_u(t)\right\} cos\, 2\pi f_c t \\ + \left\{-\widehat{I_u}(t) - \frac{1}{2}\widehat{Q_u}(t)\right\} sin\, 2\pi f_c t.\end{aligned} \tag{10}$$

I-data and Q-data can be extracted by multiplying $cos\, 2\pi f_c t$. In the case of LSB, the transmission signal is expressed as

$$\begin{aligned}S_l(t) = \left\{I_l(t) + \frac{1}{2} Q_l(t)\right\} cos\, 2\pi f_c t \\ - \left\{-\widehat{I_l}(t) - \frac{1}{2}\widehat{Q_l}(t)\right\} sin\, 2\pi f_c t.\end{aligned} \tag{11}$$

Figure 7 shows Q-SSB modulation circuit. Here, the modulation signal on the I-data is $I(t)$, and the modulation signal on the Q-data is $Q(t)$. USB is adopted as the sideband. As shown from Figure 7, Q-data is halved after QPSK mapping, and $S(t)$ is configured as (10).

Figure 8 shows the amplitude combinations of IQ data on the receiver side.

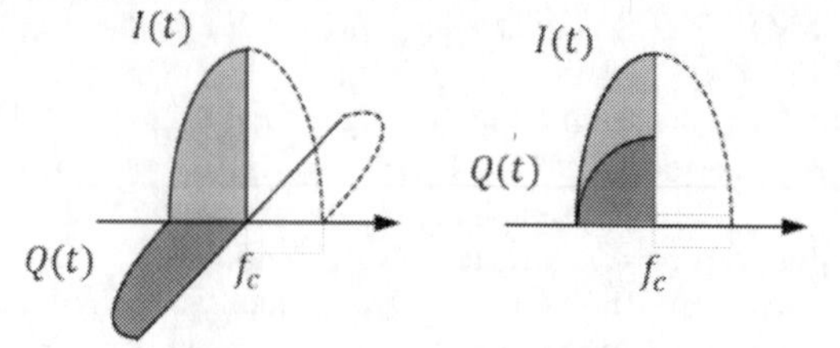

(a) Conventional method (b) Proposed method

Figure 6. Comparison between conventional method and proposed method

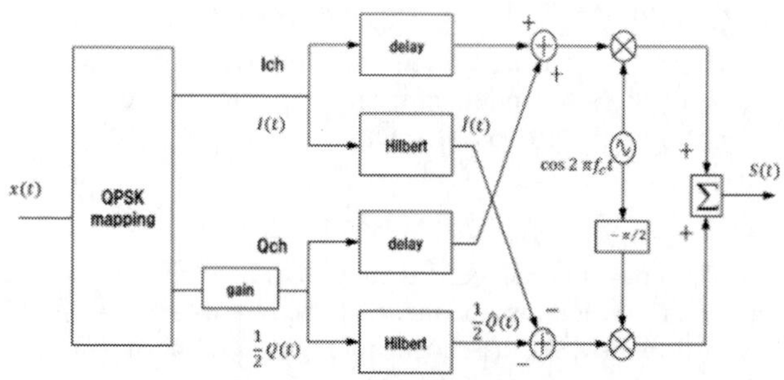

Figure 7. Q-SSB modulation circuit

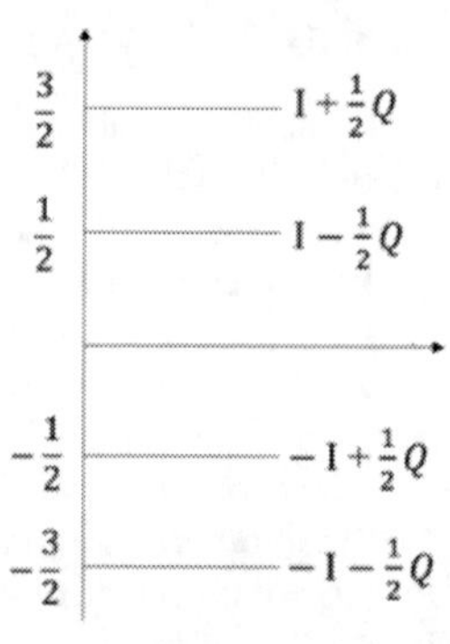

Figure 8. Amplitude of quadrature SSB received signal

As mentioned in the introduction, our system estimates the amplitude of $\left\{I_u(t)+\frac{1}{2}Q_u(t)\right\}$ on the receiver side. Since our system introduces QPSK modulation, the value of I-data and Q-data is 1 or -1. So, the amplitude of $\left\{I_u(t)+\frac{1}{2}Q_u(t)\right\}$ is represented as in Figure 8. The quadrature signals can be demodulated by the distinction of each amplitude in Figure 8.

B. The method of multiplexing Q-SSB NOMA modulation

In the previous section, we described the modulation method of SSB signal. However, it is a method to suppress the sideband on the opposite side, putting information on LSB or USB with one carrier wave.

In this paper, we put different information on LSB and USB at the same carrier frequency and perform data transmission by multiplexing method. From (10) and (11), the signal obtained by adding different information on USB and LSB is represented as

$$S(t)=\left\{I_u(t)+\frac{1}{2}Q_u(t)+I_l(t)+\frac{1}{2}Q_l(t)\right\}cos\,2\pi f_c t \\ +\left\{-\widehat{I_u}(t)-\frac{1}{2}\widehat{Q_u}(t)+\widehat{I_l}(t)+\frac{1}{2}\widehat{Q_l}(t)\right\}sin\,2\pi f_c t. \qquad (12)$$

Then, the spectrum of the multiplexed SSB signal can be represented as Figure 9.

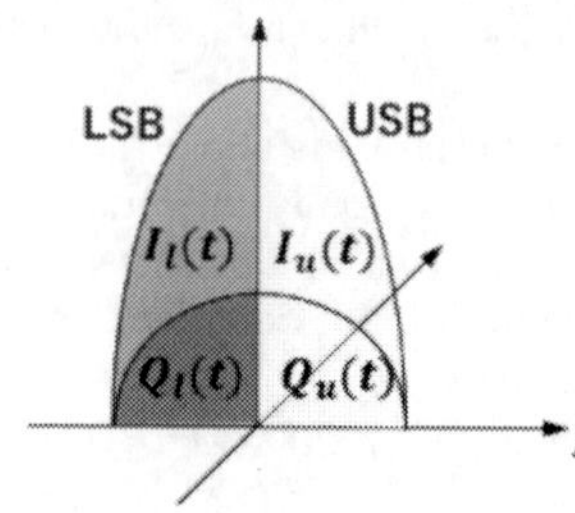

Figure 9. Spectrum of multiplexed SSB signal

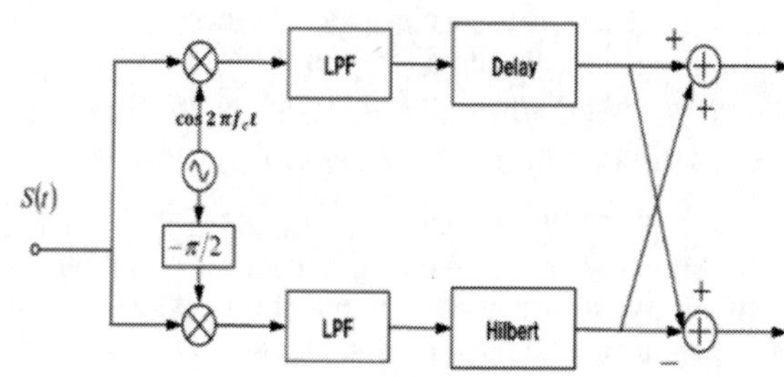

Figure 10. Demodulation circuit of multiplexed SSB signal

On the receiver side, our proposed system uses the demodulation circuit as show in Figure 10. In the upper part of Figure 10, $S(t)$ of (12) is multiplied by $cos\,2\pi f_c t$, and passed through LPF. That is represented as (13). In the lower part of Figure 10, $S(t)$ of (12) is multiplied by $sin\,2\pi f_c t$, and passed through LPF. That is represented as (14). And the signal when the Hilbert transformation is performed on (14) is represented as (15). The USB signal is extracted by adding (13) and (15), and IQ data is obtained by the amplitude estimation.

$$S_{cos}(t)=I_u(t)+\frac{1}{2}Q_u(t)+I_l(t)+\frac{1}{2}Q_l(t) \qquad (13)$$

$$S_{sin}(t)=-\widehat{I_u}(t)-\frac{1}{2}\widehat{Q_u}(t)+\widehat{I_l}(t)+\frac{1}{2}\widehat{Q_l}(t) \qquad (14)$$

$$\hat{S}_{sin}(t)=I_u(t)+\frac{1}{2}Q_u(t)-I_l(t)-\frac{1}{2}Q_l(t) \qquad (15)$$

Similarly, the LSB signal is extracted by subtracting (13) and (15), and IQ data is obtained by the amplitude estimation.

V. Performance Evaluation by Simulation

In this paper, we confirmed BER performances in both of the Q-SSB NOMA signal which have data on only USB, and the Multiplexing Q-SSB NOMA signals. And we confirmed that the BER performance of the QPSK based Q-SSB NOMA signal is superior by 3dB in CNR in comparison to the same data rate and the same occupied bandwidth of 16QAM signal.

A. Simulation specification

Table 1 shows the simulation tables used in this study. Our proposed system performs on the simulation by using MATLAB/Simulink. Figure 11 shows the block diagram of the Q-SSB NOMA system. Figure 12 shows the block diagram of the Multiplexing Q-SSB NOMA system. We have evaluated the utility of Q-SSB NOMA signal by measuring its BER performance and spectrum. We also confirmed the advantage of proposal compared to the conventional Q-SSB modulation method in Figure 6.

TABLE I. SIMULATION SPECIFICATION.

Primary Modulation	QPSK
Secondary Modulation	SSB
Data Rate	2 Mbps
Carrier Frequency	16 MHz
Data Size	Single Carrier
Transmitted Sample Rate	128Mbps
Received Sample Rate	512Mbps

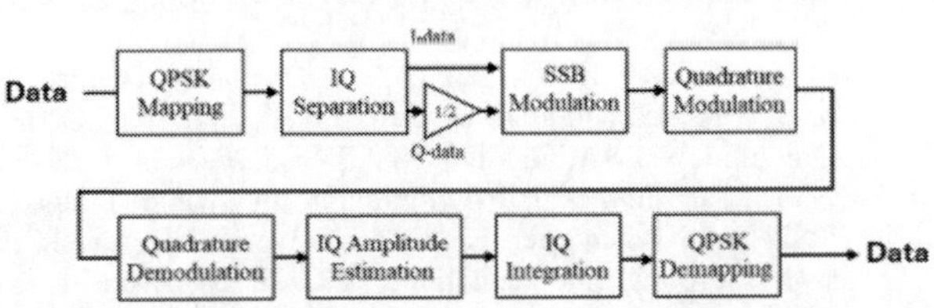

Figure 11. Block diagram of Q-SSB NOMA system

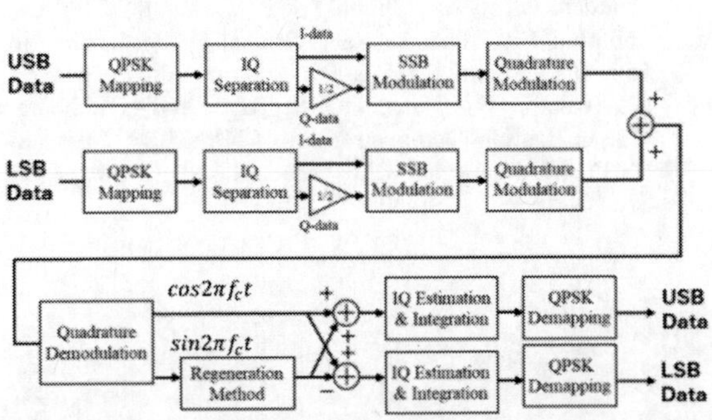

Figure 12. Block diagram of Multiplexing Q-SSB NOMA system

B. Simulation result (Q-SSB NOMA signal)

Figure 13 shows the spectrum of Q-SSB NOMA signal. Figure 14 shows the BER performance of the conventional Q-SSB modulation method (a) and our proposed Q-SSB modulation method (b) shown in Figure 6. Figure 15 compares the BER performance of DSB QPSK transmission or DSB 16QAM transmission with the BER performance of Q-SSB QPSK transmission.

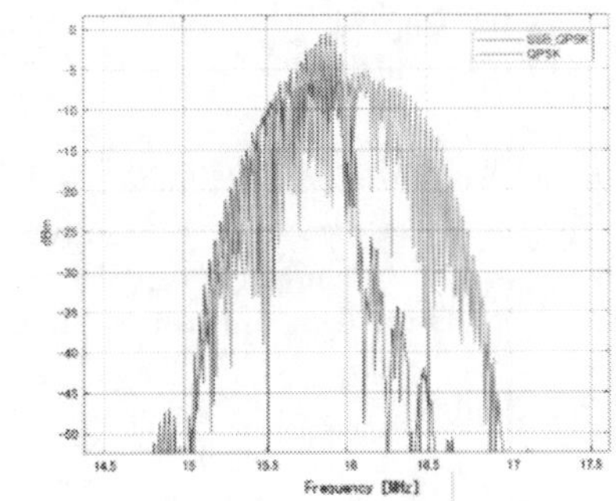

Figure 13. Spectrum of Q-SSB NOMA system

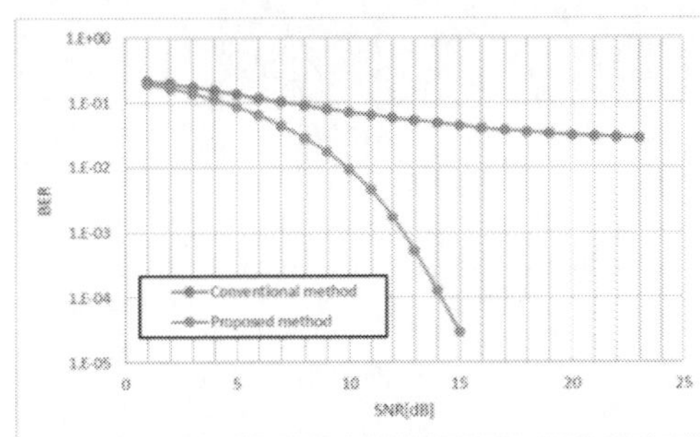

Figure 14. BER performance of conventional method and proposed method

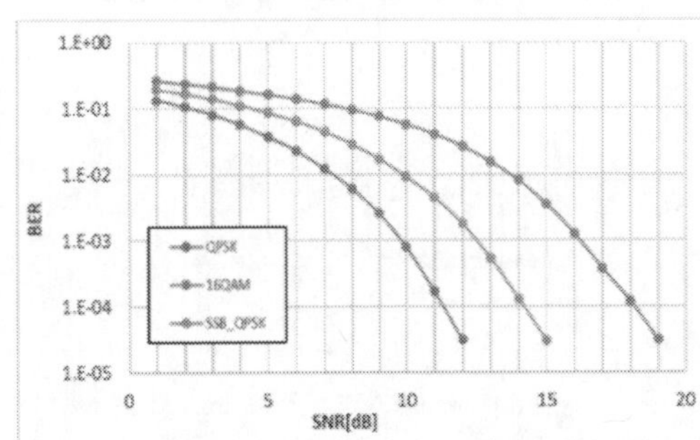

Figure 15. BER performance of Q-SSB NOMA system

As can be seen from Q-SSB NOMA modulation spectrum, compared to QPSK modulation spectrum, the part of the opposite sideband is suppressed by about 30dB by the Hilbert transformation process. And it expresses that Q-SSB NOMA signal can be transmitted using only one sideband.

As shown in Figure 14, it can be confirmed that our proposed method has the BER performance of 7.5dB better than the conventional method. This is because the conventional method uses a complicated demodulation method to remove an extra Hilbert component, whereas the proposed method can demodulate only by amplitude estimation without considering the Hilbert component.

As can be seen from 15, the SSB method that can send 4-bit data using two transmissions simultaneously has the BER performance of 3.5dB better than the DSB method that sends 4-bit data using 16QAM. The reason why the BER performance of Q-SSB QPSK transmission is 2.5dB worse than DSB QPSK transmission is considered to be the penalty when IQ data transmitted by NOMA is separated by the amplitude estimation method.

C. Simulation result (Multiplexing Q-SSB NOMA signal)

Figure 16 shows the spectrum of Multiplexing Q-SSB NOMA signal. Figure 17 compares the BER performance of the Q-SSB signal with data only on USB and the BER performance when each of USB and LSB signals are extracted from Multiplexing Q-SSB signal.

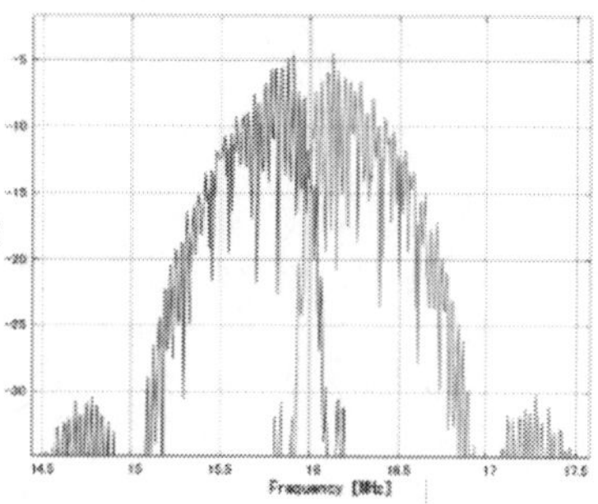

Figure 16. Spectrum of Multiplexing Q-SSB NOMA system

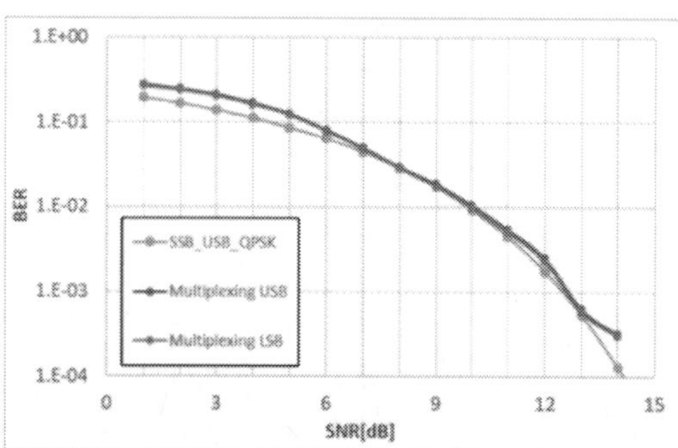

Figure 17. BER performance of Multiplexing Q-SSB NOMA system

As can be seen from Figure 16, each sideband part suppresses the opposite sideband by the Hilbert transformation process, so that two QPSK transmissions can be performed simultaneously using different data on USB and LSB.

In Figure 17, the BER performance of the Multiplexing Q-SSB signal may be slightly more deteriorated than Q-SSB signal with data on only one sideband. But that is due to the regenerating method to adjust Hilbert components, and their BER performances are almost not change. DSB 16QAM transmission and Q-SSB NOMA QPSK transmission sends 4 bits per symbol. Therefore, it was confirmed that the Multiplexing Q-SSB NOMA signal is superior to 16QAM transmission in terms of BER performance.

VI. Conclusion

We have proposed the Q-SSB NOMA modulation scheme to generate the quadrature SSB modulation signal with half of frequency band. It has been confirmed that under AWGN channel environment the BER performance of the QPSK based Q-SSB NOMA signal is superior by 3.5dB in CNR in comparison to the same data rate and the same occupied bandwidth of 16QAM signal. We are going to improve better the BER performance of the QPSK based Q-SSB NOMA signal. Additionally, we proposed improving the frequency efficiency of single carrier transmission. Therefore, we are going to improve the frequency efficiency of multicarrier transmission by combining the OFDM method and the Q-SSB modulation method.

References

[1] M. Mustafa, "Four Single-Sideband M-QAM Modulation using Soft Input Soft Output Equalizer over OFDM," 28th ITNAC, 2018.

[2] Y. Jiang, Z. Zhou, M. Nanri, G. Ohta, T. Sato, "Performance Evaluation of Four Orthogonal Single Sideband Elements Modulation Scheme in Multi-Carrier Transmission Systems," 2011 IEEE Vehicular Technology Conference, 2011.

[3] B. Pitakdumrongkija, H. Suzuki, S. Suyama, and K. Fukawa, "Coded Single-Sideband QPSK and Its Turbo Detection for Mobile Communication Systems," IEEE Transactions on Vehicular Technology, VOL. 57, NO.1, pp.311-323, January 2008.

[4] S. A. Mujtaba, "A Novel Scheme for Transmitting QPSK as a Single-Sideband Signal," IEEE GLOBECOM 1998, pp.592-597,1998.

[5] K. Senda and H. Otsuka, "Transmission Performance of Superposed Modulation Using QPSK and 1024-QAM in Downlink NOMA," IEEE VTS APWCS 2019.

[6] J. G. R. C. Gomes and A. Petraglia, "A switched-capacitor DSB to SSB converter using a recursive Hilbert transformer with sampling rate reduction," ISCAS 2000, pp.315-318, 2000.

[7] X. Wang and M. Hanawa, "Sideband Suppression Characteristics of Optical SSB Generation Filter with Sampled FBG Based 4-taps Optical Hilbert Transformer," 15th APCC, pp.622-625, 2009.

[8] K. Takao, N. Hanzawa, S. Tanji, and K. Nakagawa, "Experimental Demonstration of Optically Phase-Shifted SSB Modulation with Fiber-Based Optical Hilbert Transformers," OFC/NEOEC, 2007.

A Vehicle Position Estimation Method Combining Roadside Vehicle Detector and In-Vehicle Sensors

Shunya Yamada
Graduate School of Informatics
Nagoya University
Nagoya, Japan 464–8601
Email: s_yamada@ertl.jp

Yousuke Watanabe
Institutes of Innovation for Future Society
Nagoya University
Nagoya, Japan 464–8601
Email: watanabe@coi.nagoya-u.ac.jp

Hiroaki Takada
Institutes of Innovation for Future Society
and graduate School of Informatics
Nagoya University
Nagoya, Japan 464–8601
Email: hiro@ertl.jp

***Abstract*—To improve highway traffic safety and traffic flow, it is important to properly manage merging at junctions. Accurate vehicle positions and velocities are necessary to achieve this, but existing sensors have both advantages and disadvantages. Roadside vehicle detectors are very accurate, but only available at fixed points. By contrast, in-vehicle Global Navigation Satellite System (GNSS) sensors can be used anywhere except in tunnels, but are less accurate. However these sensors can compensate for each other's weak points. In this paper, we proposed a vehicle position estimation method that combines roadside vehicle detector and in-vehicle sensors. This gathers data from roadside vehicle detector and in-vehicle sensors via different wireless networks, applies Kalman filters to calculate accurate position and velocity. When exchanging information over wireless networks, communication delays occur and data arrival sequence is not guaranteed. Our method can retroactively calculate vehicle position in the presence of delays below a maximum acceptable threshold. The results of simulation experiments show that our method can estimate vehicle positions more accurately than using data from either sensor alone.**

Keywords–Sensor fusion, Position estimation, Communication delays, DSRC, Intelligent transportation system.

I. Introduction

At highway junctions, vehicles merging into the main lane are increasingly causing the traffic congestion in that lane [1], and the 20-30% of highway truck accidents occur at or near junctions [2]. Thus, appropriately managing traffic and controlling merging at junctions is important for improving both highway safety and traffic flow.

Several previous studies have investigated proper traffic management and merging control at junctions. Cui et al. [3] proposed a system for detecting collisions by estimating the vehicle arrival time at junctions. Their system obtain the vehicle positions and velocities from a monocular camera installed at the junction and uses these to estimate the arrival times. Milanes et al. [4], local control system installed near the junction receives position and velocity information from approaching vehicles and send them a low-risk merging strategies. Chou et al. [5] proposed a merging method based on Vehicle-to-Vehicle (V2V) communication. Vehicles approaching the junction use this to exchange their positions and velocities, then the vehicles in the main lane create gaps for entering vehicles before they have even reached the merging point. Hirai et al. [6] proposed such a system that used roadside vehicle detection sensors, installed before merging points. Roadside vehicle detection sensors are often used to get presence of vehicles and vehicles' velocities on the lane in order to estimate traffic flows (see Figure 1). In Hirai's approach, these are used to acquire vehicles' velocities and estimate their arrival times at the merging points. When a vehicle on the on–ramp will arrive at almost the same time as a vehicle in the main lane, the system alerts the vehicle in main lane, enabling to prepare for merging even if its driver has not seen the vehicle on the on–ramp. Giving drivers longer to prepare makes the process safe. Japan's government started the field tests of autonomous driving in Tokyo waterfront area [7] and roadside vehicle detection sensors' information can be available in the filed tests. Proper traffic management and merging control at junctions are considered by participating companies in the filed tests.

Figure 1. Roadside vehicle detection sensor.

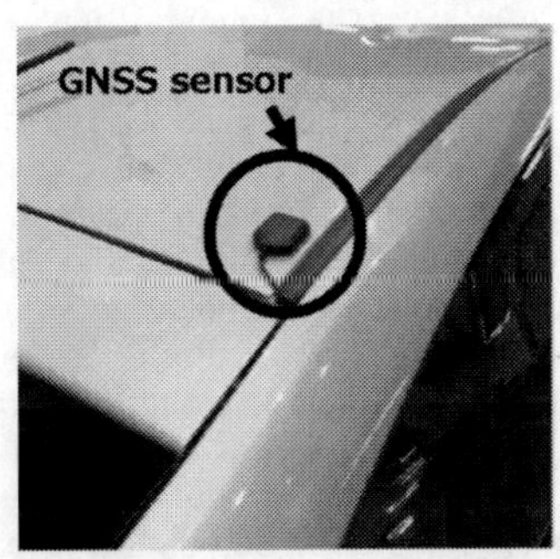

Figure 2. General-purpose GNSS sensor.

All of these merging methods depend on vehicle position and velocity information to properly manage traffic and control

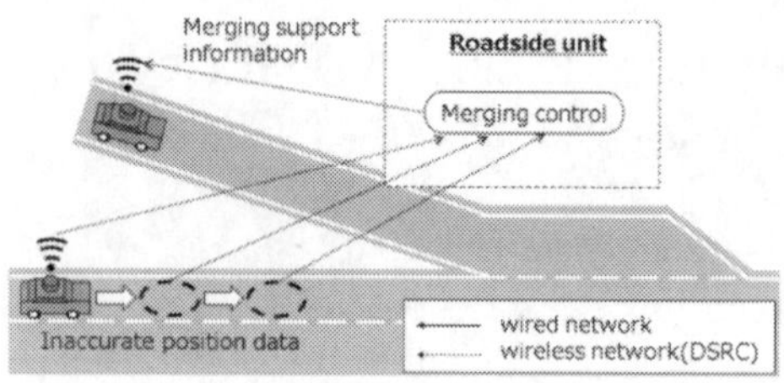

Figure 3. Existing approach1: Using GNSS sensors.

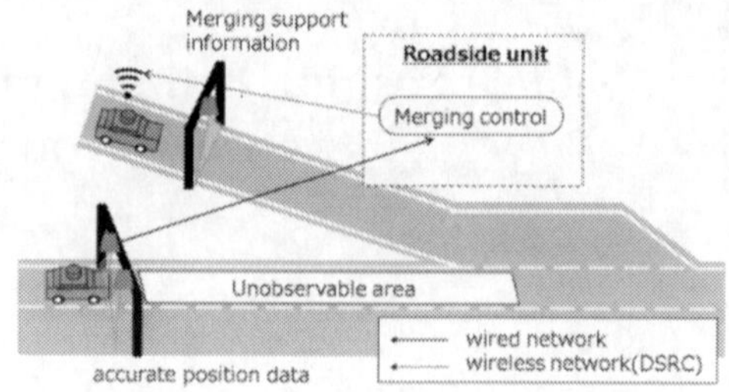

Figure 4. Existing approach2: Using roadside vehicle detection sensors.

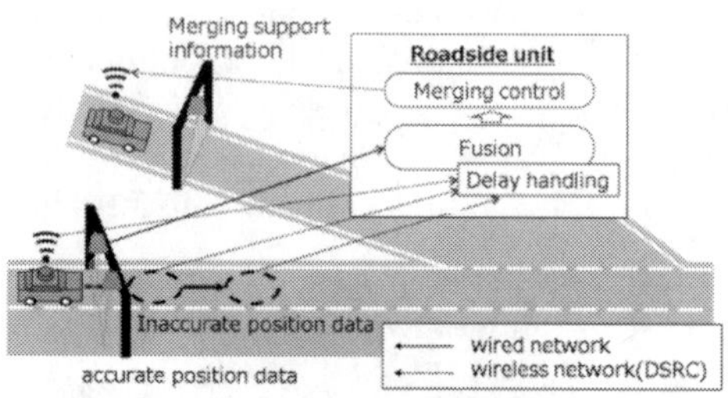

Figure 5. Proposed approach: Combining both sensors.

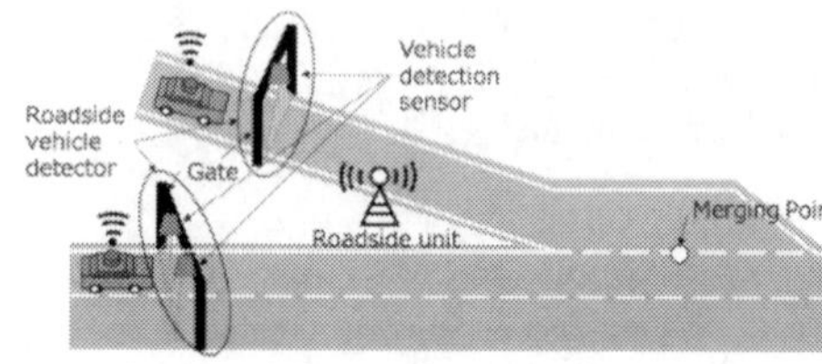

Figure 6. Merging support system overview.

merging at junctions. The location estimation method using a camera needs to be installed so that occlusion does not occur, so the place where it can be used is limited. Although accurate vehicle velocities can be obtained from speed sensors, vehicle positions can be incorrect. These are often acquired from position estimation methods using a Light Detection and Ranging (LiDAR) or in-vehicle Global Navigation Satellite System (GNSS) sensors. Since the position estimation method using a LiDAR can estimate the position more accurately than GNSS sensors, autonomous vehicles often use it for position estimation. However, a cost of LiDAR is much higher than general-porpose GNSS sensors and a LiDAR will not be installed immediately in conventional vehicles. GNSS sensors are often used to get position and accurate time by receiving signals emitted from satellites. These can function anywhere except in tunnels. Signals received from satellites contain noise. Since high-precision GNSS sensors can correct noise [8], they can obtain accurate positions but they are very expensive. GNSS sensors mounted on vehicles are almost general-purpose products (see Figure 2). They are cheep but positions measured via them can, depending on the location, differ from the true position by more than 10 meters. It has been confirmed that properly manage traffic and control merging control at junctions cannot be performed when vehicles' position errors are large [5]. The system using roadside vehicle detection sensors' estimates the vehicle arrival times accurately when the sensor is close to the merging point. However, the error increases with the distance between the sensor and the merging point. Moreover, establishment cost is high and multiple installations are not reasonable because roadside vehicle detection sensors are usually attached to poles installed at roadsides and gates across the road (see Figure 1).

The errors in GNSS-based vehicle positions are almost constant, except in areas where the environment is changing rapidly. On the other hand, the errors in the positions estimated by roadside vehicle detection sensors are small, as long as the sensor is close to the merging point, but they increase with the sensor's distance from the merging point, leading to large errors in the estimated vehicle arrival times. Thus, we consider an approach that combines the positions obtained from GNSS and roadside vehicle detection sensors. In this way, we obtain accurate positions near the roadside vehicle detection sensors but the error does not increase too much when the roadside vehicle detection sensor is further from the merging points. Position estimation method using both GNSS and roadside vehicle detection sensors has not been considered because roadside vehicle detection sensors are infrastructure sensors and cannot be easily used unlike GNSS sensors. For example, these have been managed by National Police Agency in Japan and data from these can only be acquired at specific authorized locations.

In addition, Dedicated Short-Range Communications (DSRC) or Long Term Evolution (LTE) are used for V2V and Vehicle-to-Infrastructure (V2I) communications. However, exchanging information via such wireless networks leads to communication delays. According to Dey et al. [9], these are approximately 1.5[s] for LTE and 100[ms] for DSRC (for communication between a vehicle traveling at 80[km/s] and a roadside unit). These delays also mean the data arrival times are not guaranteed. Thus, we believe that we obtain more accurate vehicle positions by combining data from GNSS and roadside vehicle detection sensors and compensating for communication delays.

In this paper, we propose a vehicle position estimation method that combines data from roadside vehicle detector and in-vehicle sensors. This can retroactively calculate prior vehicle positions in the presence of delays below the maximum acceptable threshold. This paper makes the following two main contributions.

1) A vehicle position estimation method that combines data from roadside vehicle detector and in-vehicle sensors.
2) A communication delays compensation method.

1) In our system, a vehicle detection sensor is installed before the merging point and a roadside unit is installed near the junction. In-vehicle sensor information is used to estimate its position and velocity. In addition, a roadside vehicle detection sensor is also used to estimate the vehicle position based on the sensor position and vehicle velocity. The two estimates are combined using a statistical approach proposed by Duffin [10]. Previous studies used only one of position information obtained from GNSS and roadside vehicle detection sensors (see Figures 3 and 4). However, our method estimates positions using both position information (see Figure 5).

2) Vehicle positions at earlier times are retroactively calculated when older data arrives, up to the predetermined maximum communication delay. When the roadside unit does not receive information from a vehicle, it estimates the vehicle's position based on the most recent information received from it. Modified Kalman filters that take communication delays into accounts has been proposed [11]. The second contribution of this paper is applying the modified Kalman filter to the scene of merging support.

This paper is organized as follows. Section II describes the assumptions made in this study. Section III introduces the proposed method. Section IV evaluates the method using simulations, and then Section V presents results. Section VI concludes the paper.

II. ASSUMPTIONS

In this study, vehicle detection sensors (mounted in gates) are installed before the merging point and a roadside unit is located near the junction (see Figure 6). All vehicles have GNSS devices, speed sensors, and DSRC communication devices. The communication range of DSRC is fixed. Its communication area is limited in a hot spot. On the other hand, DSRC has the advantage that the number of vehicles simultaneously communicated with a roadside unit does not become overcapacity because of the limited communication area. Vehicles approaching the junction send their current position and velocity, as well as the time the data was acquired, to the roadside unit via DSRC. This information is repeatedly sent at regular intervals within DSRC range and started to send before the vehicle passes through the gate.

The vehicle positions and velocities are given in terms of the average value and standard deviation. The vehicle detection sensors are assumed to obtain the positions of the vehicle's center. The system clocks in the vehicles, roadside vehicle detector, and roadside units are assumed to be synchronized. There is some delay in the communications between vehicles and roadside units. On the other hand, the communication delays between the roadside vehicle detector and roadside unit are assumed to be negligible because the communication between them is via wire and dedicated connection. Finally, we consider lateral movement but not vertical movement.

Figure 7 shows the environmental model used in this study. Here, the vehicle drives from the start point toward the merging point. A roadside vehicle detector is installed at $x = x_0^{rvd}$[m]. The vehicle sends information about its position (namely the average x_t^{gps}[m] and standard deviation σ_t^{gps}[m]) and velocity (average v_t[km/s] and standard deviation σ_{v_t}[km/s]) to the roadside unit. Meanwhile, the roadside vehicle detector sends the position of the vehicle's center (average x_0^{rvd}[m] and standard deviation σ_0^{rvd}[m]) and the detection time t_0[s] to the roadside unit when the vehicle passes through the gate.

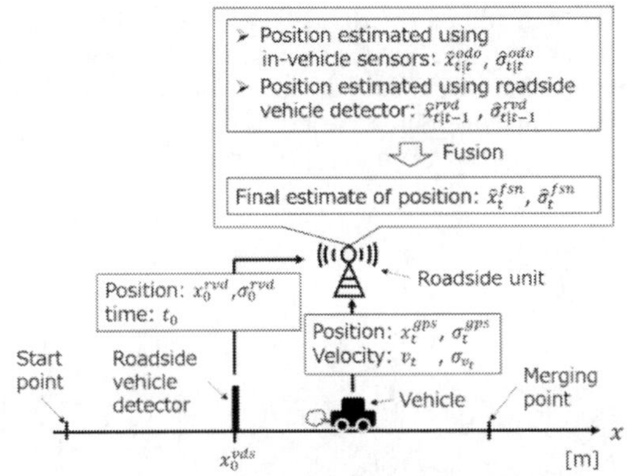

Figure 7. Illustration of the position estimation model and variable definitions.

The roadside unit estimates the vehicle's position, both using the information received from the vehicle (average $\hat{x}_{t|t}^{odo}$[m] and standard deviation $\hat{\sigma}_{t|t}^{odo}$[m]) and using that from the roadside vehicular detector (average $\hat{x}_{t|t-1}^{rvd}$[m] and standard deviation $\hat{\sigma}_{t|t-1}^{rvd}$[m]). Then, it combines these two estimates to obtain the final vehicle position (average $\hat{x}_t^{fsn}$[m] and standard deviation $\hat{\sigma}_t^{fsn}$[m]).

The assumptions in this study came from actual field test of Japan [7]. Support for autonomous driving by providing information for automatically adjusting the speed and timing of entering the main line at highway junctions has been considered in the field tests [12]. These information is provided from roadside units installed near the vehicle detection sensors via DSRC. Roadside units estimate the speed and timing to safely join the main lane from the vehicle velocity obtained from the vehicle detection sensors. Furthermore, there are already previous studies on time synchronization [13]. Therefore, these assumptions are realistic.

III. PROPOSED METHOD

In this section, we described our proposed position estimation approach, followed by our method of compensating for communication delays.

A. Position Estimation

Vehicle approaching the merging point send their position and velocity information to the roadside unit via DSRC. This applies Kalman filters to the data to estimate each vehicle's position before it passes through the gate. When the vehicle passes through the gate, the roadside unit also receives the estimated position of vehicle's center from roadside vehicle detector. The roadside unit produces a final estimate of vehicle's position by combining its estimated center and velocity with the Kalman filters' prediction using a statistical approach proposed by Duffin [10].

Figure 8 presents a flow diagram showing the steps performed to estimate the vehicle's position when it passes through the gate at time t_0[s]. Here, the vehicle's position is estimated by applying Kalman filters to the position and velocity information received from it until passes through the gate. Kalman filters are often used to estimates the exact state based on inaccurate, noisy information, hence, we use it here to estimate the vehicle position from noisy position and velocity information.

Kalman filters are divided into prediction and correction steps. During the prediction step, the vehicle's position is estimated based on the estimate from the previous time step and the current vehicle velocity information. The correction step adjusts this estimated position using the current vehicle position information. The specific equations are as follows.

Prediction step:

$$\hat{x}^{odo}_{t|t-1} = \hat{x}^{odo}_{t-1|t-1} + \frac{5}{18} v_t dt, \tag{1}$$

$$\left(\hat{\sigma}^{odo}_{t|t-1}\right)^2 = \left(\hat{\sigma}^{odo}_{t-1|t-1}\right)^2 + \left(\frac{5}{18}\sigma_{v_t} dt\right)^2. \tag{2}$$

Correction step:

$$\hat{x}^{odo}_{t|t} = \hat{x}^{odo}_{t|t-1} + k_t\left(x^{gps}_t - \hat{x}^{odo}_{t|t-1}\right), \tag{3}$$

$$\left(\hat{\sigma}^{odo}_{t|t}\right)^2 = (1-k_t)\left(\hat{\sigma}^{odo}_{t|t-1}\right)^2, \tag{4}$$

$$k_t = \frac{\left(\hat{\sigma}^{odo}_{t|t-1}\right)^2}{\left\{\left(\hat{\sigma}^{odo}_{t|t-1}\right)^2 + \left(\sigma^{gps}_t\right)^2\right\}}. \tag{5}$$

where $\hat{x}^{odo}_{t|t-1}$[m] and $\hat{\sigma}^{odo}_{t|t-1}$[m] are the average and standard deviation of the vehicle position, respectively, generated by the prediction step for timestep t [s], $\hat{x}^{odo}_{t|t}$[m] and $\hat{\sigma}^{odo}_{t|t}$[m] are the average and standard deviation of the vehicle position, respectively, generated by the correction step for timestep t [s], v_t[km/s] and σ_{v_t}[km/s] are the average and standard deviation of the vehicle velocity, respectively, generated by the correction step for timestep t [s], k_t is the Kalman gain at timestep t[s], and $\frac{5}{18}$ is a term to convert the vehicle velocity from [km/h] to [m/s].

The roadside unit receives the position of the vehicle's center from the roadside vehicle detector at time t_0[s], then combines this with the velocity information received from the vehicle, and the Kalman filters' prediction step in order to estimate the vehicle's position. The specific equations are as follows.

Position estimation:

$$\hat{x}^{rvd}_{t} = \hat{x}^{rvd}_{t-1} + \frac{5}{18} v_t dt, \tag{6}$$

$$\left(\hat{\sigma}^{rvd}_{t}\right)^2 = \left(\hat{\sigma}^{rvd}_{t-1}\right)^2 + \left(\frac{5}{18}\sigma_{v_t} dt\right)^2. \tag{7}$$

where $\hat{x}^{rvd}_{t|t-1}$[m] and $\hat{\sigma}^{rvd}_{t|t-1}$[m] are the average and standard deviation of the vehicle position predicted by the Kalman filters at timestep t [s], and v_t [km/s], σ_{v_t}[km/s] are average and standard deviation of the vehicle velocity at timestep t [s], and $\frac{5}{18}$ is a term to convert a vehicle velocity from [km/h] to [m/s].

The vehicle position (average $\hat{x}^{rvd}_{t_0}$[m] and standard deviation $\hat{\sigma}^{rvd}_{t_0}$[m]) at timestep t_0[s] is defines as the position received from the roadside vehicle detector, and hence is given by

$$\hat{x}^{rvd}_{t_0} = x^{rvd}_0, \tag{8}$$

$$\hat{\sigma}^{rvd}_{t_0} = \sigma^{rvd}_0. \tag{9}$$

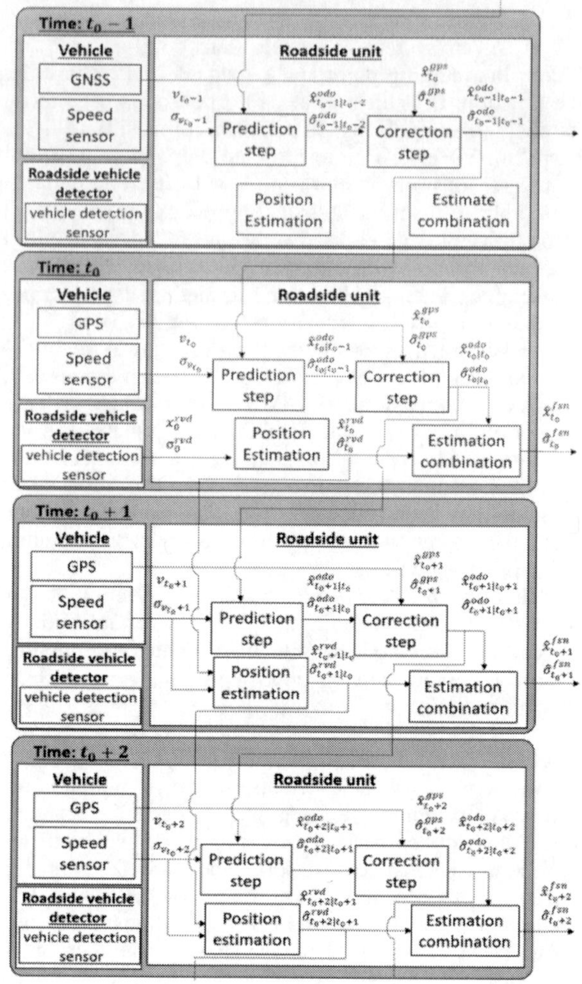

Figure 8. Flow diagram showing the steps performed to estimate the vehicle's position.

where x^{rvd}_0[m] and $\sigma^{rvd}_{t_0}$.[m] are average and standard deviation, respectively, of the vehicle position received from the roadside vehicle detector.

Finally, the two vehicle position estimates are combined using a statistical approach proposed by Duffin [10], which is based on Bayes' Rule and Kalman filters. This approach simply combines the two Gaussian distribution as follows.

Estimate combination:

$$\hat{x}^{fsn}_{t} = \hat{x}^{odo}_{t|t} + \frac{\left(\hat{\sigma}^{odo}_{t|t}\right)^2}{\left(\hat{\sigma}^{odo}_{t|t}\right)^2 + \left(\hat{\sigma}^{rvd}_{t}\right)^2}\left(\hat{x}^{rvd}_{t} - \hat{x}^{odo}_{t|t}\right), \tag{10}$$

$$\left(\hat{\sigma}^{fsn}_{t}\right)^2 = \left\{1 - \frac{\left(\hat{\sigma}^{odo}_{t|t}\right)^2}{\left(\hat{\sigma}^{odo}_{t|t}\right)^2 + \left(\hat{\sigma}^{rvd}_{t}\right)^2}\right\}\left(\hat{\sigma}^{odo}_{t|t}\right)^2. \tag{11}$$

where $\hat{x}^{fsn}_{t}$[m] and $\hat{\sigma}^{fsn}_{t}$[m] are average and standard deviation of the vehicle position obtained by combining the two estimates.

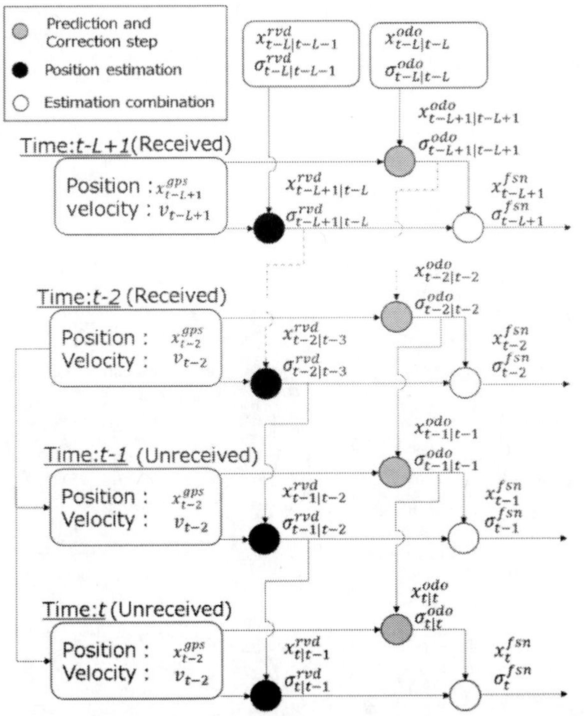

Figure 9. Overview of our communication delays compensation method.

B. Communication delays compensation

Since communication delays inevitable occur when exchanging information over wireless networks, it is necessary to take account for them when estimating the vehicle positions. Here, we use Kagami et al.'s approach, which involves modified Kalman filters that accounts for communication delays [11]. This method retroactively calculates prior positions and velocities when older data is received, up to a predetermined maximum communication delay. However, the modified Kalman filters' model Kagami et al.'s proposed is a multidimensional state space model. In this study, the communication delays compensation is only used the concept and Kalman filters' model was changed to a one-dimensional CV (Constant Velocity) model.

Figure 9 illustrates our method of compensating for communication delays. Here, L [s] is the maximum communication delay, $t - L$ [s] is L timesteps after the vehicle passed through the gate, and the roadside units did not receive any position and velocity information from the vehicle at timesteps $t - 1$ and t [s]. The data is received at timestep $t - 2$[s], and the roadside unit uses this to retroactively calculate the vehicle positions and velocities at timesteps $t - 1$ and t [s], working back from the present time to the predetermined maximum communication delay.

The vehicle position is estimated using (1)–(11) at each time. The vehicle's position is estimated based on the estimate from the previous time step and the each time vehicle position and velocity information. Finally, the two vehicle position estimates are combined.

IV. EVALUATION EXPERIMENTS

In this section, our vehicle position estimation method is evaluated using a series of simulations, conducted both with and without communication delays. Here, we used Matlab R2019a. Table I shows that the specifications of PC used for simulation.

TABLE I. SPECIFICATIONS OF THE PC USED FOR THE SIMULATIONS.

CPU	Intel Core i9-9900X @ 3.50GHz
Memory	64 GB
Storage	Samsung MZVLB1T0HALR-00000

TABLE II. PARAMETERS OF THE GAUSSIAN WHITE NOISE MODEL.

GNSS error	σ_w
Low	3
Medium	6
High	9

TABLE III. SPECIFICATIONS OF THE GNSS USED IN THE EXPERIMENT.

GNSS chip	UBX-M8030-KT (u-blox)
Receiver type	GPS, QZSS, GLONASS
Tracking sensitivity	-167[dBm]
Horizontal position accuracy	2.0[m]
Internal antenna	Dielectric antenna (25x25x4[mm])

TABLE IV. PARAMETERS OF THE GAUSS–MARKOV RANDOM PROCESS MODEL.

	σ_g	σ_r	β
Case 1	0.2020	0.0027	1/600
Case 2	0.1030	0.3160	1/600

A. Environment without communication delays

In this experiment, the position estimation accuracy was evaluated in an environment where the communication delays were assumed to be negligible. Here, our proposed method (labeled as "Fusion" below) was compared with one that simply applies Kalman filters to the in-vehicle sensor data (labeled as "GNSS only").

In this simulation, a vehicle drove from the start point at $x = -100$[m] toward the merging point at a speed of 80 [km/h]. The roadside vehicle detector was installed at $x = 0$[m]. The standard deviations of the vehicle's center position and velocity were set to s $\sigma_0^{rvd} = 0.5$[m] and $\sigma_{v_t} = 5$[km/s]. The vehicle sent its position and velocity to the roadside unit every 100[ms], and the roadside unit also estimated the vehicle's position every 100[ms]. The vehicle acquired its position from a GNSS device, and we considered the two models of GNSS position error, namely a Gaussian white noise model and a Gauss–Markov random process model, as used by a previous study [5]. There are described below, and the simulation was repeated six times for each GNSS position error models.

1) Gaussian white noise model: This is given by

$$x_t^{gps} = x_t + w_t. \tag{12}$$

where x_t is the actual vehicle position and w_t is Gaussian white noise, i.e., $w_t \sim N(0, \sigma_w)$. Here σ_w set as in Table II. σ_w in Table II are set from a trial experiment using a general-purpose GNSS sensor. The specifications of the GNSS used in the experiment is Table III. When position data were acquired using the sensor at multiple points in Nagoya University, the most low value was $\sigma_w \approx 3$, the most high value was $\sigma_w \approx 9$. Thus the σ_w is set as 3 in the low GNSS error and the σ_w is set as 9 in the high GNSS error. As an intermediate value

TABLE V. COMPARISON OF POSITION ESTIMATION METHODS.

Gaussian white noise model (Low GNSS position error)	Average [m]	Standard deviation [m]
GNSS only	0.298	0.182
Fusion	0.238	0.030
Gaussian white noise model (Medium GNSS position error)	Average [m]	Standard deviation [m]
GNSS only	0.360	0.290
Fusion	0.260	0.052
Gaussian white noise model (High GNSS position error)	Average [m]	Standard deviation [m]
GNSS only	0.467	0.461
Fusion	0.274	0.085
Gauss–Markov random process model (Case 1)	Average[m]	Standard deviation[m]
GNSS only	1.681	0.907
Fusion	1.280	0.591
Gauss–Markov random process model (Case 2)	Average [m]	Standard deviation [m]
GNSS only	0.691	0.467
Fusion	0.477	0.315

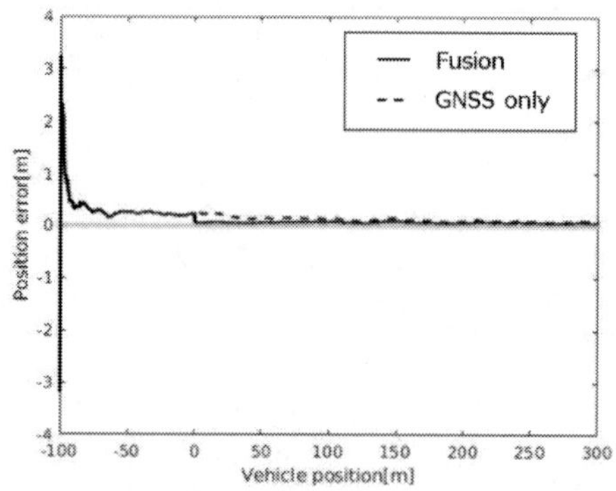

Figure 10. Position error versus true position (Gaussian white noise model with low GNSS position error).

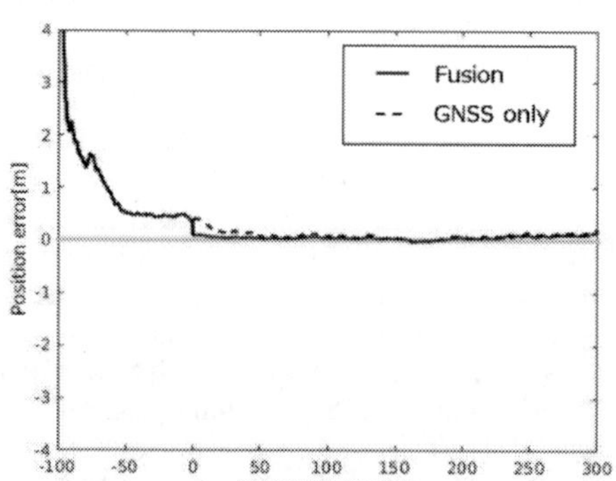

Figure 11. Position error versus true position (Gaussian white noise model with medium GNSS position error).

between the high and low GNSS error, σ_w is set as 6 in the medium GNSS error.

2) Gauss–Markov random process model: This is given by the following equations [14]:

$$m_t = e^{-\beta dt} m_{t-1} + g_t, \quad (13)$$

$$n_t = m_t + r_t, \quad (14)$$

$$x_t^{gps} = x_t + 0.9 n_t. \quad (15)$$

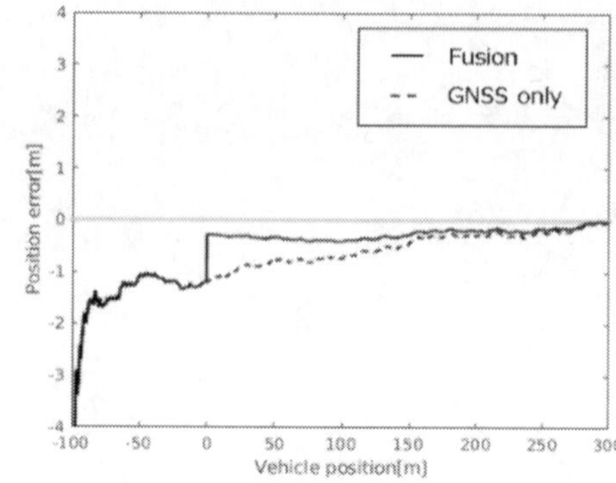

Figure 12. Position error versus true position (Gaussian white noise model with high GNSS position error).

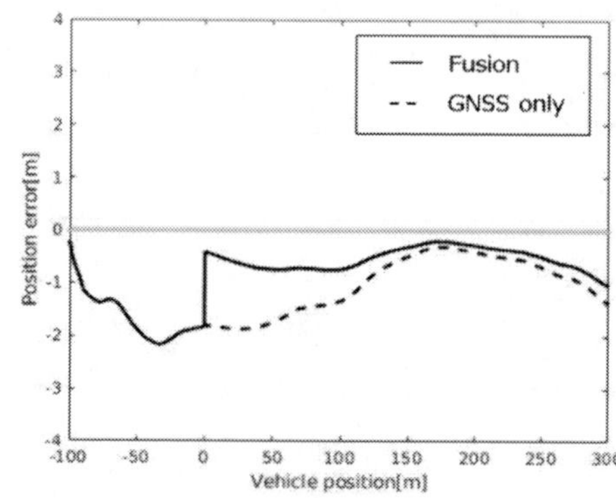

Figure 13. Position error versus true position(Gauss–Markov random process model, Case 1).

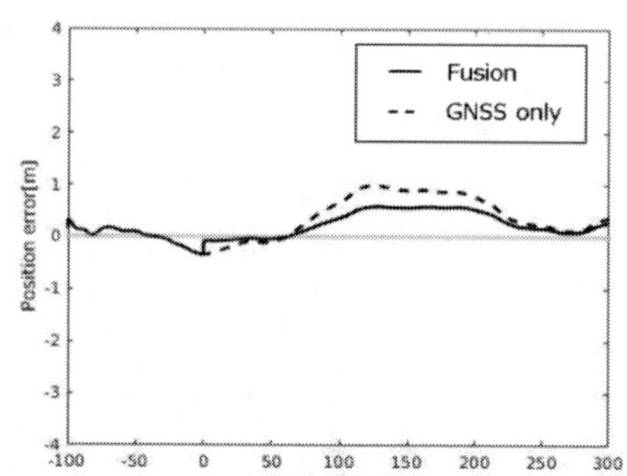

Figure 14. Position error versus true position(Gauss–Markov random process model, Case 2).

Here, represents time–correlated noise with time constant β and Gaussian white noise g_t, i.e., $g_t \sim N(0, \sigma_g)$. In addition, n_t is the total noise , composed of m_t and uncorrelated noise r_t, i.e., $r_t \sim N(0, \sigma_r)$. As in the previous study [5], σ_g, σ_r, and β were set as in Table IV. The case2 GNSS error is worse than the case1 in the paper [5].

B. Environment with communication delays

In this experiment, our communication delays compensation method is evaluated by comparing the performance our method (called "Fusion with DC" below) with those of two

TABLE VI. EVALUATION OF OUR COMMUNICATION DELAYS COMPENSATION METHODS.

	Average [m]	Standard deviation [m]
GNSS only without DC	-2.420	0.612
Maximum communication delay of 0.10[s]	Average [m]	Standard deviation [m]
GNSS only with DC	-0.471	0.527
Fusion with DC	-0.248	0.065
Maximum communication delay of 0.12[s]	Average [m]	Standard deviation [m]
GNSS only with DC	-0.410	0.411
Fusion with DC	-0.246	0.059
Maximum communication delay of 0.14[s]	Average [m]	Standard deviation [m]
GNSS only with DC	-0.380	0.362
Fusion with DC	-0.234	0.063

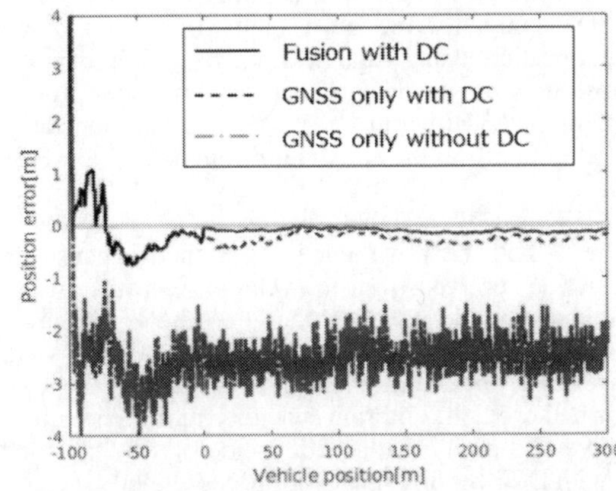

Figure 15. Evaluation of our communication delays compensation method (maximum communication delay of 0.10[s]).

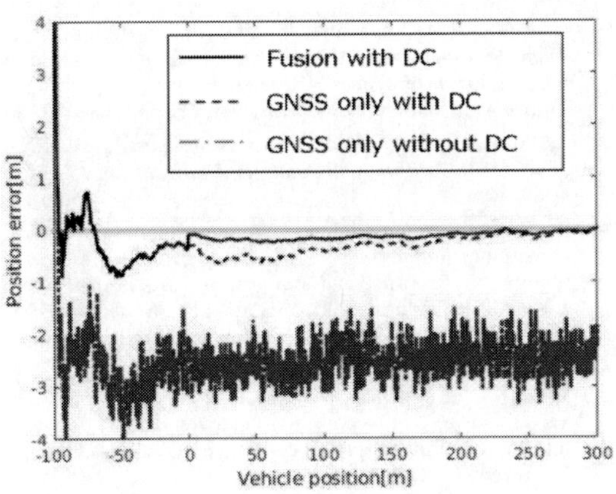

Figure 16. Evaluation of our communication delays compensation method (maximum communication delay of 0.12[s]).

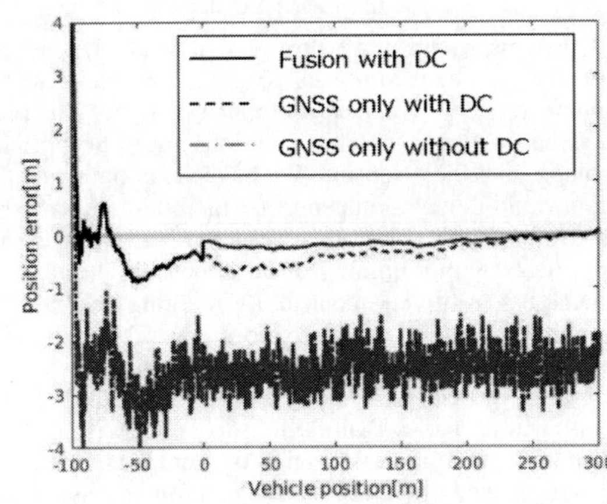

Figure 17. Evaluation of our communication delays compensation method (maximum communication delay of 0.14[s]).

other methods.

The first method (labeled as "GNSS only without DC") estimates the vehicle's position by applying Kalman filters to the in-vehicle sensor data without compensating for communication delays. This only uses the most recent position and velocity information received, ignoring older, delayed data. The second method (labeled as "GNSS only with DC") is similar, but adds communication delay compensation.

Here, the communication delays were represented by Gaussian white noise, i.e., $N(\bar{d}, \sigma_{\bar{d}}^2)$ $\bar{d}$ was set to 96.130[ms] (following previous study [9]) and $\sigma_{\bar{d}}$ was set to 2[ms]. We considered three possible maximum communication delays, namely 0.10, 0.12, and 0.14[s], and repeated each simulation six times.

V. Results

A. Position estimation

The simulation results are shown in Table V, and Figures 10-14 shows how the position error changed with the vehicle's position. Here, the horizontal axis represents the true vehicle position, while the vertical axis represents the position error, namely the difference between the true and estimated vehicle positions. When the position error is positive (negative), the vehicle's estimated position is ahead of (behind) its true position.

As Table V shows the average and standard deviation of the position error are both lower for our "Fusion" method than for "GNSS only." In Figures 10-14, we see that , when the vehicle passed through the gate and it became possible to obtain its position accurately, the position error of the "Fusion" method dropped sharply, becoming much lower than that of "GNSS only." This demonstrates that the proposed position estimation method can be significantly more accurate than "GNSS only."

B. Communication delays compensation

The simulation results are shown in Table VI, while Figures 15-17 show how the position error changed with the vehicle's position, the horizontal axis represents the true vehicle positions, while the vertical axis represents the position error, defined as before.

As Table VI shows, both the average and standard deviation of the position error were lower for our "Fusion with DC" method than for the other approaches. In addition, the errors were lower for "GNSS only with DC" than for "GNSS only without DC," and were significantly lower for "Fusion with DC" than for the other methods when the maximum communication delay time was 0.14 [s]. We believe this is because the amount of data that had to be discarded, due to not being received within the maximum communication delay time, decreased as the maximum communication delay time increased.

In Figures 15-17, the position error is always negative for the "GNSS only without DC" method because the latest information received from the vehicle was out-of-data due to communication delays. The fact that the errors are smaller for both "GNSS only with DC" and "Fusion with DC" confirms that our communication delays compensation method performed well. In addition, the fact that the position errors are lower for our "Fusion with DC" method than for "GNSS only with DC" confirms that our proposed method can estimate the vehicle position more accurately than "GNSS only" in an environment with communication delays.

VI. CONCLUSION

In this paper, we have proposed a vehicle position estimation method that combines roadside vehicle detector and in-vehicle sensors. We have demonstrated that the proposed method can estimate vehicle positions more accurately than only using in-vehicle sensors. We have also confirmed that our communication delay compensation method can perform well. Since our method can estimate vehicle positions accurately in environments with communication delays, it is more suitable for managing traffic and controlling merging at junctions.

In future work, we will explore several topics. First, in order to evaluate our proposed method in practice, we will have to consider vertical movement. Since LTE introduces longer communication delays than DSRC does, we will also need to confirm that our communication delay compensation technique can perform well for LTE. Third, communication delays are influenced by various factors, such as the number of vehicles, building, and so on, so we will need to confirm that our communication delay compensation method is also effective in practice. Finally, the proposed method can be applied while the delay occurs according to a specific distribution. The communication delay distribution tendency changes drastically with the number of increasing vehicles. Thus, it is necessary to consider a method that can handle it even if the communication delay distribution tendency is changed.

ACKNOWLEDGMENT

This work was supported by JST-OPERA Program Grant Number JPMJOP1612, Japan.

REFERENCES

[1] T. Abbas, L. Bernado, A. Thiel, C. F. Mecklenbräuker, and F. Tufvesson, "Measurements based channel characterization for vehicle-to-vehicle communications at merging lanes on highway," In *Proceedings of the 5th International Symposium Wireless Vehicular Communications(WiVeC) June 2–3, 2013, Dresden, Germany.* IEEE, Jun. 2013, pp.1–5, ISBN: 978-1-4673-6339-6, URL: https://ieeexplore.ieee.org/abstract/document/6698241 [retrieved: 12, 2019].

[2] B. N. Janson, W. Awad, J. Robles, J. Kononov, and B. Pinkerton, "Truck accidents at freeway ramps: data analysis and high-risk site identification," *Journal of Transportation and Statistics*, vol. 1, pp. 75–92, January, 1998, ISSN: 1094-8848.

[3] H. Cui et al., "Early ramp warning using vehicle behavior analysis," *Soft Computing*, vol. 22, pp. 1421–1432, March, 2018, ISSN: 1432-7643.

[4] V. Milanes, J. Godoy, J. Villagra, and J. Perez, "Automated On-Ramp Merging System for Congested Traffic Situations," *IEEE Transactions on Intelligent Transportation Systems*, vol. 12, pp. 500–508, June, 2011, ISSN: 1524-9050.

[5] F. C. Chou, S. E. Shladover, and G. Bansal, "Coordinated merge control based on V2V communication," In *Proceedings of the Vehicular Networking Conference (VNC) December 8–10, 2016, Ohio, USA.* IEEE, Dec. 2016, pp.1–8, ISBN: 978-1-5090-5197-7, ISSN: 2157-9865 , URL: https://ieeexplore.ieee.org/document/7835933 [retrieved: 12, 2019].

[6] S. Hirai et al., "AHS Safety Service Utilizing an ITS On-Board Unit for Driving Support in Merging Sections," *14th World Congress on ITS*, pp. 1–8, October, 2007.

[7] "Start of Field Operational Tests of Autonomous Driving in Tokyo Waterfront Area," URL: http://www.soumu.go.jp/menu_news/s-news/01kiban14_02000404.html [retrieved: 12, 2019].

[8] Y. Morales and T. Tsubouchi, "DGPS, RTK-GPS and StarFire DGPS performance under tree shading environments," In *Proceedings of IEEE international conference on integration technology(ICIT) March 20–24, 2007, Shenzhen, China.* IEEE, Mar. 2007, pp.519–524, ISBN: 1-4244-1091-6, URL: https://ieeexplore.ieee.org/abstract/document/4290370 [retrieved: 12, 2019].

[9] K. C. Deya, A. Rayamajh, M. Chowdhury, P. Bhavsar, and J. Martin, "Vehicle-to-vehicle (V2V) and vehicle-to-infrastructure (V2I) communication in a heterogeneous wireless network - Performance evaluation," *Transportation Research Part C*, vol. 68, pp. 168–184, April, 2016.

[10] W. Anderson and R. Duffin, "Series and parallel addition of matrices," *Journal of Mathematical Analysis Applications*, vol. 26, pp. 576–594, 1969.

[11] S. Kagami and M. Ishikawa, "A sensor selection method considering communication delays," In *Proceedings of IEEE International Conference on Robotics and Automation(ICRA) April 26–May 1, 2004, LA, USA.* IEEE, May. 2001, pp.206–211, ISBN: 0-7803-8232-3, ISSN: 1050-4729, URL: https://ieeexplore.ieee.org/document/13071529 [retrieved: 12, 2019].

[12] "Start of joint research on information provision to support autonomous driving," URL: http://www.nilim.go.jp/lab/bcg/kisya/journal/kisya20180119.pdf [retrieved: 12, 2019].

[13] F. Sivrikaya and B. Yener, 'Time synchronization in sensor networks: a survey," *IEEE network*, vol. 18, pp. 45–50, August, 2004.

[14] Rankin J, "An error model for sensor simulation GPS and differential GPS," In *Proceedings of of IEEE Position Location and Navigation Symposium(PLANS'94) April 11–15, 1994, Las Vegas, USA.* IEEE, Apr. 1994, pp.260–266, ISBN: 0-7803-1435-2, URL: https://ieeexplore.ieee.org/document/303322 [retrieved: 12, 2019].

Delay-Conscious Defense Against Fingerprinting Attacks

Jingyuan Liang
Cleveland State University
Cleveland, Ohio, USA
Email: j.liang18@vikes.csuohio.edu

Chansu Yu
Cleveland State University
Cleveland, Ohio, USA
Email: c.yu91@csuohio.edu

Kyoungwon Suh
Illinois State University
Normal, Illinois, USA
Email: kwsuh@ilstu.edu

Abstract—**In the past few years, many defense mechanisms have been proposed against website fingerprinting attacks. Walkie-Talkie (WT) built on top of Tor network is known to be one of the most effective and efficient defense mechanisms. However, we observed that WT significantly increases page loading times (time overhead) while adding little bandwidth overhead compared to other approaches. We analyze the cause of the increased page loading time and present a defending approach called Tail Timeout (TT), which addresses the problem, by introducing a timeout mechanism limiting the maximum time for which a pending request can block subsequent requests. Our experimental results indicate that the proposed TT defense can significantly reduce the page loading time while keeping similar defense performance in terms of true positive and true negative ratios achieved by WT.**

Keywords–Website fingerprinting; Censorship; Tor; Machine learning; User perceived experience.

I. INTRODUCTION

Internet censorship is on the rise [1]–[5]. Earlier, it was a simple surveillance of information in plaintext [6], [7]. Then, censors simply blocked the encryption layer when encryption was not widely-deployed [8]. Now, censors face the choice of what to do with the data that they cannot fully understand, and they usually cannot afford a complete block [9]–[11].

One of the popular approaches adopted by censors is known as website fingerprinting [12]–[14]. It uses features of packets in a network communication to infer the contents in the communication, or more precisely, to match the communication to one of several known feature models. Most popular features that have been exploited are: unique packet lengths, packet length frequency, packet ordering, and interpacket timing [15]. Machine learning approaches, such as k-Nearest Neighbors [16] can be used to conduct the fingerprinting attack. Once identified, the censor may decide to block the network connection completely. However, considering the fact that the identification of such connections is not guaranteed to be accurate, it is also possible that the censor may start deteriorating the quality of service by, for example, randomly dropping packets, or throttling the traffic [8], [17].

In this paper, we propose TT defense against website fingerprinting attacks, as an extension of WT [18] defense, which works on top of Tor [19]. WT is known to add little bandwidth overhead compared to other approaches, while keeping a moderate defending performance. We find that WT increases webpage loading time substantially, which is already high since it uses the Tor network. The page loading time may get larger unbearably if the censor decides to randomly drop packets as discussed earlier. TT defense addresses the problem by limiting the resource wait time. Our experimental study shows that WT increases page loading time by 50% or more in 22% of top 100 websites. On the other hand, in the case of TT of 1,000 msec, it occurs in only 7% of websites. Note that the defense efficiency of TT is on par with WT, but alleviates the time overhead problem.

This paper is organized as follows: Section II describes background and related work on fingerprinting attacks and the issues raised; Sections III and IV describe the TT defense methodology, implementation and setup in our experiments, respectively; Section V presents our experiment results; Section VI provides conclusions and future work.

II. BACKGROUND

To combat against website fingerprinting attacks, many efforts have been made on improving the Tor network itself or developing ones on top of Tor [20]. This is because Tor itself is already proven to be resilient to website fingerprinting attacks to some degree [21], [22]. Although Tor itself is not a complete standalone solution in combating website fingerprinting attacks, the fact that Tor network traffics are packed into fixed-length cells and sent over circuits built on-the-fly together with various control cells provides some degree of defense. Major media websites, such as BBC News, also adopted Tor, to ensure that their contents can be distributed to audiences without censorship [5]. Other defenses against website fingerprint attacks are to reschedule the packets (or other transmission units, such as Tor cells), or to insert padding units to confuse the attacker. An example of defenses using the rescheduling approach is Shmatikov's adaptive padding [23], and one using the inserting approach is Wright's traffic morphing [24]. The former approach adds a delay ("time overhead") because a unit can no longer be sent immediately once generated and needs to wait for scheduling, and the latter approach wastes network bandwidth ("bandwidth overhead") because of the padded units that do not carry useful information [25]. In addition, they only defend in a single aspect and may not be able to stand against modern attacks any more. More recent proposals for defenses against website fingerprinting attacks (BuFLO [26], Tamaraw [25], and WT [18]) use both rescheduling and padding. For example, BuFLO renders different websites produce the exact same packet sequence, defeating any possible classifier, but it increases both bandwidth and time overhead as mentioned above.

WT is known to be one of the most effective and efficient defense mechanisms. It addresses the bandwidth overhead problem by changing HTTP to a half-duplex communication protocol, in which only one party transmits data until all data held on this party get processed. With this modification, as much as possible requests or responses are combined into a single burst, within which there are only transmissions in the same direction (i.e., either all requests or all responses), reducing the total number of bursts and thus leading to a smaller amount of padding units. Bandwidth overhead is less of a concern when there exists a vast amount of bandwidth available. Rather, time overhead in WT is a concern because it directly affects the quality of service and is easily misinterpreted as service unavailability.

III. Delay-Conscious Defense

WT works on top of Tor. With Tor, the adversary can only see (or infer) a sequence of fixed-length cells and their directions when users are browsing a website. The adversary calculates the fingerprints of such cell sequences for a list of popular websites and/or websites to be monitored, and stores the fingerprints in advance. When users are browsing the web, the adversary tries to match the cell sequence observed from users against the dataset of known fingerprints, attempting to identify the website users are browsing. Considering that the cells are fixed-length and encrypted, what the adversary can see are a number of alternating (as in direction) batches, and the number of cells in each batch, as fingerprints. WT combines some of the batches by delaying sending data (until the responses to the previous batch are completely received), reducing the number of batches. Furthermore, WT then adds padding data to each batch, attempting to make cell sequences more similar to each other. Since the number of batches is already reduced, and padding is needed only for each batch, the amount of padding data is limited.

The proposed mechanism, TT, is an improvement over WT. It excludes the slow resources from WT scheduling, to minimize the delay caused by such scheduling. However, the time needed for a certain resource request is not known at the time of request. What we can do is to remove it from the pool of pending requests when it has stayed there for certain tail time (t). Precisely speaking, the proposed mechanism is that, as long as there is a previous request to the server with pending response, which was sent no more than t seconds ago, no further request is sent, and they are queued to be sent later; as soon as all pending requests either get responses or become older than t seconds, all queued requests can be sent at once in one burst, then wait for the burst for their responses; and t is a parameter, to be adjusted. Once the pool of pending requests is empty, that is, requests either received a response, or have been removed because it passed t, the next batch of requests can be sent.

The number of such slow resources is usually less than 10% according to our study on top 100 websites. Considering that only a small number of requests trigger such scenarios, we expect that this change will not significantly increase the number of bursts, thus not improving the fingerprintability as demonstrated in our experimental evaluation.

A. *WT and TT Implementation*

We implemented WT and TT based on the Mozilla Firefox browser using an browser add-on. The originally published WT / half-duplex implementation was made by modifying the Mozilla Firefox source code. The patch no longer applies in current versions of Firefox because the relevant part in Firefox code has been rewritten; we decided to keep the Firefox platform, but reimplemented the procedure. To ensure that our solution is future-proof, we made our implementation using the webRequest WebExtensions API in Mozilla Firefox, instead of patching the codebase of Mozilla Firefox itself. We also included the support for a user-configurable tail timeout value.

We implement WT's half-duplex communication by changing the way the client's browser works. The destination server does not need to make any change to accommodate the change at the browser side; the client simply does not talk when the destination server is talking. We use the webRequest API, which allows extensions to attach event listeners to the various stages of making an HTTP request, and the event listeners receive detailed information about the request and can modify or cancel the request. To achieve the half-duplex communication, the add-on keeps track of all requests, and blocks requests from being sent unless there are not any other requests on the way according to the original WT half-duplex communication design. In order to implement the TT as described in this section, we record the timestamp for each request when a request is released from the blocked status; when the current time goes past *tail timeout* seconds after the recorded timestamp of a request, the request is no longer considered on the way even if it is, and does not block other requests anymore.

IV. Experiment Setup

In our experiment with the defense implementation described above, we accessed top 100 websites and captured traces of Tor cell sequences during website accesses. We then conducted attacks against the traces to compare the attack accuracy between scenarios with WT or TT used, or TT with different timeout values used. Further we also measured the time needed to load those websites in the WT and TT scenarios, and compared them with the loading time without defenses.

A. *Data Set*

We fetched Alexa's top website list [27], which was also used by Wang et. al. [18] in the WT research, as well as other researchers working on the same area [28], as of January 24, 2019, and removed duplicated subdomains (such as `tmall.com` and `login.tmall.com`) and localization domains (such as `google.com` and `google.co.in`) from the list. We access the main page using HTTP protocol (which redirects to the HTTPS version in many websites) to start the browsing session for each site.

To build the Tor cell sequence data sets, from the list after duplication removal, we use the top 100 websites as monitored websites, with each website visited 50 times. Then we take the next 5000 websites, each accessed once, as unmonitored websites. We run the open world scenario in our experiment, meaning that the attempted attack is trained on a part of monitored data and tested on mixed unmonitored and another part of monitored data; the attack is expected to identify whether the tested traces are from the monitored websites and if one trace is from a monitored website, which website it is from. In contrast, a closed world scenario is when a the trace being tested is always known to be from one of the monitored websites, and all those monitored websites have been seen in the training set by the attack. For each visit, we try one access with unmodified Firefox, another with WT and three accesses using tail timeout values of 1,000, 2,000 and 5,000 milliseconds, respectively.

For each access, we start a Firefox instance controlled by Selenium [29] through geckodriver [30]. The Firefox instance is configured by Selenium to use a SOCKS proxy listened by a modified Tor instance, which emits cell information. The Firefox instance also gets a WT/TT implementation extension installed (other than the access without WT/TT), with tail time value configured. At the same time, Tor cell capture and web browsing to the intended target start together. After 15 seconds, the Firefox instance is terminted and the captured cell sequence is saved to a file as a part of the data set.

Note that in [18], the collection of Tor cells during web browsing sessions with WT was done by doing TCP packet captures. They then reassemble TCP packets into TCP streams, and finally analyze TLS records and guess Tor cells based on record lengths. This is also the approach an actual attacker have to use, since all they can see are the packets, however there is no guarantee that the original cells can perfectly reconstructed. We adopted a different approach by modifying Tor and having it emit individual cell information directly. Although this approach is not practical for an attacker in real world, it would provide the most accurate cell sequences, allowing us to focus on evaluating the fingerprinting attacking and defending algorithms operating on cell sequences. Note that we are working on a higher layer before an outgoing SENDME is added and after an incoming SENDME is removed, so we do not need to think about SENDME removal. This would make attacking even easier in the experiment, and eliminate noises that can occur in real world attacking.

According to [18], there needs to be a padding step to make traffic through WT actually not fingerprintable. There were several factors to consider in the padding step, including difficulties in implementation for real time packet streams, but in consistence with the original research by Wang et. al., we only do simulated padding on the cell sequence data set built above to construct a "padded" data set. We follow the padding procedure described by Wang et. al. [18] to align the cell sequence being padded with a pre-selected decoy sequence by bursts. Then, for each burst (incoming and outgoing), if the number of cells is lower in the cell sequence to be padded than the decoy sequence, we add padding cells in the cell sequence to be padded inside the burst to make the number of cells equal to the number of cells in the burst in the decoy sequence at the same position. Specifically, we make the added cells uniformly distrubuted between the first cell and the last cell in the burst on the timeline, and for decoy sequence selection, we choose the largest sequence in the same data set for all sequences in the data set.

B. Performance Measures

To evaluate the defenses with and without the TT modification, we follow the approach taken to evaluate the original WT and measure the true positive rate (TPR), false positive rate (FPR), true negative rate (TNR) and false negative rate (FNR), on the cell sequences both before and after applying the padding step.

We run k-Nearest Neighbors (k-NN) classifier-based attack [16] on the cell sequences, which is shown in [18] by Wang et. al. to achieve much better performance compared to previous attack methodologies including SVM [12] and CUMUL [15]. There are also newer attacks, such as k-fingerprinting [31] and p-FP [28], which outperforms k-NN, while we still chose k-NN to ensure results comparable with the original WT research. During the attack, 1,225 features are extracted for each trace, and initial weights for those features are randomly chosen between 0.5~1.5.

To measure the page loading time, independent from the 50 visits on each website collecting Tor cell sequences, we access each of the 100 websites five times and record the loading time values, and caluclate the average to build a list of page loading time for the 100 websites, for each TT configuration. For each access, we browse the website and record the timestamps of `navigationStart`, `domInteractive` and `domComplete` events in `window.performance.timing`. If the page does not finish loading within a certain time period, which is 120 sec when doing overall measurement and 300 sec when inspecting individual websites, or an error occurs during loading, the data is marked as such and may be excluded from final processing. Otherwise, we calculate (`domComplete` − `navigationStart`) as the page loading time.

V. Results and Discussion

As described above, evaluated data during experiments include time needed to load the pages, and defense effectiveness, as evidenced by attack accuracy on defensed datasets. To better discuss the reason why page loading time is improved, we further looked into two cases to identify the source of delay.

A. Page Loading Time

As described before, we measured website loading times from experiments with 70 websites selected out of the top 100 websites. The 30 websites were excluded because of unstable data and excessive amount of network errors, which usually happen on foreign websites without a good connectivity to the Internet. With each TT configuration, each site is accessed five times and the average value of the loading time is taken.

Figure 1 shows the overview of the loading times of websites before and after the TT change, and a significant improvement can be observed. More specifically, WT increases the website access time by 50% or more in 22% of the websites in our dataset. On the other hand, in the case of TT of 1,000 milliseconds, it occurs in only 7% of websites.

For comparison, we also captured data in Figure 2 where the `domInteractive` event is used in place of `domComplete`. Unlike `domComplete`, which fires when the whole page completes loading including all the resources, `domInteractive` comes earlier when the necessary information needed to complete the DOM tree is ready, which is usually just the document and synchronous scripts, but without any styling information or media resources. It is expected that the slowdown of WT compared to unmodified Firefox is less significant, since the total amount of data and requests are both lower, which can also been seen in the chart, while the use of TT still provides some speed up. WT increases the website access time by 50% or more in 12% of cases. On the other hand, in the case of TT of 1,000 milliseconds, it occurs in only 2% of websites.

Looking into the data, we specifically noticed the major improvement on some popular content-oriented websites. For example, on `cnn.com` and `nytimes.com`, as well as `sina.com.cn`, the loading times are reduced by a maximum

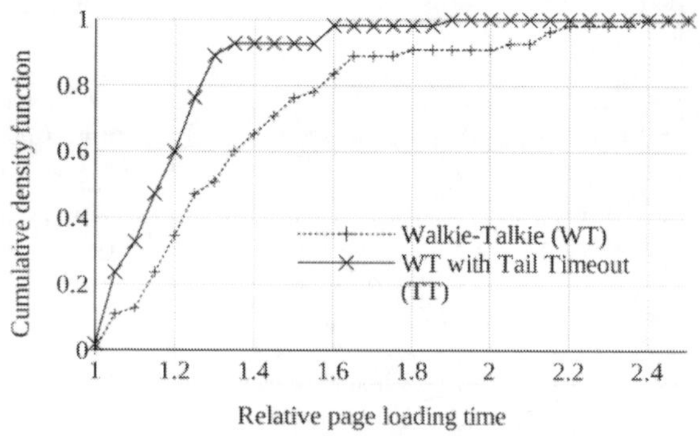

Figure 1. Page Loading Time Comparison (`domComplete` event used; page loading time values in X-axis are normalized to unmodified Firefox, i.e., loading time of 1 in X-axis means an equal loading time of the same website in unmodified Firefox, Y-axis shows the ratio of websites which finished loading by the given loading time in each scenario; timeout = 1,000 ms)

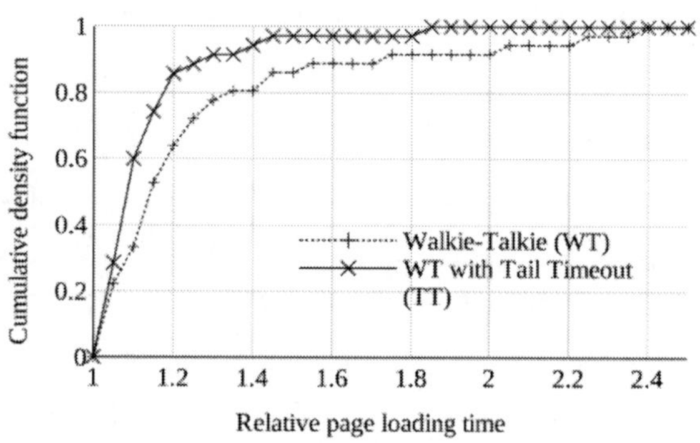

Figure 2. Page Loading Time Comparison (`domInteractive` event used; normalized to unmodified Firefox; timeout = 1,000 ms)

of 30~50%, as shown in Table I. On `nytimes.com`, the webpage could not finish loading within 300 seconds when using WT and we terminated page loading at 300 seconds. Also as expected, within the range of tail timeout values we tested, smaller value reduces page loading time.

TABLE I. LOADING TIME (DOMCOMPLETE EVENT, SECONDS) OF CERTAIN WEBSITES AT SOME DIFFERENT TAIL TIMEOUTS

Website	Unmodified	WT	TT 1,000	TT 2,000	TT 5,000
cnn.com	46.758	123.441	59.231	67.160	121.596
nytimes.com	26.262	> 300	30.335	37.370	41.306
sina.com.cn	35.094	75.404	42.075	46.530	66.359

B. *Waterfall Charts*

To further identify the source of the delay, we captured the timing information during page loading. For each request, we capture the following four timestamps during page loading.

- Requested time: the time when the browser initially wants to process the request
- Beginning time: the time when the request is released by the add-on from the "blocked" status
- Ending time: the time when the request is taken out of the "on-the-way" pool, or responded time, whichever earlier
- Responded time: the time when the response of the request is received, or the request is otherwise finished

The timing information is recorded into logging data in the WT/TT implementation add-on to the Firefox browser when requests are processed by the add-on. Between the beginning time and ending time, requests are made by the browser with its original scheduling mechanisms.

We tested `nytimes.com` and `cnn.com` for page loading, and plotted the timing data for `cnn.com` in Figure 3 and that for `nytimes.com` in Figure 4. For the sake of brevity, only some requests may be shown for multiple requests in the same half-duplex burst with similar timing characteristics, and only first few bursts are shown.

We can notice that in Figures 3a and 4a, when no TT is applied, certain requests, such as requests 7, 15 and 16 in `cnn.com` and requests 6 and 7 in `nytimes.com`, took a long time to finish, while other requests in the same burst finished within one or two seconds. The slow requests held all following requests so they cannot be sent, causing a significant delay. Recall that in Table I, smaller tail timeout values result in shorter overall page loading times. We see it here that when a long loading time happens, only a few "bottleneck" requests are blocking the whole browsing session. By using a smaller tail timeout value, the maximum delay that can be caused by a request is limited, and a shorter overall time can be expected.

We further tracked down the particular request 7 on `cnn.com`. By looking at the page source code of `cnn.com`, we noticed that request 7 was introduced in the HTML document with a `<script>` tag with the `async` attribute set. Request 7 points to https://native.sharethrough.com/assets/sfp-creative-hub-listener.js and Sharethrough is an advertisement platform. As we pointed out before, the resource fetched by the request is exactly for advertisements, and should have a relatively lower priority.

Web developers of `cnn.com` correctly specified the lower priority for these resources by using the `async` attribute, then by design, the browser tends to load these resources at a later time, and gives priority to other resources. However with WT's half-duplex communication, no other requests can be sent. This situation can be resolved only when the browser finishes the low priority request, probably after an internal timeout, or with the designed TT in the add-on, when the timeout passed, which can be earlier than the internal timeout, saving some page loading time. Similar results can be concluded from several other requests in the same shape.

In addition to the lower priority requests, there can also be requests to a slow remote server that take a relatively long time. This scenario was not observed in our experiment, but we can predict that such scenarios can happen and cause a similar delay.

C. *Defense Effectiveness*

We also want to verify that TT does not increase the fingerprintability on the traffic. We follow the approach taken to evaluate the original WT, to run k-NN attacks on the cell sequences using WT and TT, with padding (actual working scenario) and without padding (as contrast), and measure the

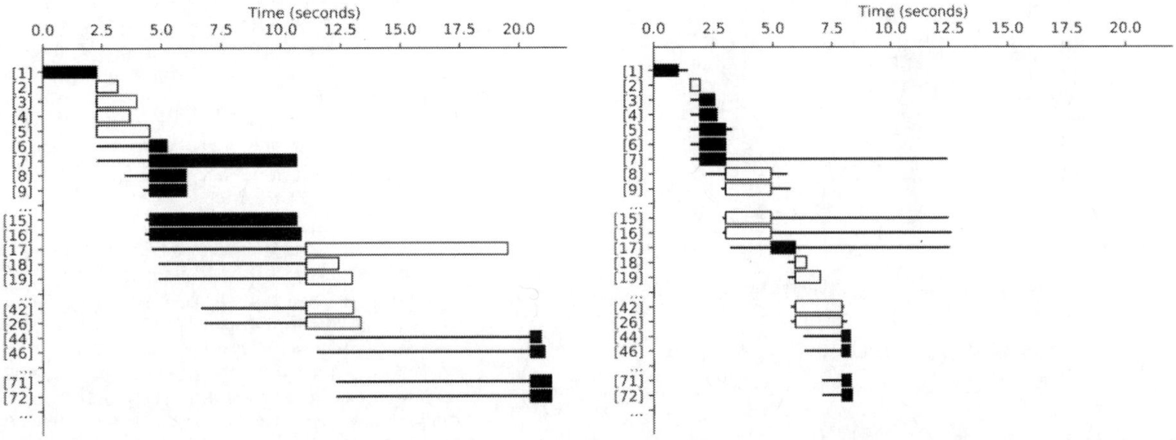

(a) Original WT (b) TT of 1 second

Figure 3. Loading `cnn.com` main page with original WT and with TT of 1 second. See [32] for URLs. (The beginning and the end of a slim line denote the Requested time and Responded time, respectively. A black or white bar shows the beginning and end times of a request during the page loading process, respectively. Neighboring requests with bars in the same color (e.g., [6]~[16]) are in the same burst. In (b), the burst containing requests [18]~[26] is not held by requests [7], [15] and [16] for long time anymore.)

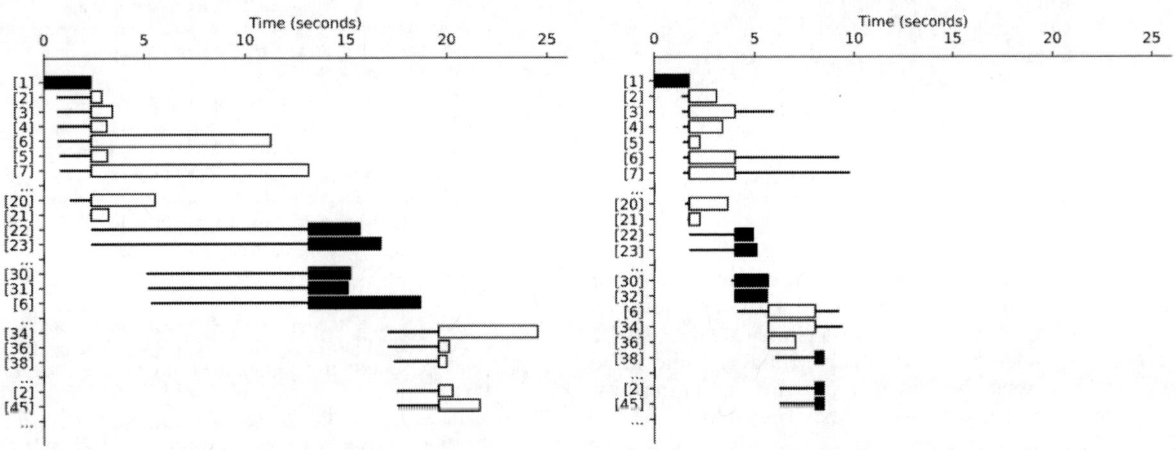

(a) Original WT (b) TT of 2 second

Figure 4. Loading `nytimes.com` main page with original WT and with TT of 2 second. See [32] for URLs. (In (b), The burst containing requests [22]~[30] is not held by requests [6] and [7] for long time anymore.)

true positive rate (TPR), false positive rate (FPR), true negative rate (TNR) and false negative rate (FNR).

In the evaluation, we count the number of true positives (TP), false positives (FP), true negatives (TN), false negatives (FN) given by the attack on the dataset, as well as total number of actual positives (P) and actual negatives (N). We use TPR = TP / P, FPR = FP / N, TNR = TN / N, FNR = FN / P. For attempted *k*-NN attacks against data sets, as described previously, we plot the TPR in Figure 5 and the TNR in Figure 6. Note that tail timeout value is applicable to TT (without and with padding) only.

In Figure 5, it is observed that TT shows a comparable defense to WT while padding improves the defense by 15~21% in both WT and TT. In Figure 6, it is observed TT (padding) shows 3~5% better defense than WT (padding) while they perform worse than the Unmodified Firefox without padding, which means to block more websites unnecessarily.

Considering TT is an extension to WT, and WT has already been evaluated with other defenses and shown a decent performance, we believe that TT is providing a good website fingerprinting defense comparable to WT.

VI. Conclusion and Future Work

In this paper, we presented a new delay-conscious defense mechanism based on WT against website fingerprinting attacks. We demonstrated that WT could significantly increase the page loading time for many popular websites, such as `cnn.com` and `nytimes.com` in practice. By analyzing the websites experiencing inflated page loading time under WT, we found that the contents marked with low priority, such as online Ads

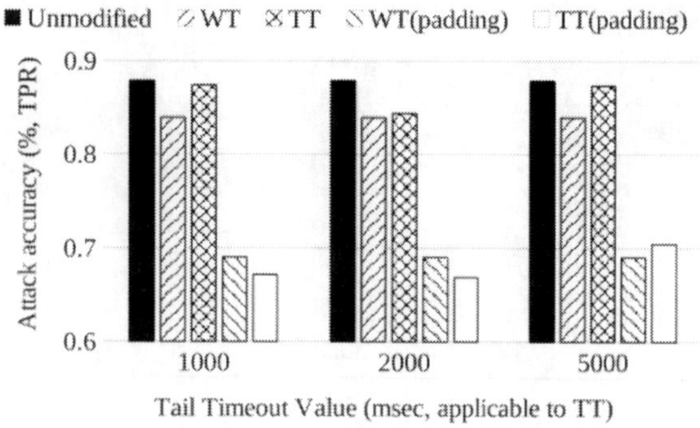

Figure 5. Attack accuracy - True Positive Rate (TPR)

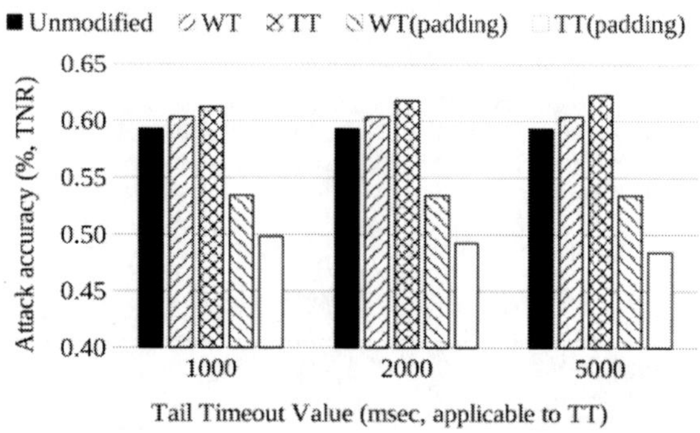

Figure 6. Attack accuracy - True Negative Rate (TNR)

could incur such delays in practice. To address the problem of increased page loading time, we proposed a TT defense as an extension of WT. Our experimental results indicate that the TT extension can significantly reduce the page loading time while keeping similar defense performance in terms of true positive and true negative ratios achieved by the original WT.

In our research, we arbitrarily selected the tail timeout values to test (1,000, 2,000, etc. milliseconds). We demonstrated that TT works with these values, while we have not identified an approach to determine the optimum values. At the same time, identifying the optimum values is currently not our goal. We are leaving this as future work, as well as investigating the trade-off between the defense effectiveness and user experience.

In the future, we also plan to try other attack models, such as naïve Bayes or the more trending deep learning based classifiers [28], [33], or on larger datasets, to evaluate the performance of TT. In addition, we plan to apply TT extension to other defense mechanisms, such as LLaMa [34] that potentially increase page load times due to the same head-of-line issue.

REFERENCES

[1] R. Deibert, J. Palfrey, R. Rohozinski, J. Zittrain, and J. G. Stein, Measuring Global Internet Filtering. MITP, 2008.

[2] C. S. Leberknight, M. Chiang, H. V. Poor, and F. Wong, "A taxonomy of internet censorship and anti-censorship," in Fifth International Conference on Fun with Algorithms, 2010.

[3] P. Winter and S. Lindskog, How the Great Firewall of China is blocking Tor. USENIX-The Advanced Computing Systems Association, 2012.

[4] Z. Wang, Y. Cao, Z. Qian, C. Song, and S. V. Krishnamurthy, "Your state is not mine: a closer look at evading stateful internet censorship," in Proceedings of the 2017 Internet Measurement Conference. ACM, 2017, pp. 114–127.

[5] "Bbc news launches 'dark web' tor mirror," BBC News, Oct 2019. [Online]. Available: https://www.bbc.com/news/technology-50150981

[6] J.-P. Verkamp and M. Gupta, "Inferring mechanics of web censorship around the world." in FOCI, 2012.

[7] R. Clayton, S. J. Murdoch, and R. N. Watson, "Ignoring the great firewall of china," in International Workshop on Privacy Enhancing Technologies. Springer, 2006, pp. 20–35.

[8] S. Aryan, H. Aryan, and J. A. Halderman, "Internet censorship in iran: A first look," in Presented as part of the 3rd USENIX Workshop on Free and Open Communications on the Internet, 2013.

[9] K. Ko, H. Lee, and S. Jang, "The internet dilemma and control policy: political and economic implications of the internet in north korea," The Korean journal of defense analysis, vol. 21, no. 3, 2009, pp. 279–295.

[10] J. Holowczak and A. Houmansadr, "Cachebrowser: Bypassing chinese censorship without proxies using cached content," in Proceedings of the 22nd ACM SIGSAC Conference on Computer and Communications Security. ACM, 2015, pp. 70–83.

[11] C. Brubaker, A. Houmansadr, and V. Shmatikov, "Cloudtransport: Using cloud storage for censorship-resistant networking," in International Symposium on Privacy Enhancing Technologies Symposium. Springer, 2014, pp. 1–20.

[12] A. Panchenko, L. Niessen, A. Zinnen, and T. Engel, "Website fingerprinting in onion routing based anonymization networks," in Proceedings of the 10th annual ACM workshop on Privacy in the electronic society. ACM, 2011, pp. 103–114.

[13] K. P. Dyer, S. E. Coull, T. Ristenpart, and T. Shrimpton, "Peek-a-boo, i still see you: Why efficient traffic analysis countermeasures fail," in 2012 IEEE symposium on security and privacy. IEEE, 2012, pp. 332–346.

[14] P. Velan, M. Čermák, P. Čeleda, and M. Drašar, "A survey of methods for encrypted traffic classification and analysis," International Journal of Network Management, vol. 25, no. 5, 2015, pp. 355–374.

[15] A. Panchenko, F. Lanze, J. Pennekamp, T. Engel, A. Zinnen, M. Henze, and K. Wehrle, "Website fingerprinting at internet scale," in NDSS, 2016.

[16] T. Wang, X. Cai, R. Nithyanand, R. Johnson, and I. Goldberg, "Effective attacks and provable defenses for website fingerprinting," in 23rd USENIX Security Symposium (USENIX Security 14), 2014, pp. 143–157.

[17] R. Ensafi, J. Knockel, G. Alexander, and J. R. Crandall, "Detecting intentional packet drops on the internet via tcp/ip side channels," in International Conference on Passive and Active Network Measurement. Springer, 2014, pp. 109–118.

[18] T. Wang and I. Goldberg, "Walkie-talkie: An efficient defense against passive website fingerprinting attacks," in 26th USENIX Security Symposium (USENIX Security 17), 2017, pp. 1375–1390.

[19] R. Dingledine, N. Mathewson, and P. Syverson, "Tor: The second-generation onion router," Naval Research Lab Washington DC, Tech. Rep., 2004.

[20] M. Juarez, M. Imani, M. Perry, C. Diaz, and M. Wright, "Toward an efficient website fingerprinting defense," in European Symposium on Research in Computer Security. Springer, 2016, pp. 27–46.

[21] T. Wang and I. Goldberg, "Improved website fingerprinting on tor," in Proceedings of the 12th ACM workshop on Workshop on privacy in the electronic society. ACM, 2013, pp. 201–212.

[22] ——, "On realistically attacking tor with website fingerprinting," Proceedings on Privacy Enhancing Technologies, vol. 2016, no. 4, 2016, pp. 21–36.

[23] V. Shmatikov and M.-H. Wang, "Timing analysis in low-latency mix networks: Attacks and defenses," in European Symposium on Research in Computer Security. Springer, 2006, pp. 18–33.

[24] C. V. Wright, S. E. Coull, and F. Monrose, "Traffic morphing: An efficient defense against statistical traffic analysis." in NDSS, vol. 9. Citeseer, 2009.

[25] X. Cai, R. Nithyanand, T. Wang, R. Johnson, and I. Goldberg, "A systematic approach to developing and evaluating website fingerprinting defenses," in Proceedings of the 2014 ACM SIGSAC Conference on Computer and Communications Security. ACM, 2014, pp. 227–238.

[26] X. Cai, X. C. Zhang, B. Joshi, and R. Johnson, "Touching from a distance: Website fingerprinting attacks and defenses," in Proceedings of the 2012 ACM conference on Computer and communications security. ACM, 2012, pp. 605–616.

[27] [Online]. Available: http://s3.amazonaws.com/alexa-static/top-1m.csv.zip

[28] S. E. Oh, S. Sunkam, and N. Hopper, "p1-fp: Extraction, classification, and prediction of website fingerprints with deep learning," Proceedings on Privacy Enhancing Technologies, vol. 2019, no. 3, 2019, pp. 191–209.

[29] "Selenium - web browser automation." [Online]. Available: https://www.seleniumhq.org

[30] "mozilla/geckodriver: Webdriver for firefox." [Online]. Available: https://github.com/mozilla/geckodriver/releases

[31] J. Hayes and G. Danezis, "k-fingerprinting: A robust scalable website fingerprinting technique," in 25th USENIX Security Symposium (USENIX Security 16), 2016, pp. 1187–1203.

[32] J. Liang, C. Yu, and K. Suh, "Delay-conscious defense against fingerprinting attacks," Cleveland State University, Tech. Rep., 2020.

[33] P. Sirinam, M. Imani, M. Juarez, and M. Wright, "Deep fingerprinting: Undermining website fingerprinting defenses with deep learning," in Proceedings of the 2018 ACM SIGSAC Conference on Computer and Communications Security. ACM, 2018, pp. 1928–1943.

[34] G. Cherubin, J. Hayes, and M. Juarez, "Website fingerprinting defenses at the application layer," Proceedings on Privacy Enhancing Technologies, vol. 2017, no. 2, 2017, pp. 186–203.

Implementation and Deployment of a Server at the Edge Using OpenStack Components

Carlo Vitucci
Technology Management
Ericsson AB
Stockholm, Sweden
e-mail: carlo.vitucci@ericsson.com

Tommaso Cucinotta, Riccardo Mancini, Luca Abeni
Real-Time System Laboratory (RETIS)
Scuola Superiore Sant'Anna
Pisa, Italy
e-mail: firstname.lastname@santannapisa.it

***Abstract*—As the 5th telecommunication Generation (5G) deployments are spreading around via various mobile operators, the capabilities behind 5G are becoming more and more understandable. Infrastructure vendors, operators, and end users now have a clear picture of the 5G potential and, for that reason, the research and the development of 5G are surely continuing. The one-to-one mapping between 5G and Software Defined Network - Network Function Virtualization (SDN-NFV) architecture is not in discussion, but the impact of porting SDN-NFV into the Radio Access Network (RAN) is still under investigation. Sometimes, the RAN requirements set strong limitations even in the basic hardware and software setup. For example, the most complete and very well integrated SDN-NFV infrastructure distributions require specific hardware capabilities in terms of available nodes, in contrast with the RAN requirement to be economic, power consumption limited and with limited overhead due to operating system and middleware cost. For that reason, this study uses only a minimal set of OpenStack components in order to evaluate what is the minimal hardware capability needed to set up a basic, but fully working environment for NFV, highlighting the pros and cons of embracing a solution solely based on standard OpenStack components.**

Keywords-5G; RAN; SDN-NFV, edge computing; server at the edge; Service deployment; OpenStack, E2E deployment.

I. Introduction

2019 is the year in which 5G started to be a practical and viable commercial solution available to mobile operators [1]. The importance of 5G architecture is now widely understood and shared: the new technology has the potential to drive economic growth. Its possibilities are so broad that we probably cannot even imagine what and how many new services will be possible. Today, all operators see 5G as the enabler for full connectivity between people, for the creation of the Internet of Things (IoT) and as a startup for the so-called Industry 4.0. However, although this is already very stimulating and large enough to justify the investment in the new architecture and infrastructure, 5G is beyond all of that. Smart cities, Industrial IoT, augmented reality, autonomous transport, digital health, are just some of the countless commercial opportunities that could be possible when 5G will be fully deployed. To allow such an enormous commercial opportunity to become real, it is necessary to be able to count on a very well-defined ecosystem, where a new approach to the network is needed, including (RAN), to address the wide distribution of functions, applications, and data. The distribution of services requires an End-to-End architecture (E2E) where, thanks to a high-level programmability and "software-ability" of the architecture, it will be possible to offer new advanced services to consumers by dedicating portions of the network. In this mode, it will be possible to guarantee precise levels of service quality and to respond to the increasingly demanding application needs of a wide variety of sectors (Figure 1).

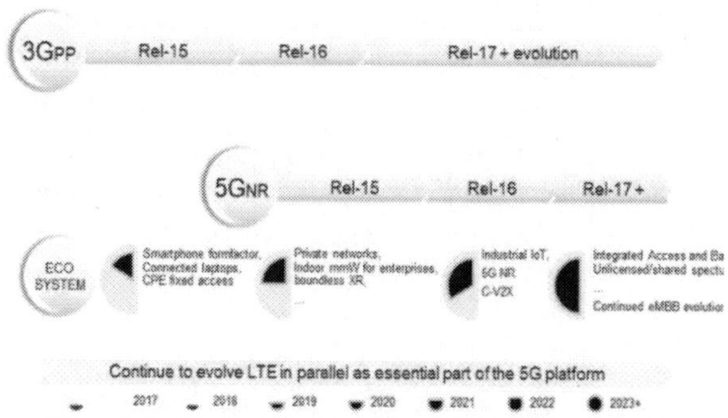

Figure 1. 5G Standards and Commercialization Time Line [2]

SDN-NFV is the most suitable system architecture to support the necessary 5G ecosystem [3]. To make it successful, however, the solution must rely on an NFV infrastructure (NFVI) optimized to support the rapid implementation of new generation services with low latency and a varied and distributed group of terminals and devices. As mentioned in our previous work [4], the infrastructure shall be designed to remove inefficiencies in the modern cloud due to a distance between the design of high-level cloud management/orchestration and low-level kernel/hypervisor mechanisms. The two worlds should talk to each other, providing richer abstractions to describe the low-level mechanisms and to automatically map higher-level descriptions and abstractions to configuration and performance tuning options available within operating systems and kernels (both host and guest), as well as hypervisors.

The rest of this paper is organized as follows. Section II introduces the Network Operating System definition and explains the decision to use OpenStack components. Section III describes the hardware environment used in the implementation phase. Section IV addresses the software environment setup. Section V goes into finer details for OpenStack components selection. Section VI and Section VII emphases the set of for network and storage respectively, while Section VIII lines out the deployment configuration actions needed. Eventually, Section IX shows the deployment sequence. Section X points to the hardware minimal capability as those used by the experiment and Section XI discusses some conclusions.

II. Network OS

The Network Operating System (NOS) is, by definition, the horizontal server network resources controller in a distributed system. It is responsible to provide a virtualized (programmable) environment and the connected control part. Describing the structure of the SDN-NFV architecture is not one of the purposes of this paper, but related references are easily available [5][6]. In the SDN-NFV architecture, the NOS is spread between NFVI and Virtual Infrastructure Manager (VIM), as graphically shown in Figure 2.

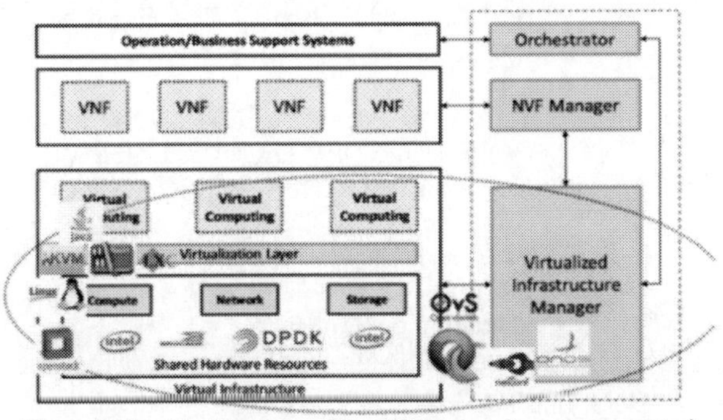

Figure 2. Graphical location of the NOS: network resources control and allocation location in the SDN-NFV architecture are spread between NFVI and VIM

"De facto", commercial solutions use OpenStack to deploy virtualized environments. OpenStack is an "always evolving" project built over several components. These can easily be added or removed from the configuration of a deployment, optionally plugging other open-source components/agents, like OpenDayLight, NetConf, OpenFlow and others [7]. For any next-generation mobile system, a mandatory requirement is to be a fully integrated ecosystem that, independently of specific vendors, can be orchestrated by a (logically) centralized controller. Assuming for the RAN the server configuration described in [3], in the following we describe an OpenStack deployment over a few different boards constituting a simple edge-computing test-bed.

III. Hardware Environment Setup

Hardware environment set up has been done considering some main rules:

1. It shall be, as much as possible, based on commercial hardware and have limited cost;
2. It shall consist of a basic set of hardware components and boards;
3. It shall be suitable for housing a NOS fully based on OpenStack components;

The first rule has been set considering the capillary, widely distributed, explosion of computer deployment close to the end user, into the edge of the network [8][9]: minimizing the cost of the deployment looks like a strong requirement for the success of the 5G implementation.

The second rule has been set to overcome the limits the most popular OpenStack distributions have. For example, Open Platform for NFV (OPNFV), a complete solution for development and evolution of NFV components across various open-source ecosystems, requires a significant number of controller and specific hardware characteristics for the system development board [10]. OPNFV is surely a complete and powerful solution, but, in this work, we are interested in understanding the bare minimum set of hardware characteristics necessary for implementing a NOS based on open software.

Figure 3. Hardware Environment Set up

The third rule is a practical decision (software availability) and it is not limiting the result achieved in the lab. With the only exception of the radio interface board, for which it is possible to use 5G-ready existing radio product solutions, the server at the edge has been built (see Figure 3) as one compute node (CP), one networking node (NET), one controller node (CTRL) and an Ethernet switch (SW). The development & deployment environment is represented by another board, the developer node, that will act also as containers repository site (DB).

TABLE I. HARDWARE COMPONENTS FOR THE NODE

Object	Vendor & Type
Motherboard	GIGABYTE H310M-A
CPU	Intel Core i3 8100
Disk	WD Green3D Nand 240 GB
RAM	DDR4 Corsair Vengeance 32 GB
Eth. daughterboard	Intel X710-DA2
Power	SFX Power 2
Router	Netgear ProFase GS108

The hardware characteristics of the nodes are summarized in Table I.

IV. SOFTWARE ENVIRONMENT SETUP

The software environment set up has been done considering only open-source components imposing minimal requirements on the needed underlying hardware. The software shall be able to run into the minimal set of boards used for the server at the edge concept and it shall be fully based on open-source packaging. For the servers at the edge, we chose to use a Linux operating system, Ubuntu [11] distribution. The Deployment Board uses a Desktop version while the other boards use a Server distribution (see Figure 4).

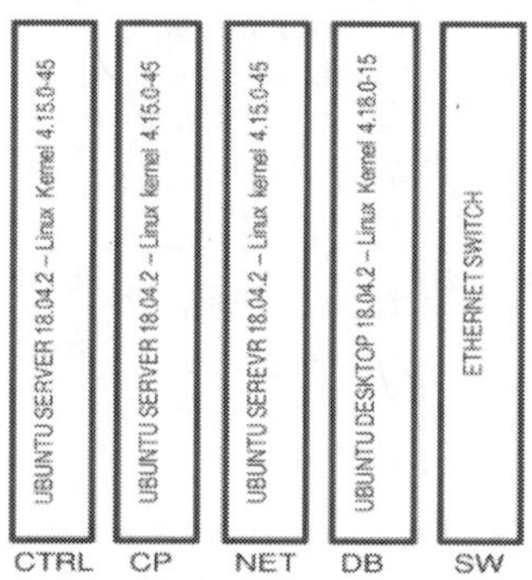

Figure 4. Hardware Environment Set up

The latest 18.04.2 Ubuntu Long Term Support (LTS) is used. Kernel version is 4.15 for server and 4.18 for Desktop. During the test phase, the node has been regularly upgraded with the Ubuntu standard updates using the apt package manager [12]. At the time when this paper has been written, the latest working update was:

DB: Linux 4.18.0-24-generic #25~18.04.1-Ubuntu SMP

OTHERS: Linux 4.15.0-28-generic #64-Ubuntu SMP

V. INFRASTRUCTURE SETUP

The most complete and up-to-date among available open-source distributions of OpenStack for the infrastructure is probably OPNFV [13], an SDN-NFV distribution fully integrated with the latest technologies, for example, Open Network Automation Platform (ONAP) [14] and Open RAN (O-RAN) [15]. However, the OPNFV hardware requirements are not suitable for an edge-computing proof of concept (PoC), as it requires a minimum of 2 controller nodes, 3 compute nodes, and a minimum of 64 gigabyte (GB) Random-Access Memory (RAM) mounted. For that reason, the PoC building of the server at the edge has been fully based on self-building OpenStack components and we started from the suggested configuration for containers handling [16].

The OpenStack components List is (Figure 5):

Basic Infrastructure components (mandatory)

- Nova, to provide compute instances;
- Glance, to provide an image service;
- Keystone, to provide Application Program Interface (API) client authentication;

Extended Infrastructure components (mandatory)

- Neutron, to provide network connectivity;
- Swift, to provide an objects store service;
- Cinder, to provide block storage and volume service;

Extended infrastructure components (optional)

- Kuryr, network plugin to provide networking services to Docker containers;

Optional enhancements

- Horizon, Dashboard to provide a web-based user interface;
- Grafana, to provide a metrics dashboard;
- Cyborg, to support possibly available accelerations: Graphics Processing Unit (GPU), Data Plane Development Kit (DPDK), etc...

Consumption services

- Tacker, to provide generic VNF Manager (VNFM) and NFV Orchestrator (NFVO);
- Kolla-Ansible, to deploy OpenStack components in Docker containers using Ansible;
- Zun, to provide API for launching and managing containers;
- Magnum, to provide container orchestration services;
- Heat, to provide template-based orchestration.

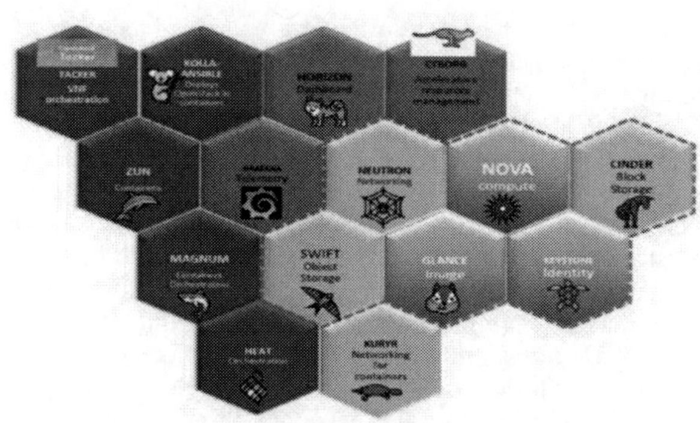

Figure 5. Selected OpenStack Package

Kolla-Ansible [17] has been conveniently used to ease the deployment of the various OpenStack components. It is worth to mention here that the selected set of OpenStack components do not constitute necessarily an optimal selection, as an evaluation or comparison of the possible optional components was not in the goal of the study described in this paper.

Kolla-Ansible comes with a minimal set of software requirements and dependencies on other software components. The list of install dependencies is available in [18].

During the set-up and configuration phase, various issues have been tackled and the following workarounds applied:

- We had to use the development version of Kolla-Ansible because the released version seemed to have issues in the container deployment phase (specifically, raising the MariaDB container didn't work).
- The Internet Protocol (IP) check for services was failing due to the lack of configured passwords. This was fixed by adding password roles in the /etc/sudoers file.
- We needed to install docker-ce instead of docker 12.1.0*. Note that the deployment board is used as a local Docker registry in our environment.
- Create a link -s -L to easy_install in /usr/local/bin/ because it doesn't exist in the installed distribution. You need to compile and install python-3.7 locally.
- During the deployment phase, Koll-Ansible uses frequently Docker commands. This might generate permission denied alarm. In order to remove that issue, it is enough to add own user to the Docker group.
  sudo gpasswd -a $USER docker
  newgrp docker
- the local Docker registry address needed to be added to the list of allowed insecure registries in the Docker daemon configuration file (/etc/docker/daemon.json).

The Docker daemon uses the HTTP_PROXY, HTTPS_PROXY and NO_PROXY environment variables. Those variables cannot be configured using the daemon.json file. They can be set in an http-proxy.conf file in the /etc/system/docker.service.d directory. The definition of the NO_PROXY allows contacting the internal Docker register without proxying.

VI. Network Setup

Kolla-Ansible needs two IP addresses per board: the networking setup for OpenStack is one of the most complicated actions to do, but Kolla-Ansible as a deployment tool is simplifying a lot. We let Kolla-Ansible set neutron for us, with the cost of the setup of two Virtual Local-Area Network (VLAN) per board. Note that our server and desktop distributions are not the same. The server is using netplan while the desktop is still counting on ifupdown. In order to manage the network using the same setting, ifupdown has been installed in our Ubuntu Server nodes. Once ifupdown has been loaded, the vlan configuration could be done by editing the /etc/network/interface file.

```
auto eno1
iface eno1 inet dhcp

auto eno1.1
iface eno1.1 inet static
        address 11.22.33.44/23
        netmask 255.255.254.0
        gateway XX.YY.ZZ.1
        vlan-raw-device eno1

auto eno1.2
iface eno1.2 inet static
        address 11.22.33.55/23
        netmask 255.255.254.0
        gateway 11.22.33.1
        vlan-raw-device eno1

auto lo
iface lo inet loopback
```

Eventually, the vlan kernel module is installed to keep network setting permanent:

sudo su -c 'echo "8021q" >> /etc/modules

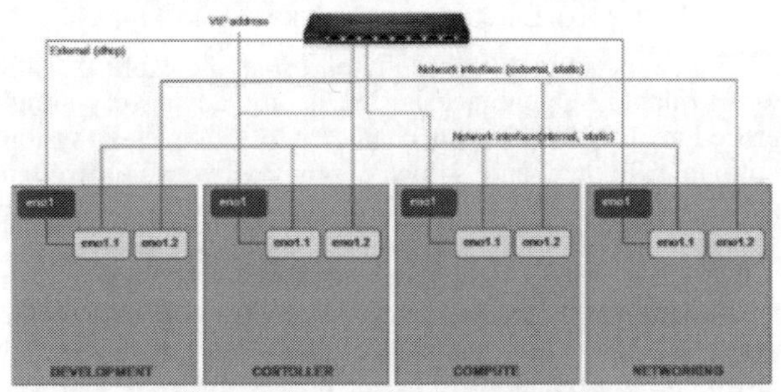

Figure 6. Server at the edge connectivity

The networking is done to have demo-networking, internal, public networking, external and VIP networking, neutron keepalive control, as shown in Figure 6.

VII. Storage Setup

Swift requires block devices to be available for storage. To prepare a disk for using a swift storage device, a special partition name and filesystem label needed to be added. Moreover, before running Swift, we had to generate rings, which are binary compressed files that at a high level let the various Swift services know where data is in the cluster. Cinder also needs a dedicated Logical Volume Management (LVM) physical volume group. Note the partition for swift and Cinder are strongly recommended (see Figure 7).

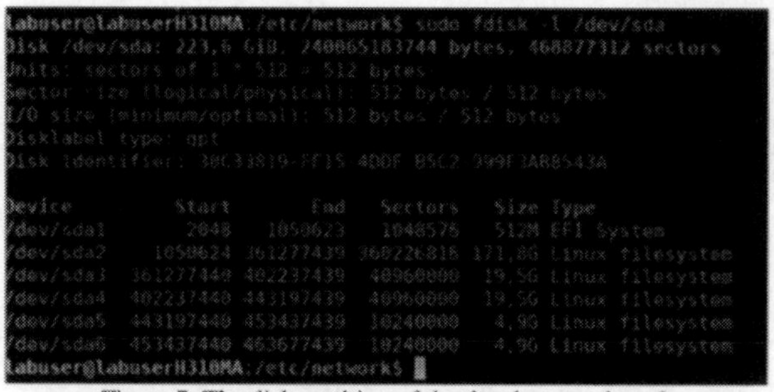

Figure 7. The disk partition of the development board

The Swift and Cinder disk partitions are required where the system storage is hosted; as described in the infrastructure setup, this is the development board in this study. Note that the size of the partitions is not optimized, and the correct size should be defined or investigated in advance for the product deployment case. Most likely, a real production environment needs bigger disks/partitions.

VIII. Kolla-Ansible Configuration Files

The most attractive benefit of using the Kolla-Ansible tool to deploy OpenStack is that it provides a very simple procedure to identify and characterize the overall system, both in hardware and software point of view. OpenStack package components set, network setup, hardware inventory and storage definitions are defined and managed using only two files: the so-called "globals.yml" and the "multinode.yml" configuration file. Both of them are available as a template in the Kolla-Ansible distribution/installation file. To match the real hardware setup and use the selected OpenStack components, the customization of them is straightforward: remove or add a comment to existing lines.

"multinode.yml" is the Ansible inventory file and configures the connection parameters for the hosts (i.e., IP/hostname, username, and password) and its services need to be installed in each of them. This is done by defining which groups each host belongs to. The most important groups are control, network, compute, monitoring and storage. Kolla-Ansible will take care of installing the required services to each host depending on the groups they belong to. In order to match the hardware setup as described before, the multimode configuration looks like below:

```
[control]
11.22.33.11 ansible_user=user_name
ansible_password=user_passwd ansible_become=true
[network]
11.22.33.22 ansible_user=user_name
ansible_password=user_passwd ansible_become=true
[compute]
11.22.33.44 ansible_user=user_name
ansible_password=user_passwd ansible_become=true
[monitoring]
#select the control
11.22.33.44
[storage]
localhost        ansible_connection=local
become=true
[deployment]
localhost        ansible_connection=local
become=true
```

The "globals.yml" configuration file is used for network configuration, OpenStack package definition, certification, repository, and storage assignment. According to the software setup defined previously, for the PoC of the server at the edge, it looks like below:

```
# You can use this file to override _any_ variable
throughout Kolla.
# Additional options can be found in the
# 'kolla-ansible/ansible/group_vars/all.yml' file.
Default value of all the
# commented parameters are shown here, To override
the default value uncomment
# the parameter and change its value.
###############
# Kolla options
###############
# Valid options are [ COPY_ONCE, COPY_ALWAYS ]
#config_strategy: "COPY_ALWAYS"
# Valid options are ['centos', 'debian',
'oraclelinux', 'rhel', 'ubuntu']
kolla_base_distro: "ubuntu"
# Valid options are [ binary, source ]
kolla_install_type: "source"
# Valid option is Docker repository tag
openstack_release: "rocky"
# Location of configuration overrides
#node_custom_config: "/etc/kolla/config"
# This should be a VIP, an unused IP on your
network that will float between
# the hosts running keepalived for high-
availability. If you want to run an
# All-In-One without haproxy and keepalived, you
can set enable_haproxy to no
# in "OpenStack options" section, and set this
value to the IP of your
# 'network_interface' as set in the Networking
section below.
kolla_internal_vip_address: "XX.YY.ZZ.VIP"
```

Where Kolla_internal_vip_address could be, for example, 11.22.33.99.

```
################
# Docker options
################
# Below is an example of a private repository with
authentication. Note the
# Docker registry password can also be set in the
passwords.yml file.
docker_registry: "XX.YY.ZZ.DEV:5000"
#docker_namespace: "regionone"
#docker_registry_username: "sam"
#docker_registry_password:
"correcthorsebatterystaple"
```

In our case, docker_registry is hosted on the development board, for example, 11.22.33.55.

```
##############################
# Neutron - Networking Options
##############################
# This interface is what all your api services will
be bound to by default.
# Additionally, all vxlan/tunnel and storage
network traffic will go over this
# interface by default. This interface must contain
an IPv4 address.
# It is possible for hosts to have non-matching
```

```
names of interfaces - these can
# be set in an inventory file per host or per group
or stored separately, see
#
http://docs.ansible.com/ansible/intro_inventory.htm
l
# Yet another way to workaround the naming problem
is to create a bond for the
# interface on all hosts and give the bond name
here. Similar strategy can be
# followed for other types of interfaces.
network_interface: "eno1.1"
# These can be adjusted for even more
customization. The default is the same as
# the 'network_interface'. These interfaces must
contain an IPv4 address.
#kolla_external_vip_interface: "{{
network_interface }}"
api_interface: "{{ network_interface }}"
#storage_interface: "{{ network_interface }}"
#cluster_interface: "{{ network_interface }}"
#tunnel_interface: "{{ network_interface }}"
#dns_interface: "{{ network_interface }}"
# This is the raw interface given to neutron as its
external network port. Even
# though an IP address can exist on this interface,
it will be unusable in most
# configurations. It is recommended this interface
not be configured with any IP
# addresses for that reason.
neutron_external_interface: "eno1.2"
# Valid options are [ openvswitch, linuxbridge,
vmware_nsxv, vmware_nsxv3, vmware_dvs, opendaylight
]
# if vmware_nsxv3 is selected, enable_openvswitch
MUST be set to "no" (default is yes)
#neutron_plugin_agent: "openvswitch"
# Valid options are [ internal, infoblox ]
#neutron_ipam_driver: "internal"
###################
# OpenStack options
###################
# Use these options to set the various log levels
across all OpenStack projects
# Valid options are [ True, False ]
#openstack_logging_debug: "False"
# Valid options are [ none, novnc, spice, rdp ]
#nova_console: "novnc"
# OpenStack services can be enabled or disabled
with these options
enable_cinder: "yes"
enable_cinder_backend_lvm: "yes"
enable_collectd: "yes"
enable_gnocchi: "yes"
enable_grafana: "yes"
enable_heat: "yes"
enable_horizon: "yes"
enable_horizon_magnum: "yes"
enable_horizon_tacker: "yes"
enable_horizon_zun: "yes"
enable_influxdb: "yes"
enable_kuryr: "yes"
enable_magnum: "yes"
enable_swift: "yes"
enable_telegraf: "yes"
enable_tacker: "yes"
enable_zun: "yes"
########################
# Glance - Image Options
########################
glance_backend_ceph: "no"
glance_backend_swift: "yes"
glance_enable_rolling_upgrade: "no"
#################################
# Cinder - Block Storage Options
#################################
cinder_backup_driver: "swift"
#################################
# Swift - Object Storage Options
#################################
swift_devices_match_mode: "strict"
swift_devices_name: "KOLLA_SWIFT_DATA"
```

IX. Deployment Sequence

Once the environment is ready, the deployment is straightforward. The very first time it is suggested to use the "pull" command before "deploy" to populate the local registry with the needed containers. In fact, the local registry is still empty. Pull will fail, pointing to the container still missing. The missing container could be easily added following the sequence:

```
docker pull
"this_openstack_component:rocky"
docker image tag
"this_openstack_component:rocky"
11.22.33.55:5000/this_openstack_componen
t:rocky
docker push
11.22.33.55:5000/this_openstack_componen
t
```

once the local repository is completed, the "pull" command becomes optional and deploy is possible using only three commands: bootstrap-servers, prechecks and deploy.

Figure 8. The Kolla-ansible deploy successfully result

```
sudo ./kolla-ansible -i multinode
bootstrap-servers
sudo ./kolla-ansible -i multinode
prechecks
(sudo ./kolla-ansible -i multinode pull)
sudo ./kolla-ansible -i multinode deploy
```

The result is shown in Figure 8.

After the deployment, a few commands are needed for the very first set up of the manager, like the definition of allowed volume size, basic test container image, and environment definitions.

```
./kolla-ansible -i multinode post-deploy
source /etc/kolla/admin-openrc.sh
./init-runonce
```

At the end of the sequence, the deployment has been done and the server is ready and can be used.

Figure 9. OpenStack Horizon Dashboard

Figure 9 shows the result of the deployment using the OpenStack standard dashboard (Horizon).

X. RESULT

It is interesting to analyze the distribution of the container executed by Kolla-Ansible deploy action. That investigation is useful to understand which and how resources are consumed by the infrastructure itself and so how heavy could be the cost of the SDN-NFV in the radio node. The "docker ps" is a command that could be used per any board to collect the list of running containers (see Figure 10).

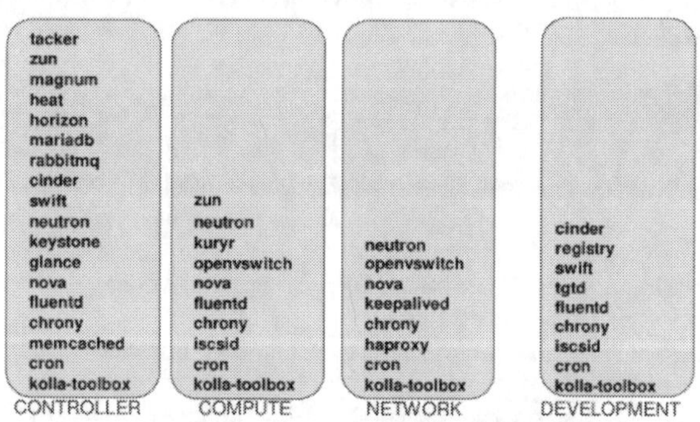

Figure 10. OpenStack Components distribution

The controller is the most populated board. This is not a problem. The experiment goal was to understand the minimal set of hardware resources needed by the Server at the edge of the network, but the Compute board usage is the most critical, since the Radio Interface boards could be connected to the node as "radio devote" compute board (as described in [3]). For that reason, this study is not focusing to the Controller or Network board resources usage, but to the Compute board. Central Processor Unit (CPU), RAM and Disk usage in compute board have been measured. The CPU load is normally less than 1%, disk usage is around 17GB (8% of available storage) and RAM usage is about 770 megabyte (MB) of the available 32GB. A comparison with minimal hardware requested by OPNFV is interesting:

TABLE II. COMPUTE BOARD MINIMAL HARDWARE REQUIREMENTS

Object	*Test Lab*	*OPNFV*
CPU socket	1	2
Disk (GB)	20	256
RAM (GB)	0,7	16

Managing and supervising containers is done using standard OpenStack Horizon and Grafana Dashboards.

XI. CONCLUSION

Working directly with OpenStack components instead of using an SDN-NFV package distribution, like OPNFV, allowed us to have a better idea of the minimal hardware resources setup at the cost of the maintenance. It is not so simple to verify the compatibility between different OpenStack components versions and which patches/modifications might be needed. The availability and correctness of Opensource documentations, in our point of view, need to improve. Components cross-reference dependencies, patches and exception descriptions are not always easy to find and clear. Whenever available, most of the documentation referred to old Linux/OpenStack releases. It looks like different projects are moving forward totally independently from each other, with the result that document begins to be obsolete within 6 months and the interplay among different components needs plenty of documentation review and corrections. This impacted on the extended time needed to achieve a correct set up of the software environment in the experimental study, and that is surely not an optimal condition. If the cost of the maintenance is so relevant, then integrated SDN-NFV distributions have their own meaning from a product point of view. Yet, they are too expensive in terms of the minimal set of hardware resource requirement. However, components like ONAP, O-RAN or the latest delivery of Kubernetes well integrated with the NOS have a huge value. This results probably in enough reasons for considering SDN-NFV integrated distributions while searching for a more product-oriented solution. The Opensource community should try to have a minimal distribution package for the SDN-NFV integrated distribution, more careful to the value of the hardware resources availability. Indeed, this will be a key factor to use SDN-NFV very close to the End User.

REFERENCES

[1] Ericsson, "Ericsson Mobility Report," Jun 2019, Rev. A, available from https://www.ericsson.com/en/mobility-report/ reports/june-2019 [retrieved: Sep, 2019].

[2] M. Branda, "Acceleration of the 5G NR global standards gains industry momentum," Sep, 2016, OnQ Blog, Qualcomm, available from https://www.qualcomm.com/news/onq/2016/09/27/acceleration-5g-nr-global-standard-gains-industry-momentum [retrieved: Sep, 2019].

[3] C. Vitucci and A. Larsson, "Flexible 5G Edge Server for Multi Industry Service Network," International Journal on Advances in Networks and Services, Vol. 10, no. 3-4, 2017, pp. 55.65, ISSN: 1942-2644.

[4] T. Cucinotta, L. Abeni, M. Marinoni and C. Vitucci, "The importance of being OS-aware in Performance Aspects of Cloud Computing Research," in Proceedings of the 8th International Conference on

Cloud Computing and Services Science (CLOSER 2018), Mar, 2018, pp. 626-633

[5] 5GPPP Architecture Working Group, "View on 5G Architecture," version 2.0, December 2017, available from https://5g-ppp.eu/wp-content/uploads/2018/01/5G-PPP-5G-Architecture-White-Paper-Jan-2018-v2.0.pdf [retrieved: Nov, 2018].

[6] ETSI paper, "Network Functions Virtualisation (NFV); Use Cases," ETSI GS NFV 001, v.1.1.1, 2013, available from https://www.etsi.org/deliver/etsi_gs/nfv/001_099/001/01.01.01_60/gs_nfv001v010101p.pdf [retrieved: Sep, 2019]

[7] OpenStack Foundation, OpenStack Community Software Reference Page, available from https://www.openstack.org/software/ [retrieved: Sep, 2019]

[8] R. Vilalta, A. Mayoral, R. Casellas, R. Martínez and R. Muñoz, "Experimental demonstration of distributed multi-tenant cloud/fog and heterogeneous SDN/NFV orchestration for 5G services," 2016 European Conference on Networks and Communications (EuCNC), Athens, 2016, pp. 52-56

[9] H. M. Abdel-Atty, R. S. Alhumaima, S. M. Abuelenin and E. A. Anowr, "Performance Analysis of Fog-Based Radio Access Networks," in IEEE Access, vol. 7, 2019, pp. 106195-106203.

[10] OPNFV Licensed webpage, "OPNFV Fuel Installation instruction", chapter 2.4 Hardware Requirements, available from https://opnfv-fuel.readthedocs.io/en/latest/release/installation/installation.instruction.html [retrieved; Jan, 2020]

[11] Canonical Ltd. Ubuntu, Ubuntu reference page, available from https://ubuntu.com/ [retrieved: Sep, 2019]

[12] Ismail Baydan, "Apt ad Apt-Get Tutorial With Examples", Poftut online tutorial, latest update by Nov. 2019, available from https://www.poftut.com/apt-and-apt-get-tutorial-with-examples/ [retrieved: Jan, 2020]

[13] OPNFV Project a Series of LF Projects, OPNFV reference page, available from https://www.opnfv.org/ [retrieved: Jan, 2020]

[14] ONAP a Series of LF Projects, ONAP reference page, available from https://www.onap.org/ [retrieved: Jan, 2020]

[15] O-RAN Alliance e.V., "Operator Defined Next Generation RAN Architecture and Interfaces", 2019, available from https://www.o-ran.org/ [retrieved: Jan, 2020]

[16] OpenStack Foundation, "Container Optimized sample configuration", available from https://www.openstack.org/software/sample-configs/#container-optimized [retrieved: Jan, 2020]

[17] OpenStack Foundation, "Deploys OpenStack in Containers using Ansible", available from https://www.openstack.org/software/releases/stein/components/kolla-ansible [retrieved: Jan, 2020]

[18] OpenStack Foundation, "Quick Start how to deploy OpenStack using Kolla and Kolla-Ansible on bare metal servers or virtual machine", available from https://docs.openstack.org/kolla-ansible/ocata/user/quickstart.html [retrieved: Jan, 2020]

Provisioning Using Opendaylight OVSDB Into Openstack: Experiments

Alexandru Eftimie,
University POLITEHNICA of Bucharest, Bucharest, Romania
Department of Telecommunication, University "Politehnica" of Bucharest, , Romania
E-mail: alexandru.eftimie@gmail.com

Eugen Borcoci
University POLITEHNICA of Bucharest, Bucharest, Romania
Department of Telecommunication, University "Politehnica" of Bucharest, , Romania
E-mail: eugen.borcoci@elcom.pub.ro

Abstract **– Network function virtualization (NFV) and Software Defined Networking (SDN) are complementary technologies that support flexible development or virtual machines in various environments, e.g., multi-tenant / multi-domain. While SDN separates the architectural control plane, versus data plane, NFV implements a lot of functions (that traditionally have been performed by dedicated boxes), by software – using virtualized network functions (VNF). There are still open research issues in both SDN and NFV, especially related to their cooperation and integration. This paper presents an experiment of deploying networks and virtual machines (VMs) using Openstack and Open vSwitch Database Management Protocol (OVSDB) from Opendaylight project. The study is oriented towards implementation aspects. Its main objective is to deploy an Openstack controller, an Opendaylight controller and two compute nodes and to create on top of existing infrastructure several networks and illustrate how this is automatically achieved and how overlay networks can coexist. The paper describes step by step how to configure controllers, how connectivity is achieved and how OpenFlow is used to forward packets.**

Keywords-Openstack; Network Function Virtualization; Software Defined Network; OpenFlow.

I. INTRODUCTION

In traditional networking architecture, the IP datagrams are carried and processed by network nodes that are individual boxes, each performing a specific function, such as forwarding, switching, filtering, firewall. These network boxes bring costs, capital expenditure (CAPEX) and operating expenses (OPEX), and there is no flexibility in using them as the network is growing and, most important, changing.

Software Defined Networking (SDN) separates network control and data forwarding functions leading to centralized and programmable network control. SDN architecture has several main components such as: data plane consisting in network resources for forwarding traffic; control plane implemented as SDN controller, which manages the network resources; network applications plane. The interface between the forwarding and the control plane is the "*southbound*" interface, and the interface between the control plane and applications is the *"northbound"* [1].

Network function virtualization (NFV) aims to implement by software many functions, that traditionally have been implemented as expensive hardware-software combinations. Recent standards define the NFV architecture and also how to implement different virtualized network functions (NFV) in a virtual environment – to replace the traditional dedicated boxes which performed individual functions. The SDN and NFV are complementary techonologies, usable independently or in cooperation. While NFV replaces hardware network elements, SDN deals with replacement of network protocols, bringing centralized control. [2]

By decoupling the two planes (SDN) and by using the function virtualization (NFV) many borders of traditional networks can be overcome. All functions that are currently delivered by hardware boxes will be implemented in software, the deployments can be done automatically, on demand or by reacting to network changes.

This paper is organized in three sections. Section number II is an introduction to the main technologies used and is describing the relevance of NFV and SDN. Section III will go thorugh all the implementation steps and details demonstrating the cooperation between the technologies and describing the results.

II. NETWORK FUNCTION VIRTUALIZATION (NFV) and SOFTWARE DFINED NETWORK (SDN) INTEGRATION

This section will summarize some aspects of Network Function Virtualization and Software Defined Network and introduce the SDN-NFV approach.

A. Network Function Virtualization

In traditional networks that do not yet benefit from virtualization, network features are implemented as a combination of software and hardware that are specific to a manufacturer; these are called network nodes. Virtualization of network functions is a step forward in the telecommunications environment by introducing differences in the way services are delivered compared to the current practice. These differences can be described as the following:

- Decoupling hardware from software;
- Flexible implementation of network feature;
- Dynamic operations.

Implementation, control and management of network functions are required in the context of NFV-enabled network nodes for various optimization purposes. Thus, many challenges relate to the algorithm and design of the system in terms of implementation of functions. One of these challenges is the automatic provision of network and processing resources based on the use of the underlying resources involved. A similar and probably the most important challenge is the placement and automatic allocation of VNFs, because their placement and allocation significantly influence service performance. Both automatic supply and placement require a global view of resources and a unified control and optimization system with various optimization engines running in it [2].

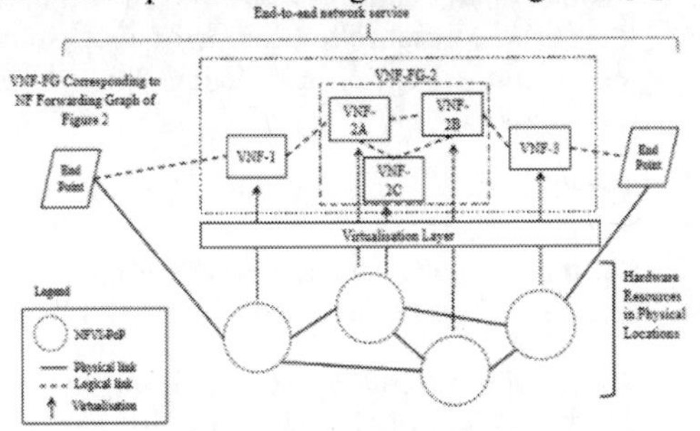

Figure 1: Example of end-to-end network service using VNFs and forwarding graph *[2]*

The end-to-end network services can be composed of several VNFs, organized in forwarding graphs (VNF-FG), as depicted in Figure 1. Terminals and network functions are nodes and correspond to equipment, applications, or even physical servers.

B. *Software Defined Network*

By separating control plane from data plane, the network switches become mainly forwarding devices. However, the SDN flow concept (and the flow tables installed in the SDN switches by the controller), allows a large range of processing actions to be executed upon the packets of a flow matching the flow tables. So, an SDN switch can be more powerful than a traditional router. A simplified view of SDN architecture is shown in Figure 2.

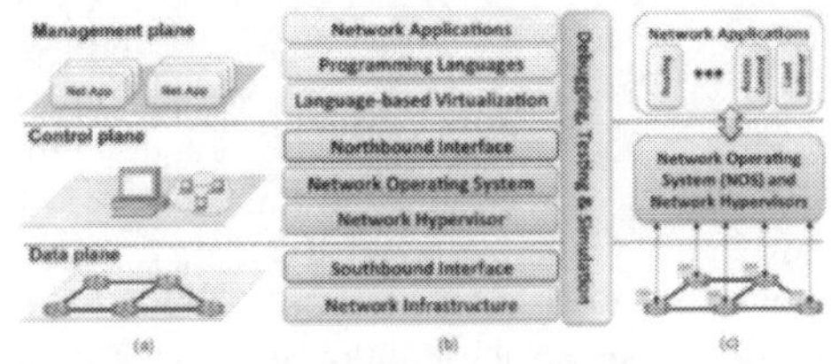

Figure 2: SDN Arhitecture *[3]*

The Opendaylight project [4] is an open source SDN platform that uses open protocols to provide centralized control and monitor of network devices. Like many other SDN controllers, Opendaylight supports OpenFlow, offering network ready solutions for installation as part of the platform.

The core of the Opendaylight platform is the Model-Drive Service Abstraction Layer (MD-SAL). In Opendaylight, network-based devices and network applications are represented as objects or models; SAL is a mechanism for data exchange and adaptability between YANG models, representing network devices and applications. YANG models provide generalized descriptions of capabilities of a device or application without the need to know specific details of their implementation [5] [4].

C. *Integration*

In the SDN-NFV approach the network functions are implemented as software modules, running on virtual machines with the control of a hypervisor, which allows the flexibility of supplying computing and network resources. Thus, because the computational capacity can be increased when needed, there is no need for over-provisioning. . On the other hand, service chaining in SD-NFV benefits from from improvement. For geographically spread networks, updating devices requires a high cost. Additionally, errors may occur in update operations, and reconfiguration may lead to disruption of the entire network.

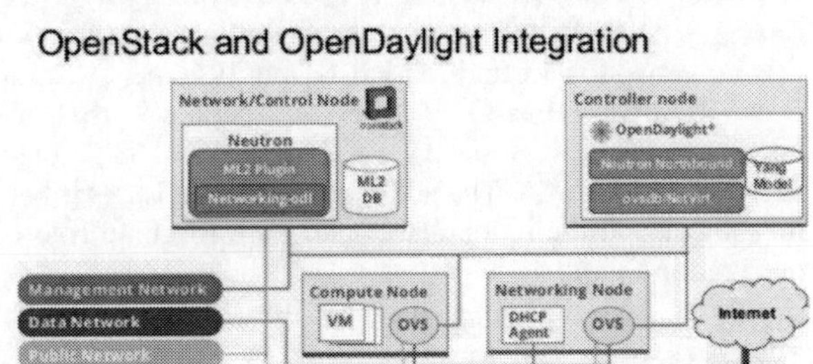

Figure 3: Openstack – Opendaylight integration *[6]*

However, with SD-NFV, service providers can create new connections without radically changing hardware.

With intelligent service linkages, the complexity of resource delivery is significantly reduced. The SD-NFV architecture is still in the research phase; one possible integration is represented in Figure 3; a single control and orchestration framework is required to integrate the SDN controller, routing elements and virtual network functions. Moreover, due to the functionality dynamic feature and the provision of resources, this SD-NFV framework must provide coordinated control status [1] [7]. The Modular Layer 2 (ML2) plugin is a framework allowing OpenStack Networking to simultaneously utilize the variety of layer 2 networking technologies found in real-world data centers.

III. OVSDB WITH OPENSTACK USE CASE

Openstack offers open APIs to support a wide range of applications and infrastructures, including Neutron API and Neutron / Multi-Layer 2 (ML-2) for networking. Neutron offers a "low-level" interface and was not designed to manage the data center substrates. The ML-2 Neutron has been designed to expose data center switch capabilities, but there is currently a limitation to some virtual and physical switches. (Opendaylight - Cloud and NFV)
Opendaylight is an open source framework for migrating to a SDN network architecture [8].

This section will cover all the steps done to configure and deploy an Openstack environment using OVSDB project from Opendaylight. This environment will be used to deploy network and instances on various compute node and to show how tunnels are automatically configured and how OpenFlow is used for forwarding the traffic [6].

A. *Arhitcture and IP addressing schema*

For this experiment, a Fedora 32-bit image was used, with an average resource allocation as there will be several machines in place. For the experiment creating and managing the network using an Openstack controller and ODL controller through OpenFlow, 3 virtual machines were chosen. A virtual machine will act as a controller and two will be compute nodes. The used hypervisor is the Oracle Vm Virtual Box that was configured with two private networks, VirtualBox Host-Only Ethernet Adapter and VirtualBox Host-Only Ethernet Adapter 2, that are allocating IP addresses via DHCP from 192.168.56.0/24 and 192.168.57.0/24. The addressing scheme is described in Table 1 and the interconnect and each machine role is depicted in Figure 4.

After booting the VM's the IP addressing is the following along with the roles inside the Openstack/ODL architecture:

TABLE I ADDRESSING SCHEME OF THE THREE VMS

VM	Role	Interface p7p1	Interface p8p1
Fedora 1	Controller node	192.168.56.117	192.168.57.113
Fedora 2	Compute node	192.168.56.118	192.168.57.114
Fedora 3	Compute node	192.168.56.119	192.168.57.115

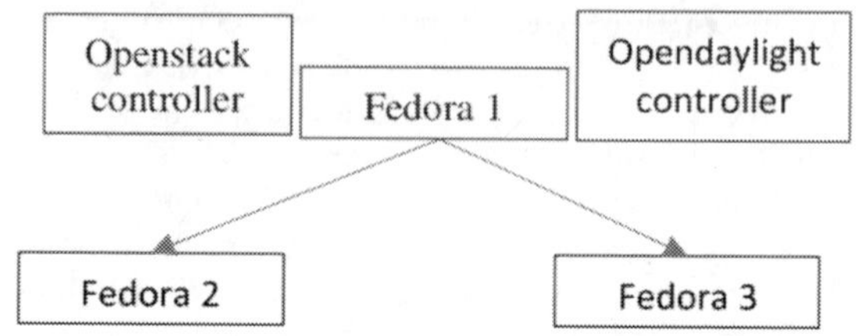

Figure 4: Roles of VMs

To prepare the setup for deployment, there are several steps required:

a) Start the OVS service - although this service should start automatically when running the devstack configuration script of Openstack, we can start the service using the following command:

```
[fedora@fedora1 ~]$ sudo /sbin/service openvswitch start
Redirecting to /bin/systemctl start openvswitch.service
```

b) Configure the /etc/hosts file to reflect the host and IP addressing of the lab. This file will look the same on all three machines:

```
[fedora@fedora1 ~]$ sudo vi /etc/hosts
127.0.0.1 fedora1 localhost localhost.localdomain localhost4 localhost4.localdomain4
192.168.56.117 fedora1
192.168.56.118 fedora2
192.168.56.119 fedora3
::1 localhost localhost.localdomain localhost6 localhost6.localdomain6
```

c) Change the hostname on the VMs and reboot for the changes to take effect:

```
[fedora@fedora1 ~]$ cat /etc/hostname
[fedora@fedora1 ~]$ sudo hostname -b fedora2
[fedora@fedora1 ~]$ sudo shutdown -r now
```

B. *Starting the Opendaylight controller on the Openstack controller*

Configuration must be checked to be sure that the OpenFlow version used is 1.3 as all the scripts will ask for this version:

```
[fedora@fedora1 ~]$ cd opendaylight/
[fedora@fedora1 opendaylight]$ grep ovsdb.of.version configuration/config.ini
ovsdb.of.version=1.3
```

Next action required is to launch the Opendaylight controller, using:

```
./run.sh -XX:MaxPermSize=384m -virt ovsdb -of13
```

Once started the deployment is done automatically and it will be finished when the FlowConfiv provider, GroupConfig provider, MeterConfig Provider and the Statistics Provider are started

```
2019-05-07 12:21:34.153 CEST [pool-2-thread-5] INFO o.o.controller.frm.flow.FlowProvider - Flow Config Provider started.
2019-05-07 12:21:34.159 CEST [pool-2-thread-5] INFO o.o.c.frm.group.GroupProvider - Group Config Provider started.
2019-05-07 12:21:34.226 CEST [pool-2-thread-5] INFO o.o.c.frm.meter.MeterProvider - Meter Config Provider started.
2019-05-07 12:21:34.247 CEST [pool-2-thread-4] INFO o.o.c.m.s.manager.StatisticsProvider - Statistics Provider started.
```

The controller will start listen on TCP port 6633:

```
[fedora@fedora1 ~]$ lsof -iTCP | grep 66
java 1223 fedora 41u IPv6 20211 0t0 TCP *:6633 (LISTEN)
java 1223 fedora 57u IPv6 20216 0t0 TCP *:6653 (LISTEN)
```

C. *Configure Openstack controller*

Openstack must be configured and the controller must be started using Devstack tool. It is required to keep the ODL controller started and a new SSH connection is made to Fedora 1. On Fedora 2 and 3 it can be done from same command line.

a) Edit the local.conf file according to our IP addressing schema – I will copy here only the most important elements that need configuration:

```
[[local|localrc]]
LOGFILE=stack.sh.log
SCREEN_LOGDIR=/opt/stack/data/log
LOG_COLOR=False
OFFLINE=True
#RECLONE=yes
HOST_IP=<IP-ADDRESS-OPENSTACK-CONTROLLER>
HOST_NAME=fedora1
SERVICE_HOST_NAME=${HOST_NAME}
SERVICE_HOST=<IP-ADDRESS-OF-OPENSTACK-CONTROLLER>
url=http://<IP-ADDRESS-OF-ODL-CONTROLLER>:8080/controller/nb/v2/neutron
```

```
[fedora@fedora1 devstack]$ grep 192.168.56 local.conf
HOST_IP=192.168.56.117
SERVICE_HOST=192.168.56.117
url=http://192.168.56.117:8080/controller/nb/v2/neutron
```

SERVICE_HOST and the IP address from the url will always point to the controller, all other elements will be configured with local information. Having these changes made, Openstack can be started by running the stack.sh script and the installation is done automatically. During the installation it can be observed that in the ODL command line there are several messages showing the communication between ODL and Openstack [9]:

```
2019-05-07 12:35:54 Starting Neutron
2019-05-07 12:35:56 Waiting for Neutron to start...
2019-05-07 12:36:04 {"versions": [{"status": "CURRENT", "id": "v2.0", "links": [{"href": "http://192.168.56.117:9696/v2.0", "rel": "self"}]}]}Added interface d0ced68a-2350-4516-9908-a073fe208af2 to router 9a89b604-750f-4f7b-a440-ce22e78321e1.
```

```
osgi> 2019-05-07 12:35:59.978 CEST [http-bio-8080-exec-1] INFO o.o.c.u.internal.UserManager - Local Authentication Succeeded for User: "admin"
2019-05-07 12:35:59.980 CEST [http-bio-8080-exec-1] INFO o.o.c.u.internal.UserManager - User "admin" authorized for the following role(s): [Network-Admin]
```

Open vSwitch after the compute nodes are stacked:

```
[fedora@fedora1 devstack]$ sudo ovs-vsctl show
3cc9dac3-9fa6-4c69-acc1-a2d463396fc8
    Manager "tcp:192.168.56.117:6640"
        is_connected: true
```

```
    Bridge br-int
        Controller
"tcp:192.168.56.117:6633"
            is_connected: true
        fail_mode: secure
        Port "vxlan-192.168.56.118"
            Interface                "vxlan-
192.168.56.118"
                type: vxlan
                options:           {key=flow,
local_ip="192.168.56.117",
remote_ip="192.168.56.118"}
```

One thing to note is that the manager is configured automatically, and it always points to the ODL controller. The connection is done to OVSDB socket 192.168.56.117: 6640. Also, the br-int bridge is created on all 3 instances - the controller is the same machine as the IP address 192.168.56.117, but the connection is made on port *6633* that indicates the **connection to OpenFlow**. During tests it has been noticed that it is mandatory to have the status of "is_connected" to be true. If it is not present, OVS is configured, but the connection is not available (no errors are being throwned, needs manual check). Same procedure needs to be done on Fedora 2 and Fedora 3.

D. *Provisioning*

Before starting to provision the infrastructure it must be checked if there are three hypervizors registered with Nova:

- Populate the proper Keystone credentials for service client commands using the openrc file:

```
[fedora@fedora1 devstack]$../openrc admin
admin
```

- Check hypervizor's list:

[fedora@fedora1 devstack]$ nova hypervisor-list

ID	Hypervisor hostname
1	fedora1
2	fedora2
3	fedora3

- Run the add.imgage.sh script - this is required because the virtual machine we're working on is a Fedora 32-bit architecture and default Cirrus image is not 32 bit, so we add an image with x386 architecture in Glance (cirros-0.3.1-i386)

```
[fedora@fedora1          devstack]$          cat
./addimage.sh
```

```
[fedora@fedora1 devstack]$ ./addimage.sh
Added new image with ID: a335d33d-fee1-
41be-8be9-458cd3f7e309
/home/fedora/devstack
```

- On this infrastructure 6 overlay network will be build, using GRE and VxLAN encapsulation:

```
neutron    net-create    gre1    --tenant_id
$(keystone tenant-list | grep '\sadmin' |
awk '{print $2}') --provider:network_type
gre --provider:segmentation_id 1300
neutron subnet-create gre1 10.100.1.0/24 -
-name gre1
```

A summary of those networks will look like this:

id	name
45cf5f88-1d60-46da-a651-a3df32bc217c	gre1
4e5c0d59-e903-47a1-8bbc-3691351eb4ce	vxlan-net1
7e634fbe-ebcf-47a3-80af-7054ad4fb4fb	gre2
9574dfb9-4e52-4243-8b5e-10f1b44bfab1	private
b980e7ba-c495-44ae-8dc8-7066ac7fd941	gre3
d56a4ac9-34f0-45d2-be92-2d9d7ae83153	public
ef07fbf4-1b98-42ff-92c4-87dcb79dcaff	vxlan-net3
f2b32863-39d1-459c-97c5-7f9212e618e0	vxlan-net2

- Starting instances on compute nodes:

To create VM on the command line, the following commands were used, specifying which networks are to be attached. There is also the option to use the "availability zone" option to specify which compute nodes will host the VMs

```
nova boot --flavor m1.tiny --image $(nova
image-list | grep $IMAGE'\s' | awk '{print
$2}')  --nic  net-id=$(neutron  net-list  |
grep vxlan-net1 | awk '{print $2}') vxlan-
host1 --availability_zone=nova:fedora2
```

ID	Name	Status
e02df395-d234-4995-bf69-2db77cb7d3ec	admin-private1	ACTIVE
278619f0-9a5d-4f0d-a336-16d0d282c4a6	gre-host1	ACTIVE
30e30c81-c7a0-46d7-869f-4229ef5e0690	gre-host2	ACTIVE
5c808b8a-5c80-4c39-9464-4b25c2fe4c34	vxlan-host1	ACTIVE
6d26fc2a-bb45-4eef-903f-7f115ac4198a	vxlan-host2	ACTIVE

One can observe on Fedora 2 that GRE and VxLAN tunnels have been automatically created between neighboring switches. We get a full mash between VM in this way and control their creation by specifying the location for each instance.

```
[fedora@fedora3 devstack]$ sudo ovs-vsctl
show
```

```
3cc9dac3-9fa6-4c69-acc1-a2d463396fc8
    Manager "tcp:192.168.56.117:6640"
        is_connected: true
    Bridge br-int
        Controller
"tcp:192.168.56.117:6633"
            is_connected: true
        Port br-int
                type: internal
            Interface "tap86dfa951-8b"
        Port "vxlan-192.168.56.117"
            Interface                  "vxlan-
192.168.56.117"
                type: vxlan
                options:           {key=flow,
local_ip="192.168.56.119",
remote_ip="192.168.56.117"}
        Port "gre-192.168.56.118"
            Interface "gre-192.168.56.118"
                type: gre
                options:           {key=flow,
local_ip="192.168.56.119",
remote_ip="192.168.56.118"}
        Port "tapc42b0d97-43"
            Interface "tapc42b0d97-43"
        Port "vxlan-192.168.56.118"
            Interface                  "vxlan-
192.168.56.118"
                type: vxlan
                options:           {key=flow,
local_ip="192.168.56.119",
remote_ip="192.168.56.118"}
        Port "gre-192.168.56.117"
            Interface "gre-192.168.56.117"
                type: gre
                options:           {key=flow,
local_ip="192.168.56.119",
remote_ip="192.168.56.117"}
```

The network topology can also be checked via Openstack Horizon at http://192.168.56.117, using default credentials (user: admin, password: admin):

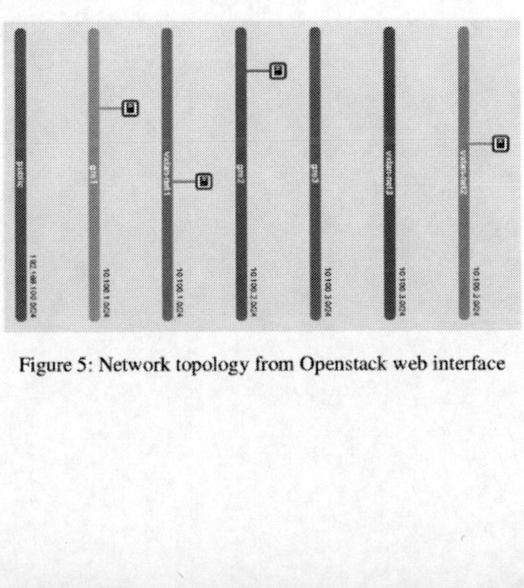

Figure 5: Network topology from Openstack web interface

In Figure 5 it can be seen the network topology obtained, each network being represented in different color and having corresponding hosts attached.

E. *End-to-end connectivity*

To understand how traffic is routed to such an infrastructure, OpenFlow inputs must be analyzed. For the present scenario, there are 3 OpenFlow tables: Table 0, Table 10, and Table 20. Table 0 is the default table. For each tunnel created, there is an OpenFlow port present in this table, and we can see that all these tunnels are finished in this table - the full mash network. Mapping between tunnels and OpenFlow ports in this table is done using "tun_id" as a key.

In addition to provisioning, which involves networking, sub-networks, encapsulation configuration, and the launch of instances on the available infrastructure that has been presented so far, functional verification requires end-to-end connectivity between the controller and the created instance. Using the "nova list" command, we visualize the created instances and choose one of these to check for connectivity. The result of this command tells us for each instance the network to which it is attached as well as its IP address.

To test connectivity, use the ping utility, but for this packets must be sent using the interface that is connected to the same network. As shown in Figure 6 the identifier of the dhcp server dealing with addressing in the gre1 10.100.1.0/24 network was used, this being the network attached to the chosen instance.

```
[fedora@fedora1 devstack]$ sudo ip netns exec
qdhcp-45cf5f88-1d60-46da-a651-a3df32bc217c    ping
10.100.1.2
PING 10.100.1.2 (10.100.1.2) 56(84) bytes of data.
64  bytes  from  10.100.1.2:  icmp_seq=1  ttl=64
time=22.3 ms
64  bytes  from  10.100.1.2:  icmp_seq=8  ttl=64
time=12.0 ms
^C
--- 10.100.1.2 ping statistics ---
8 packets transmitted, 8 received, 0% packet loss,
time 7008ms
rtt min/avg/max/mdev = 0.392/7.810/22.338/7.077 ms
```

Figure 6 PING experiment - SUCCESS

To understand how traffic flows there were selected from the OpenFlow tables all entries used to forward the traffic:

```
Tabela 0:
cookie=0x0, duration=7472.684s,
table=0, n_packets=120,
n_bytes=11850, send_flow_rem
in_port=8,dl_src=fa:16:3e:f5:2c:a0

Tabela 10:
cookie=0x0, duration=921.617s,
table=10, n_packets=210,
n_bytes=20446, send_flow_rem
tun_id=0x514,dl_dst=fa:16:3e:e0:2e:b
8 actions=output:11,goto_table:20

Tabela 20:
cookie=0x0, duration=7587.297s,
table=20, n_packets=238,
n_bytes=22652, send_flow_rem
tun_id=0x514,dl_dst=fa:16:3e:f5:2c:a
0 actions=output:8
```

Figure 7: OpenFlow tables

In Figure 7 are represented a couple of entries from tables 0, 10 and 20. Those tables are used to forward packets between the tables or directly to the physical port.

IV. CONCLUSION

This paper presented an experiment using Openstack and Opendaylight framework used to provision and manage an infrastructure. As a proof of concept connectivity end to end between newly deployed VM and controller was successful and RTT achieved comparing to the one between two Fedora machines shows that the performance is not the same, but similar – the amount of resource allocated per machine was limited and the connectivity between instance and controller requires additional encapsulation. The paper can help designers to develop and implement systems based on cooperation between NFV and SDN, applicable to future IT developments and for the upcoming 5G technology. It is very important to choose wisely the operating system as there are unstable versions for such scenarios. The small setup implemented in this paper can be scaled to a data center to deploy and manage a larger number of instances and traffic.

As future work several experiments will be conducted, including building a network function chaining using similar deployments and compare from automation, resource consumption and stability perspective.

REFERENCES

[1] Y. Li and M. Chen, "Software-Defined Network Function Virtualization: A Survey," *IEEE Xplore Digital Library*, pp. 2542 - 2553, 9 December 2015.

[2] ETSI GS NFV 002 V1.1.1 (2013-10) , "Network Functions Virtualisation (NFV); Architectural Framework," *ETSI*, 2013.

[3] K. Diego , M. V. R. Fernando , E. V. Paulo, E. R. Christian, A. M Siamak and U. Steve, "Software-Defined Networking: A Comprehensive Survey," *IEEE Xplore Digital Library*, pp. 14-76, 19 Decembrie 2014.

[4] Opendaylight community, "Platform Overview," [Online]. Available: https://www.opendaylight.org/what-we-do/odl-platform-overview. [Accessed 15 December 2019].

[5] RFC 6020, "YANG - A Data Modeling Language for the Network Configuration Protocol (NETCONF)," Oct 2010. [Online]. Available: https://tools.ietf.org/html/rfc6020. [Accessed Jan 2020].

[6] Opendaylight community, "ODL Cloud and NFV," [Online]. Available: https://www.opendaylight.org/use-cases-and-users/by-function/cloud-and-nfv. [Accessed 15 December 2019].

[7] Q. Duan, N. Ansari and M. Toy, "Software-Defined Network Virtualization: An Architectural Framework for Integrating SDN and NFV for Service Provisioning in Future Networks," IEEE Network, 2016.

[8] Openstack community, "Openstack," 2018. [Online]. Available: https://docs.openstack.org/security-guide/introduction/introduction-to-openstack.html. [Accessed 15 December 2019].

[9] B. Salisbury, "Networkstatic," [Online]. Available: http://networkstatic.net/opendaylight-openstack-integration-devstack-fedora-20/#!prettyPhoto. [Accessed 15 December 2019].

Study on Use-Cases of Open Source Management and Orchestration Framework in 5G Projects

Andra Ciobanu, Cosmin Conțu, Eugen Borcoci
University POLITEHNICA of Bucharest - UPB
Bucharest, Romania
Emails: andraciobanu90@yahoo.com, cosmin.contu@elcom.pub.ro, eugen.borcoci@elcom.pub.ro

Abstract — **Open Source Management and Orchestration (OSM) is an European Telecommunications Standards Institute (ETSI) hosted project supporting the development of Open Source Network Function Virtualization (NFV) Management and Orchestration (MANO) software stack aligned with ETSI NFV. This short paper is focused on the introduction of OSM and studies some real use cases on the market and in the same time brings out a new possible use case in order to evidence its flexibility. The paper will prepare future work of the authors, to migrate from a previous approach based on only Service programming and orchestration for virtualized software networks (SONATA) framework, to the more comprehensive OSM. A comparison between OSM and SONATA is provided here.**

Keywords — Network Function Virtualization; Software Defined Networking; Cloud computing; Open Source Mano; SONATA; Orchestration; Use case

I. INTRODUCTION

Telecommunication infrastructures include a large range of specific technologies from specialized domains such as radio, access, transport, and core and (virtualized) data center networks. Designing, deploying and operating end-to-end (E2E) services on top of the above infrastructure are commonly manual and long processes performed via traditional Operation Support Systems (OSS) resulting in long lead times (weeks or months) until effective service delivery [1]. Moreover, the involved workflows are commonly hampered by infrastructures strongly coupled to physical topologies and hardware-specific constraints.

Technological advances under the ages of Software Defined Networking (SDN) [2] in cooperation with Network Function Virtualization (NFV) bring new ways in which network operators can create, deploy, and manage their services. SDN and NFV, as well as cloud/edge computing support the introduction of novel services, and systems while meeting specific requirements and objectives (e.g., a customer requesting a specific network service). Altogether, the process shall be timely, consistent, secure, and lead to cost reduction due to automation and virtualization. We refer to Network Service Orchestration (NSO) as the automated management and control processes involved in services deployment and operations performed mainly by telecommunication operators and service providers [3].

However, to realize this paradigm, there is a need to model the E2E service and have the ability to abstract and automate the control of physical and virtual resources delivering the service. The coordinated set of activities behind such process is commonly referred to as orchestration.

In this paper, a new orchestration framework has been studied and used, i.e., Open Source MANO (OSM). The reason for this is that a previous framework SONATA and project itself is today considered as a part of entire OSM; it is not going to be treated alone anymore in the future, but as an integrated part of OSM.

OSM is an ETSI-hosted open source community delivering a production-quality MANO stack for NFV, capable of consuming openly published information models, available to everyone, suitable for all Virtualized Network Functions (VNFs), operationally significant and Virtual Infrastructure Management (VIM)-independent. OSM is aligned to NFV Industry Specification Group (ISG) information models while providing first-hand feedback based on its implementation experience [4]. The first release of OSM was in October 2016 and in December 2019 they unveiled the latest release (Release SEVEN).

The main purpose of this paper is to introduce OSM, compare it with SONATA framework from previous papers, present some specific use cases in order to understand the capabilities of the framework. Future work will test the OSM scalability properties and capabilities for using it to develop and test some custom VNFs from previous papers along with developing Network Services (NSs) with OSM and OpenStack.

The paper is organized as follows: Section I is introduction. Section II is an overview of related work and architecture of OSM framework and a short parallel with SONATA framework. Section III introduces use cases. Section IV presents conclusions and future work.

II. RELATED WORK AND SHORT PARALLEL BETWEEN OSM AND SONATA

This section presents a selective view on some related work dedicated to service development and orchestration in virtualized networks and its relation to OSM architecture, when applicable and introduces SONATA which is part of OSM.

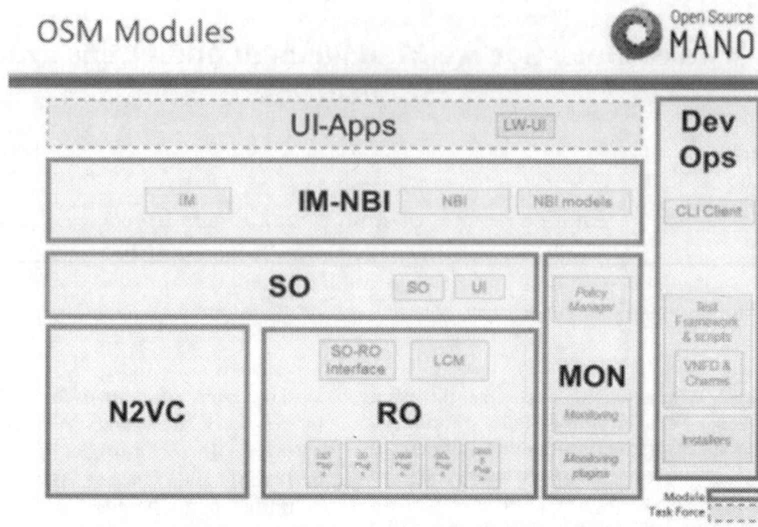

Figure 1 OSM Release Four Architecture Progression [4]

OSM is innately a modular and model driven architecture (Figure 1) and has evolved steadily to adopt cloud native design principals. The OSM community adopted rapidly this modularity, given its better fit to the growing functionality and answer to the need of efficient operation.

In the Release 4, the community rationalized the network to VNF Configuration (N2VC) module and the VNF.

Configuration and Abstraction Task Force to support rapid progress on the VNF configuration functionality. The Information Model and Northbound API were combined under one module ensuring model/interface harmony in the system and to support a growing demand for vendor/user different options.

The following OSM architectural entities (Figure 1) are shortly described below.

IM-NBI contains the information model and northbound interface.

The *Service Orchestrator (SO)* is responsible for E2E service orchestration and provisioning. The SO stores the VNF definitions and Network Services (NS) catalogs, manages workflow of the service deployment and can query the status of already deployed services. OSM integrates the rift.io orchestration engine as an SO [5].

The *Resource Orchestrator (RO)* is used to provision services and it orchestrates the resources necessary to compose a service over a particular IaaS provider in a given location. The RO component can deploy networking services over OpenStack, VMware, and OpenVIM. The SO and RO components can be jointly mapped to the NFVO entity in the ETSI MANO architecture [5].

UI-Apps module refers to the new lightweight graphic user interface (GUI) of OSM.

The *DevOps* module controls the Continuous Integration (CI) / Continuous Development (CD) pipeline optimizing the release process for the developers.

The *Network Service to VNF Communication (N2VC)* Module is responsible for the plugin framework between the SO and the VNF Configuration and Abstraction (VCA) layer [6].

The *VNF Configuration and Abstraction (VCA)* layer is responsible for enabling configurations, actions and notifications to/from the VNFs and/or Element Managers. When backed by Juju, it provides the facility to create generic or specific indirect-mode Virtualized Network Functions Managements (VNFMs), via charms that can support the interface the VNF/EM chooses to export [6]. Juju is an open source modeling tool, composed of a controller, models, and charms, for operating software in the cloud. A charm is a collection of actions and hooks that encapsulate the operational logic of an application.

The *Monitoring Module (MON)* should mostly be considered as a tool for driving monitoring configuration updates to the external monitoring tool and as a conduit for steering actionable events into the Service Orchestrator. These actionable events may be either directly triggered by running NS/VNFs or deduced by the external monitoring tools. Apache Kafka was used as the Monitoring Module message bus implementation. It is a fault-tolerant message passing system that supports a publish-subscribe model that aligns with the Monitoring Module's architecture. Messages sent to or received from the Monitoring Module core will be passed via the message bus for both internal and external components of monitoring. Apache Kafka "topics" and "partitions" are used to segregate messages to MON [6].

SONATA is the acronym name of an EU-funded project who developed an NFV platform, which offers to service developers or operator an ecosystem for managing the full lifecycle of a network service [7].

It consists of three main modules:

- *Service Development Kit (SDK)* which represents a set of models and tools that can be used to develop and test NS and VNFs.
- *Service Platform (SP)* which is responsible in orchestrating the network resources by providing a MANO framework.

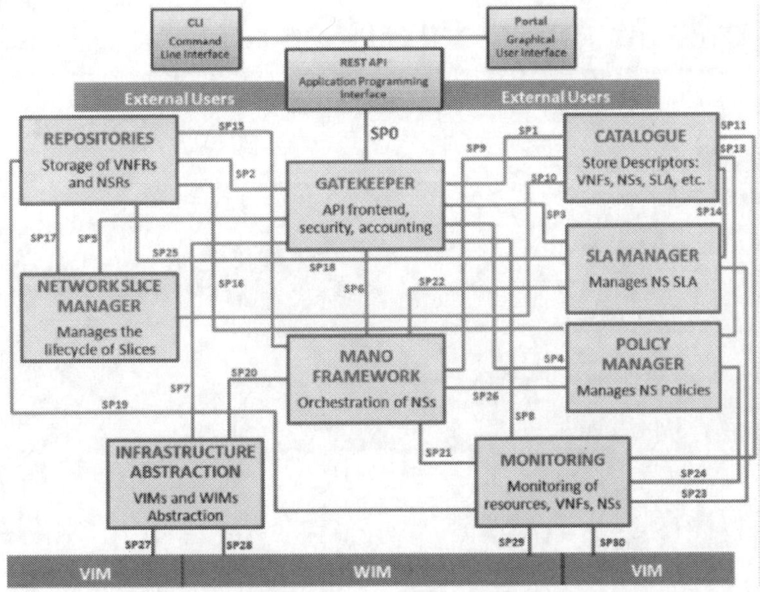

Figure 2 SONATA Service Platform Architecture [9]

- *Validation and Verification (V&V)* Platform Service which automatically manages the testing of services.

SONATA is in a direct relationship with OSM due to the integration of SONATA's emulator from the SDK module into OSM DevOps which was part of OSM Release THREE. This emulator assures an easier integration with MANO stacks due to its APIs, which resemble with the APIs offered by OpenStack [8]. Looking at Figure 2, the following components are shortly presented:

The Service Platform which may be considered as an alternative to OSM, consists of a Gatekeeper, Management and Orchestration Framework, Slice Manager, Infrastructure Abstraction, Catalogue, Repository, Policy Manager, SLA Manager, Monitoring Manager and a Portal.

Gatekeeper ensures that the Application Programming Interfaces (APIs) from the Service Platform are available to authorized users.

MANO Framework is managing the lifecycle of the Network Service active instances. It is the most important component from the Service Platform.

Network Slice Manager controls the deployment of multiple and isolated Network Services grouped in a Network Slice.

Infrastructure Abstraction is responsible of creating a unified management of all available infrastructures.

The *Catalogue* contains Virtual Network Functions (VNFs), Network Services (NS), Network Slice Templates (NSTs), etc.

Repository stores information from Network Service and Network Slice instances.

Policy Manager ensures the management of the policies used in Network Service instances.

Service Level Agreement (SLA) Manager works like a plugin and it is responsible for the lifecycle management of the SLA during the entire Network Service lifecycle.

Monitoring Manager collects data and displays the metrics through an interface.

The *Portal* is the front-end component which ensures the access to the Service Platform through an user interface.

As it was described, SONATA looks more like an OSM contributor than a competitor, having different components which are already compatible with OSM framework or which are easy to integrate. They already started a collaboration from OSM's third release (which was already stated above).

More than this short introduction and comparison, here are some pending and future works between SONATA and OSM.

SONATA is also playing a central role in a white paper that OSM is currently writing about "Experience with NFV architecture, interfaces and information models". A type of scenario is where the operator wants to cooperate with another operator to deliver the network service. For instance, it may devolve provision of the infrastructure, or of a specialist VNF, to another operator. The implication is that OSM needs an architecture that allows to orchestrate orchestrators and SONATA project contributes for this through its MANO framework. Another type of scenario involves modification to a network service, say 'video delivery'. The internal operation of the service may vary according to the specific device type, content source and so on – hence the network service may consist of an initial firewall that steers a request into the appropriate chain of VNFs. In the SONATA project, the development of their pilots is helping OSM to explore and sort out some of these scenarios.

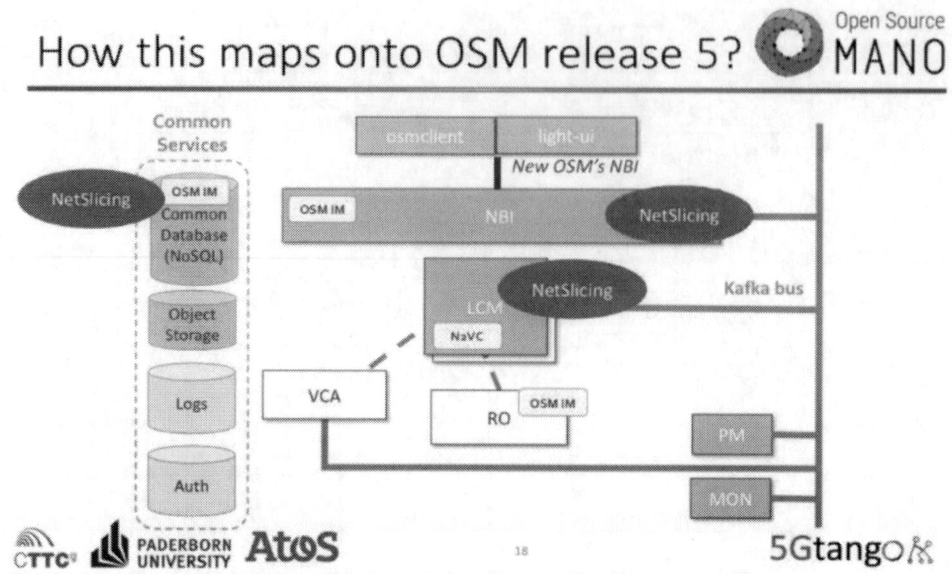

Figure 3 5GTango (SONATA) in OSM [10]

Regarding future work, there is 5GTANGO (the 5th SONATA Release) which is going to take the opportunity of the 7th OSM Hackfest to demonstrate the use of the standalone 5GTANGO V&V platform in an OSM environment. GTANGO has developed a unique V&V approach. V&V stands for verification and validation and aims at ensuring that a software application behaves according to its specification (verification) and users' needs (validation). The 5GTANGO V&V environment is a multi-MANO (targeting SONATA, OSM, ONAP) standalone test environment which streamlines the complete test chain: definition of reusable test plans across NS, reporting from the Service Platform with advanced analytics and reusable probes. Packaged with the 5GTANGO SDK, it becomes part of the developers' continuous integration (CI) framework. [14]

III. Use Cases For OSM Network Function Virtualization

Network function virtualization proposes an architecture that allows operators to virtualize network functions in a high-performing, elastic and automated way. Most of the early use cases are related to mobile networks in a move towards fifth generation (5G) technology and most implementations aim to have OpenStack as a Virtualization Infrastructure Manager (VIM), complemented with NFV orchestration platforms like the open source projects Open Source MANO (OSM) and Open Networking Automation Platform (ONAP.)

OSM can reach common goals for global service providers, leading IT/cloud players and VNF providers, but also for 5G research projects.

These 5G projects which use OSM to implement NVF MANO orchestration are very important for OSM community. Here are below, some examples of 5G projects and how OSM contributes to them:

- *5GTango* [10]: In the context of OSM, this project has contributed with a VIM emulator, advanced NFV packages formats, network slicing and many automation efforts.

- *Metro-Haul* [11]: is intended to build a smart optical metro infrastructure able to support traffic from different 5G access networks. OSM is the orchestrator in Metro-Haul, it deploys, manages and orchestrates the network services across disaggregated datacenters. It deploys VNFs across multiple datacenters in a network service; it creates L2 VLANs over the underlying network infrastructure.

There are also other 5G-oriented projects which use OSM (Matilda, 5GCity, 5G-MEDIA, 5G-TRANSFORMER).

The objective of this paper is to bring new functionalities and use cases from OSM which can be used for 5G over NFV and its application on the market in general. In order to bring new ideas, a study of the actual use cases of OSM has been done. The conclusion is that OSM is used in:

- Multi-site orchestration over disaggregated optical networks
- Urban radio infrastructure
- Media content distribution in core and edge cloud
- Computing resources management in multi-point of presence scenarios.

Next, this paper proposes an OSM approach for an Internet of Vehicles (IoV) schema in Figure [4].

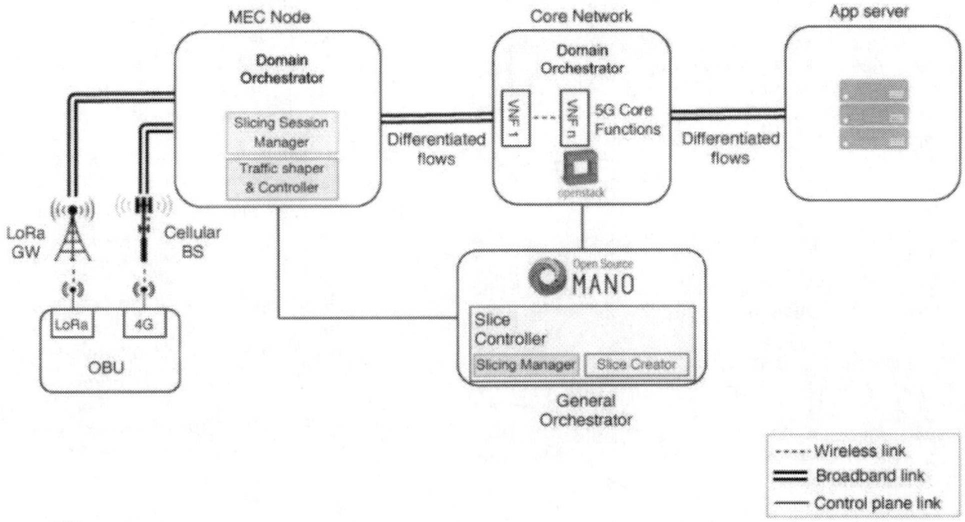

Figure 4 Implemented OSM slicing framework for vehicular applications. [13]

IoV is seen as a global network of vehicles enabled by various Wireless Access Technologies (WAT). It involves Internet and includes heterogeneous access networks. IoV can be seen a special use case of Internet of Things (IoT). IoV Target domains includes the basic vehicular services like vehicles driving and safety, but adds novel domains: traffic management, automobile production repair and vehicle insurance, road infrastructure construction and repair, logistics and transportation, etc.

IoV is a hot research domain exploiting the synergy between Cooperative Intelligent Transportation Systems (C-ITS) and the IoT, which can greatly benefit of the upcoming development of 5G technologies. [12]. The variety of end-devices, applications, and WATs in IoV calls for new networking schemes that assure the Quality of Service (QoS) demanded by the users. To this end, network slicing techniques (the slice is a dedicated, logical, isolated, virtual network sharing the same infrastructure with other slices) enable traffic differentiation with the aim of ensuring flow isolation, resource assignment, and network scalability. The development is based on a distributed Multi-Access Edge Computing (MEC) architecture, which provides flexibility for the dynamic placement of the Virtualized Network Functions (VNFs) in charge of managing network traffic. The solution is able to integrate heterogeneous radio technologies such as cellular networks and specific IoT communications with potential in the vehicular sector, creating isolated network slices without risking the Core Network (CN) scalability.

The proposal presents two orchestration tiers, complaint with ETSI NFV-Management and Orchestration (MANO):

The General Orchestrator (GO) and the Domain Orchestrator (Dos). The former is placed on the top of the system hierarchy in order to have control over the deployed slices. It consists of an OSM instance and of two micro-services in the form of VNFs: The Slicing Manager (SM) and the Slice Creator (SCr). The SM processes the slice-creation requests sent by the Slice Session Manager (SSM) placed in the MEC-node. When a request is received, the SM checks the requester subscription stored in the 5G CN's Unified Data Repository (UDR); this functionality is equivalent to the one described for the Network Slice Selection Function (NSSF) in [13].

IV. Conclusions and Future Work

Today, the OSM community is not only comprised of global service providers, leading IT/cloud players and VNF providers, but also many 5G research projects that are injecting more life, code and validation of the readiness of this NFV MANO implementation.

This study was necessary for the future work of the authors which are going to integrate OSM in the infrastructure and experiments. This integration represents an upgrade to the current infrastructure which was build using SONATA framework. After the upgrade, all experiments which were already done with SONATA will be recreated using the new infrastructure. Afterwards, new experiments containing new functionalities included in OSM will be started.

References

[1] *Blue Planet Multi-Domain Service Orchestration* [Online]. Available from: http://www.blueplanet.com/products/multi-domain-service-orchestration.html 2019.12.06.

[2] D. Kreutz, et al., "Software-defined networking: A comprehensive survey", Proc. IEEE, vol. 103, no. 1, pp. 14–76, 2015.

[3] R. Mijumbi et al., "Network function virtualization: state-of-the-art and research challenges", IEEE Commun. Surv. Tutorials, vol. 18, no. 1, pp. 236-262, 2016

[4] *OSM Release FIVE,* [Online]. Available from: https://osm.etsi.org/wikipub/index.php/OSM_Release_FIVE 2019.12.11

[5] Sagar Nangare, *Incorporation of OpenStack and Open-Source MANO (OSM) for NFV Deployments,* [Online]. Available from: https://dzone.com/articles/incorporation-of-openstack-and-open-source-mano-os 2019.12.14

[6] *OSM Release FOUR Technical Overview, May 2018,* [Online]. Available from: https://osm.etsi.org/images/OSM-Whitepaper-TechContent-ReleaseFOUR-FINAL.pdf 2019.12.15

[7] *SONATA,* [Online]. Available from: https://www.sonata-nfv.eu/ 2019.12.16

[8] *Research – OSM Public Wiki,* [Online]. Available from: https://osm.etsi.org/wikipub/index.php/Research#Sonata 2019.12.16

[9] *Service Platform,* [Online]. Available from: https://www.sonata-nfv.eu/content/service-platform 2019.12.16

[10] R. Vilalta, P. Alemany, M. Peuster, E. Schilling and F. Vicens, *"5GTANGO and OSM",* [Online]. Available from: http://osm-download.etsi.org/ftp/osm-5.0-five/5th-hackfest/5G-Day/OSM%205G%20Day%20-%20Session%203%20-%20OSM%20in%205GTANGO%20by%20Ricard%20Vilalta%20CTTC.pdf 2019.12.18

[11] Reza Nejabati, *Metro-Haul,* [Online]. Available from: http://osm-download.etsi.org/ftp/osm-5.0-five/5th-hackfest/5G-Day/OSM%205G%20Day%20-%20Session%201%20-%20OSM%20in%20MetroHaul%20by%20Abubakar%20Muqaddas%20University%20of%20Bristol.pdf 2019.12.18

[12] K. Katsaros and M. Dianati, "5G Mobile Communications. Springer"; Berlin/Heidelberg, Germany: 2017. A conceptual 5G vehicular networking architecture; pp. 595–623. [Google Scholar]

[13] Sanchez-Iborra, R.; Santa, J.; Gallego-Madrid, J.; Covaci, S.; and Skarmeta, A.' "Empowering the Internet of Vehicles with Multi-RAT 5G Network Slicing". Sensors 2019, 19, 3107.

[14] *5GTANGO presents its Validation and Verification Platform in OSM Hackfest,* [Online]. Available from: https://www.5gtango.eu/blog/69-5gtango-presents-its-validation-and-verification-platform-in-osm-hackfest.html 2019.12.15

Using the Proactive Algorithms and the User Transfer Algorithms for Load Balancing in Ultra-Dense Networks

Mohamad Salhani
Department of Communications and Networking
Aalto University
Espoo, Finland
e-mail: mohamad.salhani@aalto.fi

***Abstract*—Ultra-Dense Networks (UDNs) were introduced to improve the network coverage and support high data rate services. However, the dense deployment of small cells generates an uneven traffic distribution. The unbalanced load causes performance degradation and may be responsible for radio link failures. To address this problem, this paper proposes proactive algorithms to balance the load across the small cells based on the previous user transfer and the reactive algorithms. The proactive algorithms distribute the users, one by one, to the access points, while the reactive ones are only triggered when the load of the chosen small-cell cluster reaches a predefined threshold. The user transfer algorithms offload the small cells by transferring the extra users to the macrocells. The user transfer can be occurred before or after balancing the load by the reactive algorithms. The results indicate that the transfer_after algorithm improves the load distribution and the balance efficiency better than the proactive algorithm with the transfer_before algorithm by 3.46% and 15.71%, respectively.**

Keywords-UDN; load balancing; proactive algorithms; user transfer algorithms; reative algorithms.

I. INTRODUCTION

The rapid growth of traffic in the coming years will cause macrocell networks to evolve, becoming more tightly packed and eventually ultra-dense. To support the data demand for mobile broadband services and increase network capacity as well, the small cells will play an important role in the future 5G network and can significantly increase the capacity and throughput of the network [1]. Due to the low cost of the small cells, subscribers may have their own small cells and deploy them anywhere, even to turn on and off at any time. Therefore, the small cells will be mostly randomly distributed throughout the network [2]. Since the small cells have low transmission power, only a few users can be served by each small cell, and the mobility of users leads to an unbalanced load across the network. In addition, the preference of small cells during cell selection and reselection loads more traffic onto them; this also causes an overloaded network. When users move onto overloaded small cells, the deficit in resources results in handover failures or poor Quality of Service (QoS) [2]. Hence, some small cells do not satisfy the QoS requirements, while other neighboring small cells resources remain unused.

To balance the load and improve the performance of cellular networks, the centralized Self-Organized Network (cSON) is a promoting solution to configure and optimize the network [3]. The cSON has many features, like mobility robustness, optimization, mobility load balancing (MLB), interference management, and so on [4]. The MLB algorithm in a cSON optimizes the handover parameters and achieves Load Balancing (LB) without affecting the user (UE) experience. Thus, it is necessary to study a Load-Balancing Algorithm (LBA) that can adapt to various network environments and avoid the load ping-pongs.

The rest of this paper is organized as follows: Second II presents the related work. Section III describes the system model. The different LBAs are explained in Section IV followed by the performance evaluation in Section V. Section VI concludes the paper.

II. RELATED WORK

Researchers have proposed several solutions to address the LB problem and enhance cellular network performance. The authors in [5] proposed an MLB algorithm considering constant-traffic users with a fixed threshold to determine overloaded cells in Long Term Evolution (LTE) networks. Nevertheless, owing to the fixed threshold, the algorithm is not able to perform LB adaptive to varying network environments. In [6], a traffic-variant users LBA has been proposed considering small cells; however, this algorithm also considered a fixed threshold to identify the overloaded cells. In [2], the authors proposed an MLB algorithm considering an adaptive threshold to decide overloaded cells in a small cell network. The algorithm estimates the loads in both overloaded cells and neighboring cells, and achieves handovers based on the measurements reported by users.

The authors in [7] mathematically proved the balance efficiency of the proposed LBAs based on the overlapping zones between the intersecting small cells. The authors focused on the optimization issue of the overlapping zone selection using different approaches. The proposed LBA was small cell cluster-based and aimed first to determine the best overlapping zone among several overlapping zones and then, to select the Best Candidate user (BC) for handover in order to reduce the number of the handovers and improve the network performance. However, the proposed algorithm was reactive; it is only executed when the user density of the chosen small-cell cluster reaches a predefined threshold.

On the other hand, the load balancing by transferring users has not been highlighted enough in the recent studies. Elgendi *et al* [8] have proposed new schemes to find the optimal number of sessions to be transferred from Unlicensed Long Term Evolution (U-LTE) networks to Licensed Long Term Evolution (L-LTE) or Wi-Fi networks. They have shown that it is possible to transfer the users from programmable Base Stations (BSs) to Access Points (APs) in order to achieve a win-win outcome for both networks. Nonetheless, they have focused on the users' velocity and the distance between the user and the BS more than the data offloading. Besides, the proposed schemes have transferred a higher number of users. In contrast, the authors in [9] have proposed three user transfer algorithms to offload the small cells of UDN networks by transferring the extra users to the macrocells. They first identify the best overlapping zone among the overlapping zones and then, the BC is handed over to another AP or transferred to the BS by selective way. The results indicated that these algorithms can improve the performance of the whole UDN network.

The authors in [10] have proposed proactive LBA by initiating vertical handovers before admitting call if network resources are not substantial; however, the proactivity only concerns user-cell association policy and lacks consideration of users' mobility and content demands. Moreover, a novel proactive LB scheme was suggested in [11]. The proposed framework learns users' mobility and demands statistics jointly to proactively cache future contents during their stay at lightly loaded cells. The results indicated an improvement in the quality of experience and the load distribution compared to the state-of-the art reactive schemes.

In this paper, we propose proactive algorithms that construct clusters of the small cells and perform the LB across the APs. The proposed proactive algorithms are always on standby and ready to be triggered for distributing the new users to the small cells. To improve the LB, the proactive algorithms are followed by the transfer algorithms and the reactive algorithms, which have been proposed in [7] [9]. A comparison between all the algorithms will be achieved to figure out the best LBA. For cluster formation, we consider an overloaded small cell and two neighboring small cells. Consequently, in each cluster, the algorithm performs the LB locally and updates Cell Individual Offset (CIO) parameters of the cells.

III. SYSTEM MODEL

In this section, the system model is described and then, the measurement of the small cell load is clarified. After that, we explain the handover procedure.

A. System description

We consider a heterogeneous LTE network composed of a set of macro cells (evolved Node B (eNB)) and small cells (APs), *N*, and a set of users, *U*, as done in [2] [7]. We consider the UDN small cells with overlapping zones (Z_1, Z_2, Z_3 and Z_4) and each set of small cells constitutes a cluster. The LB is achieved in the small-cell clusters.

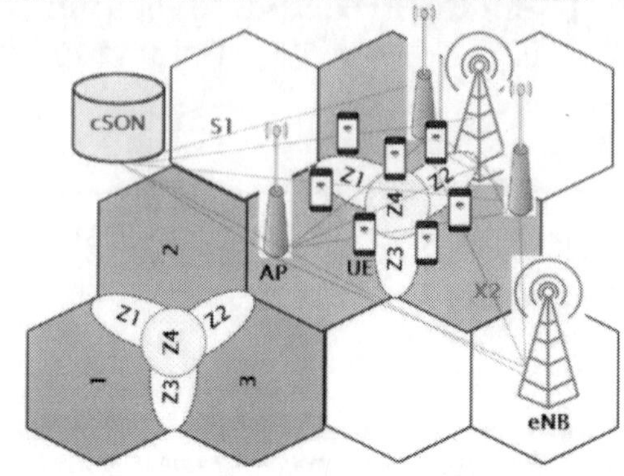

Figure 1. System model with a cSON.

In the simulation model, we considered a cluster consists of three intersecting small cells [7] [9], as depicted in Figure 1. The cells interconnect with each other via X_2 interface. This allows them to perform the needed functionalities such as handovers, load management, and so on [12]. Therefore, the users can move seamlessly among the cells. To optimize the parameters in the network, a cSON subsystem is considered [4]. The cells are connected to the cSON subsystem via S_1 interface [13]. The cSON subsystem collects the required load-related information from the network and optimizes the parameters of the cells to perform the LB process.

B. Small cells load

To measure the small cells load in each cluster, the average Resource Block Utilization Ratio, *RBUR* is calculated from the Physical Resource Blocks (*PRBs*) allocation information [2]. For a given time duration, *T*, the small cell load, ρ_i, of cell *i* at time *t*, is given as

$$\rho_i^t = \frac{1}{T.N_{PRB}} \sum_{\tau \in (t-T,\, t)} RB_i^\tau \tag{1}$$

where N_{PRB} and RB_i denote the total *PRBs* and the total allocated *PRBs* at time τ in cell *i*, respectively. Hence, the Average Cluster Load, *ACL*, is calculated as

$$ACL = (\textstyle\sum_{i=1}^{m} \rho_i)/m \tag{2}$$

where *m* is the number of the small cells constituting the cluster. In order to determine overloaded, balanced and underloaded small cells in each cluster, we introduce two adaptive thresholds; upper and lower thresholds, δ_1, δ_2, respectively, as done in [7] [9] as follows

$$\delta_1 = ACL + \alpha \times ACL \tag{3}$$

$$\delta_2 = ACL - \alpha \times ACL \tag{4}$$

where α is the tolerance parameter, which controls the width of the balance zone. A small value of α requires many handovers to reach the needed LB, and vice-versa. In this paper, α is set to 0.05, as done in [7] [9]. Equation (3) and (4) show that the thresholds are a function of *ACL* and α.

C. Handover procedure

In this paper, A3 and A4 event measurements are used to trigger a handover and select the users candidate for handovers, and the Reference Signal Received Power (RSRP) is assumed reporting signal quality for measurements, as done in [2] [14]. Actually, event A3 is widely used for triggering handovers in wireless networks [15]. In that way, event A3 is triggered and the users report the measurement results to the serving cell when the signal of a neighboring cell in a cluster is offset better than that of the serving cell. If the event A3 triggering criteria remains satisfied for longer than the Time To Trigger (TTT), the cell decides to trigger a handover. The event A3 measurement is reported if the following condition is satisfied [2]:

$$Mn + Ofn + Ocn - Hyst > Mp + Ofp + Ocp + off \qquad (5)$$

where *Mn* and *Mp* denote the average *RSRP* values. *Ofn* and *Ofp* are the frequency-specific offsets. *Ocn* and *Ocp* are the cell individual offsets for the target and the serving cells, respectively. *Hyst* is the hysteresis parameter. *Off* is the A3 event offset between the serving and the target cells. The cSON performs the LB by shifting the users in the overloaded cells to the underloaded cells. However, to balance the load, the system needs information about the edge-users distribution. For that, the event A4 is used. All the cells share the users' information with the cSON. The condition for triggering the event A4 is expressed as [2],

$$Mn + Ofn + Ocn - Hyst > Thresh \qquad (6)$$

where *Thresh* is event A4's threshold. The users that satisfy this condition report measurements for the serving and neighboring cell within the cluster in question. In this regard, each cell makes a set of edge-users based on A4 event reports. Then, the cSON collects all the edge-users' information from all the cells. The LBA in its turn selects the best candidate edge-user and transfers or hands over it to the best target cell according to the chosen LB scheme.

IV. LOAD BALANCING ALGORITHMS

In this section, we present the different LBAs that are proposed to balance the load across the small cells.

A. Proactive algorithm with (user) Rejection (ProR)

The Proactive algorithm with (user) Rejection (ProR) distributes the new users to the covering APs and rejects the extra users, as depicted in *Algorithm 1*. This algorithm is always on standby and ready to be triggered each time a new user enters the network. For each new user, the algorithm selects the best AP, which has the least load. In the ProR, the resources of the APs are considered limited; each AP has a maximum capacity, ρ_{th}. Therefore, when an AP is selected to include a new user and the load of this AP, ρ_i will not exceed ρ_{th} if it admits this user, thus the user is accepted. Otherwise, the ProR rejects the user. The distribution process is achieved for each new user moves onto the network until the user density, *D* of the chosen cluster reaches the user density threshold, D_{th}.

Algorithm 1: Proactive algorithm with Rejection (ProR)

1: Get RSRP and PRB measurements of UE j and cell i, D_{th} and UE's zone
2: **if** $D < D_{th}$ **then**
3: Find the cell that covers this UE and has the smallest ρ_i
4: **if** $\rho_i < \delta_1$ and $(\rho_i + RBUR_j) > \rho_{th}$ **then**
5: Reject this UE and update the call drop rate (PR)
6: **else**
7: Transfer the new UE to the target cell
8: Update ρ_i of the target cell
9: **end if**
10: **end if**

Algorithm 2: Proactive algorithm without rejection (Pro)

1: Get RSRP and PRB measurements of UE j and cell i, D_{th}, and UE's zone,
2: **if** $D < D_{th}$ **then**
3: Find the cell that covers this UE and has the smallest ρ_i
4: Transfer the new UE to the target cell
5: Update ρ_i of the target cell
6: **end if**

Algorithm 3: Worst Zone Algorithm (WZA)

1: Get RSRP and PRB measurements of UE j and cell i, D_{th}, UE's zone and α
2: Find the cluster with the highest user density
3: **if** $D >= D_{th}$ **then**
4: Calculate ρ for each cell i, ACL, δ_1 and δ_2
5: **if** one of the chosen cluster's cell has $\rho_i > \delta_1$ **then**
6: Calculate β_1, β_2, β_3 and β_4, and then find the worst zone
7: Apply the transfer policy
8: Calculate Δ and determine the BCj
9: **if** $\beta_{new} > \beta_{old}$ **then**
10: Transfer the BCj to the target cell (achieve a handover)
11: Update ρ for each cell i and go to step 5
12: **else**
13: **if** there are UEs of 2nd order **then**
14: Find the new BCj and execute a handover
15: Update ρ for each cell i and go to step 5
16: **else**
17: Transfer to the zone of 2nd order and go to step 7
18: **end if**
19: **end if**
20: **else**
21: **if** there is a cluster of the next order **then**
22: Go to step 3
23: **end if**
24: **end if**
25: **end if**

B. Proactive algorithm without (user) rejection (Pro)

The Proactive algorithm without (user) rejection (Pro) is similar to the ProR, as depicted in *Algorithm 2*; however, the APs are considered having enough resources to accept the new users as long as the user density of the current cluster does not exceed D_{th}. In practice, the density condition is not necessary to be checked, as this algorithm triggers for each new user. This condition is only imposed in this work to compare the results of these two proactive algorithms to the reactive and transfer algorithms with the same user density.

C. Reactive algorithms (rea)

The reactive algorithm (rea) has been proposed in [7] to balance the load across the APs. Nevertheless, this algorithm is only triggered once the user density of the cluster reaches D_{th}. To achieve the reactive algorithm, the authors have suggested three approaches based on the overlapping zones concept. In the *Common Zone (CZ) approach,* the load is only balanced via the users that are located in the CZ between the three overlapping small cells; zone 4 (Z_4), as shown in in Figure 1. The second approach is the so-called *Worst Zone (WZ) approach*. The LB in this approach is only achieved in the WZ, which has the smallest value of the Jain's fairness index, β (explained later). Note that the balance efficiency of the WZ approach has been mathematically proven in [7]. The third approach is the *Mixed Approach (MA)*. This approach is a hybrid approach that combines the CZ approach and the WZ approach. It starts balancing the load in the CZ and then, it transits into the WZ with or without returning to the CZ.

To achieve the LB, the reactive algorithm needs to identify the cluster with the highest density and then, it figures out the overlapping zone and the BC for handover. For that, it **first** starts checking the user density, D within each cluster and then, it compares the density of the cluster with the highest density to the density threshold, D_{th}. If the user density does not exceed the D_{th}, the algorithm is stopped. Otherwise, the algorithm sets the user's load, $RBUR_j$ of each user$_j$, its zone and the tolerance parameter α. Next, the algorithm calculates the load of each AP, ρ_i, and the ACL with (1) and (2), respectively. Meanwhile, the algorithm determines the state of each AP by the transfer policy. This policy verifies which AP must exclude a user (overloaded AP) and which one must include this user (underloaded AP). For that, two thresholds, δ_1 and δ_2 with (3) and (4) are needed. According to the transfer policy, an underloaded AP can accept new users and handed-over users from an overloaded AP. A balanced AP can only accept new users, while an overloaded AP does not receive any new or handed-over users. In the **second step**, the algorithm checks if there is at least one overloaded AP within the cluster with the highest user density (cluster of first order). If not, the algorithm transits into the cluster of second or third order successively and rechecks the user density condition. If this condition is not satisfied in these three clusters, the algorithm is stopped. Otherwise, the algorithm calculates the Jain's fairness index (β) [16] as

$$\beta = \frac{\left(\sum_{i=1}^{n} \rho_i\right)^2}{\left(n \times \sum_{i=1}^{n} \rho_i^2\right)} \quad (7)$$

where n is the number of the small cells that overlap on the zone in question, i.e., each overlapping zone has its own β. When all the APs have the same load, β is equal to one. Otherwise, β approaches 1/n, so $\beta \in [1/n, 1]$. The **third step** is to apply the selection policy for identifying the BC for handover. For that, the difference (Δ) between the load of the chosen overloaded AP and the ACL is calculated by

$$\Delta = \rho_{overloaded\_AP} - ACL \quad (8)$$

Of all the users located in the overlapping zone in question and connected to the chosen overloaded AP, the BC is the one for which the difference of the user's load and Δ has the smallest absolute value as follows

$$BC_j = \left|RBUR_j - \Delta\right| \quad (9)$$

The **fourth step** is to calculate the new β if the BC is handed-over. This is performed by the distribution policy to ensure that the expected handover will definitely improve the balance before achieving the handover. Thus, the handover will be carried out if and only if β_{new} is greater than β_{old}. If so, the algorithm selects this BC and the handover occurs. Otherwise, the algorithm transits into the next target zone. The target zone is one of the overlapping zones, which changes or not according to the selected LB scheme. For instance, the target zone in the WZ approach is the zone that has the smallest value of β, as depicted in *Algorithm 3*. Then, the algorithm repeats the last policies in the new target zone. The **fifth step** is to check again if there is still an overloaded AP, and also if the balance improvement is still valid. If so, the LB enhancement is evaluated again in the new target zone and so on. Otherwise, the algorithm waits for the next trigger.

D. Reactive and user transfer algorithms (rea&transfer)

The reactive algorithm with the transfer algorithms are combined (rea&transfer) in this paper in order to compare them to the proactive algorithms. In order to transfer the users from the small cells to the macrocells, two transfer algorithms are suggested as follows:

1) Transfer_After Algorithm (TAA)

The Transfer_After Algorithm (TAA) takes care of the users that should be transferred to the macrocells. This algorithm is composed of two stages. The first one is the balance stage achieved by the reactive algorithm. The second is the transfer stage, which is carried out after the balance stage. Therefore, the TAA has the same first steps of the reactive algorithm; however, when there are no more balance improvements, the transfer stage with new selection and transfer policies are initialized. In the first step of the transfer stage, the algorithm checks if at least one of the APs is overloaded, i.e., its load exceeds the ρ_{th}. If not, the algorithm is stopped. Otherwise, the second step is to achieve the new selection policy in order to determine the BC to be transferred as follows. First, the algorithm calculates the new delta as a difference between the most overloaded AP and ρ_{th} as follows,

$$\Delta_{new} = \rho_{most\_overloaded\_AP} - \rho_{th} \quad (10)$$

Second, the best candidate value $BC_{(j)}$ is calculated for each user connected to the selected AP as a difference between the user load and the new delta as follows:

$$BC_{(j)} = RBUR_{(j)} - \Delta_{new} \quad (11)$$

Of all the users connected to the AP in question, the BC is the one for which the $BC_{(j)}$ has the smallest positive value. Otherwise, the BC is the one that has the smallest negative value, if all the values of $BC_{(j)}$ are negative. The transfer from the chosen AP is repeated until the AP load becomes less than or equal to ρ_{th}. In the third step, the algorithm determines the next most overloaded AP and repeats the second step. When all the APs have checked and there is no more users for transfer, the TAA waits for the next trigger.

2) Transfer_Before Algorithm (TBA)

The Transfer_Before Algorithm (TBA) is similar to the TAA; however, the transfer stage is initialized as a first step for each AP's load exceeding ρ_{th}. Once the loads of all APs do not exceed ρ_{th} anymore or if there are no more available users to be transferred, the balance stage starts calling the reactive algorithm to continue the LB task as usual.

E. Proactive algorithms with the transfer and the reactive algorithms (Pro&transfer&rea)

In this case, the proactive algorithms are integrated with the transfer algorithms and the reactive algorithms. This means that first the Pro distributes the users to the small cells. After that, the TBA transfers the extra users to the macrocells before applying the reactive algorithms, i.e., Pro&before&rea. Instead, the TAA transfers the extra users to the macrocells after balancing the load by the reactive algorithms, i.e., Pro&after&rea. Note that the ProR does not need to be followed by the transfer algorithms or the reactive algorithms. It is itself able to balance the load without any help form these two algorithms at the price of higher rejected users.

V. PERFORMANCE EVALUATION

In the following section, we present the simulation environments and the performance evaluation metrics. Then, the simulation results are analyzed.

A. Simulation environments

We performed the simulation with a heterogeneous network with macro and small cells using *ns-3*. The proposed scenario consists of three macro cells and 10 small cells. Each set of three-hexagonal intersecting small cells forms a cluster. The user density, *D* is on average equal to six users per small cell. Therefore, the density threshold, D_{th} is equal to 18 users per cluster, as considered in [7] [9]. The users allocate multi-traffic. Each user selects a specific bit rate in the range of 0 to 350 Mbps [7] [17]. We consider a uniform deployment of small cells in order to diagnose the impact of the proposed algorithms on the network from different aspects. With regard to the users' distribution, 50% of the mobile users were randomly distributed over the whole area, and the rest were fixed and uniformly distributed over the border areas of the small cells, as listed in Table I, because the reactive algorithms hand over the users located in the overlapping zones.

TABLE I. SIMULATION PARAMETERS

Parameters	**Values**
Number of small cells	10
Tx power	24 dBm (small cell) and 46 dBm (macro cell)
System bandwidth	20 MHz
Antenna mode	Isotropic
Pathloss	$PL=147.4+43.3log_{10}(R)$
Fading	Standard deviation 4 dB, lognormal
Resource scheduling	CQA scheduler
CIO_{min} *and* CIO_{max}	-6dB, 6dB
Hysteresis	2 dB
ρ_{th}	1Gbps
BS capacity	2Gbps
D_{th}	18 user
User velocity	3.6 km/h
Mobility model	Uniform, 50% CW mobility users and 50% static users

The randomly distributed users follow the Circular Way (CW) mobility model [2] [18]. In this mobility model, the users move in a circular path with a 10m radius and a speed of 3.6 km/h. The bandwidth for each small cell was set to 20 MHz. The transmission power for the small cells and macro cells was set to 24 dBm and 46 dBm, respectively. To model the path loss, we considered Non-Line-of-Sight (NLoS) propagation loss model [2] [19]. To allocate the *PRBs* among the users in a cell, a Channel QoS-Aware (CQA) scheduler was adopted [2] [20].

B. Performance evaluation metrics

To evaluate the performance, we considered three aspects: the load distribution across the small cells, the Balance Improvement Ratio (BIR) and the Balance Efficiency (BE). To measure the load distribution, the standard deviation (σ) and the Jain's fairness index (β) with (7) are considered. The BIR is expressed as done in [7] [9],

$$BIR = \left| \frac{\sigma_{final} - \sigma_{initial}}{\sigma_{initial}} \right| \tag{12}$$

where $\sigma_{initial}$ and σ_{final} are the standard deviation of the small cells loads before and after applying the LBA, respectively. We also considered the signaling load, which is; the handover rate, HOR for the reactive algorithms, the probability of rejection (call drop rate) of the new users from the APs, PR_AP for the ProR, and the probability of rejection from the BSs and the transfer rate, PR_BS and TR for the transfer algorithms.

The BE is measured by taking into account the standard deviation and the signaling load for each algorithm [7] [9]. When applying the reactive algorithm, the BE is given by

$$BE_{rea} = 1/(\sigma_{final} \times HOR) \tag{13}$$

By applying the ProR or the Pro, the BE is expressed respectively as

$$BE_{ProR} = 1/(\sigma_{final} \times PR\_AP) \tag{14}$$

$$BE_{Pro} = 1/\sigma_{final} \tag{15}$$

Considering the transfer algorithms with or without the Pro, the BE is given by

$$BE_{Pro+transfer} = 1/(\sigma_{final} \times (HOR + TR + PR\_BS)) \tag{16}$$

C. Results analysis

To analyze the results and evaluate the performance of the different algorithms, we compare the results of the proposed combination of the proactive and transfer algorithms to the previous reactive and transfer algorithms suggested in [7] [9]. Figure 2 shows the standard deviation of the small cells loads for the different algorithms. We notice that the Pro&before&rea distributes the load across the APs better than the other algorithms except the TAA (after&rea). However, the load distribution achieved by the TAA is better only by 3.46%. Moreover, the best load distribution is achieved by the TAA using the MA. In total, the load distribution performed by the Pro&transfer&rea (the average value of the Pro&after&rea and the Pro&before&rea) outperforms the proactive algorithms (the average value of the Pro and the ProR), the transfer algorithms and the reactive algorithms by 66.62%, 22.38% and 39.17%, respectively. This demonstrates the importance of combining the proactive algorithms with the transfer algorithms and the reactive algorithms to balance the load. On the contrary, the Pro leads to the worst load distribution. In fact, the Pro distributes the new users to the APs similar to the ProR; however, the incoming users, which are not rejected when the Pro is applied, will deteriorate the LB. We also found that if the Pro&before was not followed by the reactive algorithm, the load distribution will be worse than the Pro&before&rea by 20.14%. This clearly illustrates the importance of the reactive algorithm for the transfer algorithms. Note that similar load distribution results are obtained based on the Jain's fairness index, β.

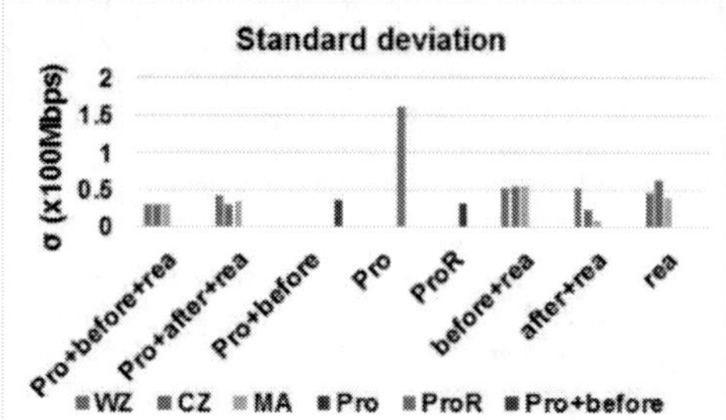

Figure 2. Standard deviation (σ) for the different algorithms.

With regard to the BIR, Figure 3 demonstrates that the best BIR is accomplished by the transfer algorithms (TAA and TBA), which is better than the Pro&transfer&rea by 13.41%. This is because the load distribution performed by the Pro&transfer&rea outperforms the one achieved by the transfer algorithms by 22.38% and then, the Pro&transfer&rea does not need to improve the balance more. For the same reason, the BIR of the reactive algorithms is higher than the Pro&transfer&rea by 11.40%.

In order to determine the best LBA, the signaling load caused by each algorithm is considered, as depicted in Figure 4. We observe that the TAA leads to the highest signaling load. This algorithm requires more signaling than the Pro&before&rea by 42.53%. In contrast, the ProR shows the smallest signaling load compared to the Pro&transfer&rea and the Pro&before, as the ProR does not achieve any handover or transfer processes. On the country, this algorithm rejects the highest rate of the new users from the APs. This rejection rate reaches 20%. In addition, the Pro&before&rea requires signaling higher than the Pro&before only by 5%, which is the value of the HOR achieved by the reactive algorithms.

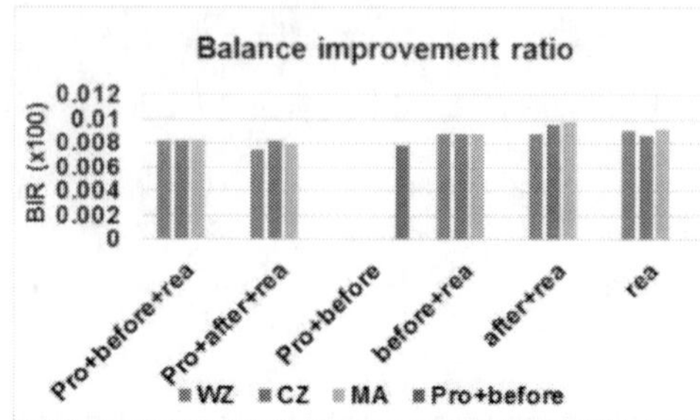

Figure 3. The balance improvement ratio for the different algorithms.

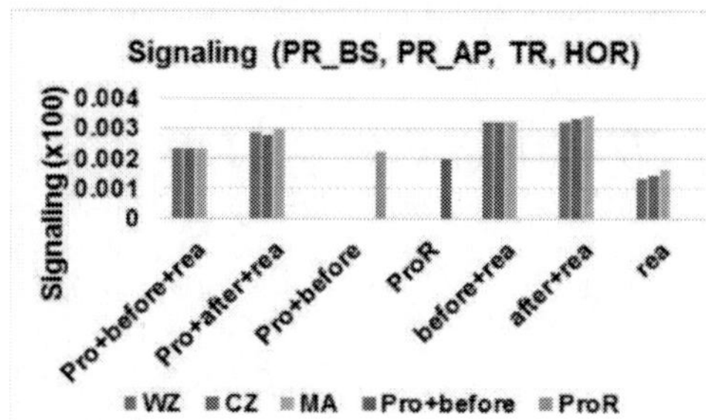

Figure 4. Signaling load for the different algorithms

With respect to the BE, we figured out that the BE of the Pro&before&rea is better than the Pro&before by 14.42%, as shown in Figure 5. This clarifies the importance for the Pro&before to be followed by the reactive algorithms. Additionally, the BE of the TAA outperforms the Pro&before&rea by 15.71%. Furthermore, the BE of the ProR and the Pro&before&rea is similar, but with a PR_AP of 20% for the ProR against a PR_BS of only 1.11% for the Pro&before&rea. However, the PR_BS of the TAA is only 0.81%. Alternatively, the signaling load caused by the TAA is higher by 42.53% than the Pro&before&rea.

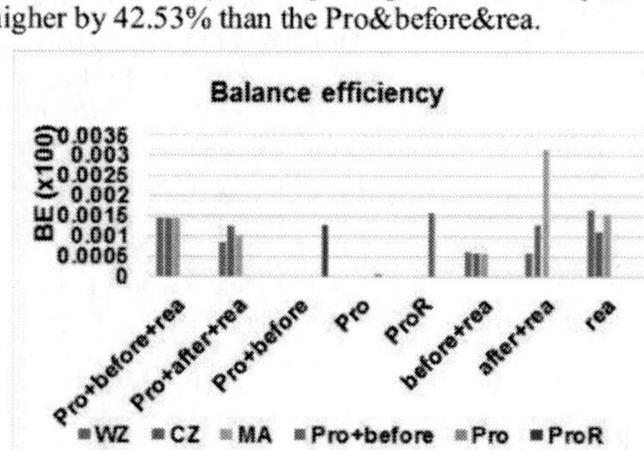

Figure 5. The balance efficiency for the different algorithms.

As a result, the ProR is a refused choice, since it leads to the highest rejection rate of all the algorithms. Thus, the Pro&before&rea and the TAA would be two promoting solutions to balance the load in UDN networks.

VI. CONCLUSION

In this paper, several load-balancing algorithms are proposed for balancing the load in UDN networks. The proactive algorithms distribute the new users, user by user, to the small cells. This can occur with or without rejecting the extra users that overload the target small cells. The user transfer algorithms can offload the small cells before or after balancing the load by the reactive algorithms. The proposed proactive algorithms with user transfer algorithms and the reactive algorithms are compared to the previous user transfer algorithm and the reactive algorithms. As a result, two promoting solutions would be used to balance the load in UDN networks. The first solution would be the transfer_after algorithm using the mixed algorithm with a probability of users rejected from the macrocells of 0.22%; however with a signaling load higher by 42.53% than the proactive algorithm with transfer_before algorithm and the worst zone algorithm. The second solution would be the proactive algorithm with the transfer_before algorithm and the worst zone algorithm with a probability of rejection from the macrocells of 1.11% and a balance efficiency smaller than that with the transfer_after algorithm by 15.17%. Future works will deal with integrating the Design Structure Matrix (DSM) method with the proposed algorithms. This would load the balance among the small cells and reduce the APs inter-communications at the same time.

REFERENCES

[1] J. Hoadley and P. Maveddat, "Enabling small cell deployment with HetNet," IEEE Wireless Commun., vol. 19, no. 2, pp. 4–5, Apr. 2012.

[2] M . M. Hasan, S. Kwon, and J. H. Na, "Adaptive mobility load balancing algorithm for LTE small-cell networks," IEEE Trans. Wireless Commun., vol. 17, no. 4, pp. 2205–2217, Apr 2018.

[3] Evolved Universal Terrestrial Radio Access Network (E-UTRAN); Self-Configuring and Self-Optimizing Network (SON) Use Cases and Solutions, document TS 36.902, 3rd Generation Partnership Project, Sep. 2010.

[4] S. Feng and E. Seidel, "Self-organizing networks (SON) in 3GPP long term evolution," Newsletter, Nomor Research GmbH, Munich, Germany, Tech. Rep., May 2008.

[5] N. Zia and A. Mitschele-Thiel, "Self-organized neighborhood mobility load balancing for LTE networks," in Proc. IFIP WD, pp.1-6, 13-15 Nov 2013.

[6] Z. Huang, J. Liu, Q. Shen, J. Wu, and X. Gan, "A threshold-based multi-traffic load balance mechanism in LTE-A networks," in Proc. IEEE Wireless Commun. Netw. Conf. (WCNC), pp. 1273–1278, Mar. 2015.

[7] M. Salhani, and M. Liinaharja, "Load balancing algorithm within the small cells of heterogeneous UDN networks : Mathematical proofs," Jounrnal of Communications, vol. 13 , no. 11 , pp. 627-634, 2018.

[8] I. Elgendi, K. S. Munasinghe and A. Jamalipour, "Traffic offloading for 5G: L-LTE or Wi-Fi," 2017 IEEE Conference on Computer Communications Workshops (INFOCOM WKSHPS), Atlanta, pp. 748-753, 2017.

[9] M. Salhani and M. Liinaharja, "Load Migration Mechanism in Ultra-Dense Networks,". In Proceedings of the 2nd International Conference on Telecommunications and Communication Engineering (ICTCE 2018). ACM, New York, NY, USA, pp. 268-274, 2018.

[10] D. Ma, and M. Ma, "Proactive load balancing with admission control for heterogeneous overlay networks. Wireless Communications and Mobile Computing," 13(18), pp.1671-1680, 2013.

[11] S. Manzoor, et al., "Leveraging mobility and content caching for proactive load balancing in heterogeneous cellular networks," Transactions on Emerging Telecommunications Technologies, p.e3739, 2019.

[12] Evolved Universal Terrestrial Radio Access Network (E-UTRAN); X2 Application Protocol (X2AP), document TS 36.423, 3rd Generation Partnership Project, Sep. 2014.

[13] "Evolved universal terrestrial radio access network (E-UTRAN); S1 application protocol (S1AP)," 3rd Generation Partnership Project (3GPP), TS 36.413, Sep. 2014.

[14] "Evolved universal terrestrial radio access (E-UTRA); radio resource control (RRC); protocol specification," 3rd Generation Partnership Project (3GPP), TS 36.331, Jan. 2016.

[15] K. Dimou, et al., "Handover within 3GPP LTE: Design Principles and Performance", VTC 2009-Fall, 2009 IEEE 70th, pp.1-5, 20-23 Sept. 2009.

[16] M. Huang, S. Feng, and J. Chen, "A Practical Approach for Load balancing in LTE Networks," Journal of Communications Vol. 9, No. 6, pp. 490-497, June 2014.

[17] P. Kela, "Continuous Ultra-Dense Networks, A System Level Design for Urban Outdoor Deployments," book 1799-4942 (electronic), Aalto University publication series DOCTORAL DISSERTATIONS 86/2017.

[18] C. Ley-Bosch, R. Medina-Sosa, I. A. González, and D. S. Rodríguez, "Implementing an IEEE802.15.7 physical layer simulation model with OMNET++," in Proc. 12th Int. Conf. Distrib. Comput. Artif. Intell., pp. 251–258, 2015.

[19] J. B. Andersen, T. S. Rappaport, and S. Yoshida, "Propagation measurements and models for wireless communications channels," IEEE Commun. Mag., vol. 33, no. 1, pp. 42–49, Jan. 1995.

[20] J. M. Ruiz-Avilés, et al., "Design of a Computationally Efficient Dynamic System-Level Simulator for Enterprise LTE Femtocell Scenarios," Journal of Electrical and Computer Engineering, vol. 2012, Article ID 802606, pp. 1–14, 2012.

Caching Data Protection Scheme for Information-Centric Wireless Sensor Networks

Shintaro Mori
Department of Electronics Engineering and Computer Science
Fukuoka University
8-19-1, Nanakuma, Jonan-ku, Fukuoka 814-0180, Japan
e-mail: smori@fukuoka-u.ac.jp

Abstract— **Internet of things is widespread in our daily life, such as smart cities (homes), health care, and our activity lifelogs. In these use cases, sensing data must be managed not only effectively but also securely. From this perspective, we adopt the information-centric network design into wireless sensor networks for efficient peer-to-peer data collection, delivery, and publication. In the study of information-centric schemes, caching technology is significantly important; thus, we focus on a secure caching mechanism to privacy and security protections. In particular, the caching data protection mechanism, i.e., to prevent cache pollution attacks, is an essential challenge for data retrieving in information-centric wireless sensor networks. In this paper, therefore, we propose a novel effective and secure caching scheme for wireless sensor networks using the information-centric network design and the blockchain technology. In particular, for caching data management, to maintain the blockchain-based ledger requires exhaustive computer calculation resources and energy consumption in mining-based verification tasks; nevertheless, resource-limited wireless node devices are not suitable. Therefore, we propose a novel light-weight verification mechanism based on proof-of-consensus, and we reveal its fundamental features using computer simulation.**

Keywords-Wireless sensor network; Information-centric network; Blockchain; Caching scheme.

I. INTRODUCTION

The growing number of devices connected to the Internet has made the ubiquitous Internet a part of all aspects of modern life. Countless new Internet-of-Things (IoT) devices are widely used by smart cities/homes, healthcare services, and other sensor and actuator solution providers. Future IoT systems are expected to communicate with each other directly, sending and receiving an enormous amount of sensing data (Figure 1). These privacy-sensitive sensing data have been under various attacks in the already deployed terminals, causing serious security concerns [1]. For example, if smart city applications are hacked and users' activities are leaked, people's personal safety can be compromised. In another example, if healthcare and smart medical devices for fitness, diet, and health monitoring do not work adequately, emergency notifications and early detection of illnesses cannot be sent. That is why Wireless Sensor Networks (WSNs) in key wireless technologies underpinning IoT services should evolve and be replaced by a modern

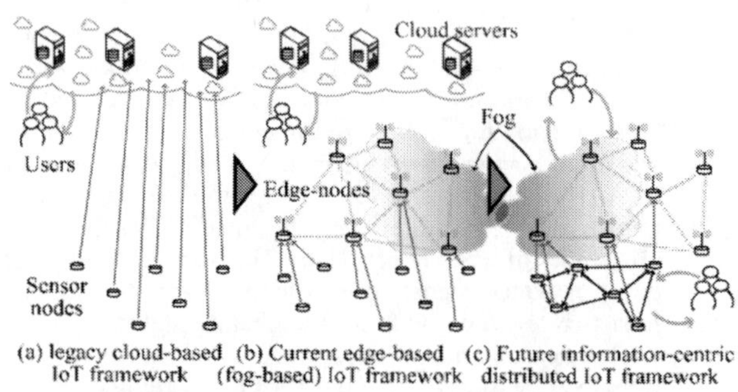

Figure 1. Transition of IoT framework architecture.

autonomous, decentralized, efficient, secure, and privacy-aware network design. These concerns motivated us to develop an effective and secure data management scheme (including storing, forwarding, and providing) based on Information-Centric Network (ICN) design and blockchain technology. In comparison with the traditional scheme, the proposed scheme has a significant characteristic and advantage that the proposed scheme can be constructed based on an overall distributed and decentralized design due to a combination of WSNs, ICN, and blockchain.

The ICN is emerging as a promising network architecture that supports efficient data provision and retrieval with in-network caching, i.e., users could obtain their desired content data from a nearby copy-holder in ICN-based systems [2]. To initiate this mechanism, users send a content request with the desired content feature in an interest packet; then, the content is sent back to the requester in a data packet when the interest packet reaches the original node or cache-available node. The reason for introducing ICN into WSNs is that the address-free structure is suitable for mobile and ad-hoc network environments, allowing ICN-WSNs to reduce the protocol overhead of data collection and retrieval in comparison with HTTP and other simplified protocols [3]. In implementation of ICN-WSN systems, the caching scheme is one of the essential technologies in the ICN framework, resulting in failed cache poisoning attacks due to the actuators performing wrong actions founded on the polluted data.

To protect the caching data of ICN-WSNs, we use the blockchain technology [4]. These three key technologies, the

WSN, the ICN, and the blockchain, work in an autonomous and decentralized environment. A blockchain-based ledger has several advantages: it can be constructed among anonymous nodes; the verification process is simple and common manner; the users can easily identify and authenticate the verified caching data without central brokers or certification authorities, and the blockchain architecture protects it from the risk of being a single point of failure when faced with malicious attacks. Moreover, when a verified block is appended into the blockchain, the users do not need any additional certification process.

A typical blockchain verification process needs exhaustive computer calculations called Proof-of-Work (PoW). Such PoWs are used, for example, by Bitcoin [5] and other crypto-currencies but cannot be applied in ICN-WSNs consisting of cheap and resource-constrained devices. Even if the proposed scheme will utilize movable vehicle nodes, such as drones and small vehicles, for data collection, accumulation, and provision, the hardware limitations can be alleviated, but the essential issues will remain. Unlike PoWs, Proof-of-Stake (PoS) utilized in Ethereum [6] does not require heavy-weight computational operations, i.e., the next block generator is selected in a pseudo-random way. However, the verification task depends on the wealth or stake of a node, i.e., the more money the node has, the higher its chances for validation, making some nodes unbalanced.

To mitigate these problems, we investigate a novel blockchain-based secure caching and data retrieving scheme for ICN-WSNs. In particular, we propose a novel light-weight verification scheme where blocks are verified while relay nodes forward unverified blocks in ad-hoc and multi-hop networks among validators in the usual WSN data transfer. In this paper, we describe the overall blueprint of our work in progress and propose a novel verification mechanism. We perform a fundamental evaluation of the proposed mechanism using computer simulation.

The remainder of this paper is organized as follows. Section II provides related work. Section III describes the proposed scheme. Section IV presents the numerical results. Finally, in Section V, we summarize our findings and conclude the paper.

II. Related Work

In legacy cloud based IoT frameworks, the authentication, authorization, and access control methods are applicable and selected as centralized controllers that currently deal with these services. While WSN systems are shifting towards decentralization, as in the edge-computing and the fog-computing, alternative security mechanisms for authentication, confidentiality, privacy, access control, resource provenance, and integrity are required [7]. Blockchain technology can address various security issues by constructing a secured and distributed ledger. Alphand et al. [8] proposed a combination scheme of the authorization blockchain and the group key for providing secure-authorized access to IoT resources. From the viewpoint of ICN caching data protection, several studies should be mentioned. Li et al. [9] proposed a blockchain-based protection scheme of the data life cycle; Guo et al. [10] investigated a public permissionless blockchain in named data networking, and Li et al. [11] proposed a trust-enhanced blockchain-based ICN architecture for content delivery.

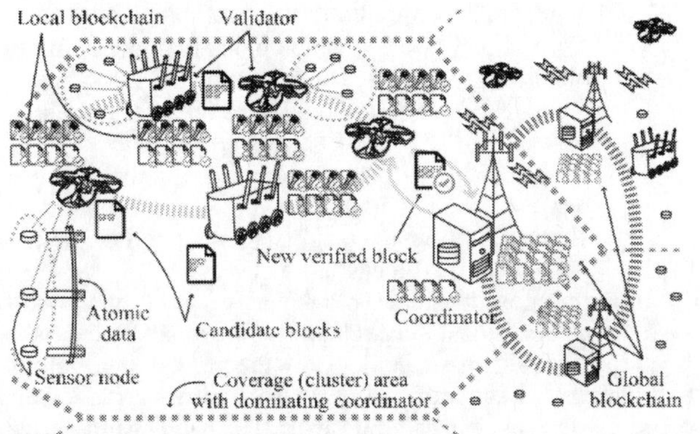

Figure 2. Overview of the proposed scheme.

On the other hand, in wireless networks, Liu et al. [12] proposed a mobile edge-computing-enabled wireless blockchain framework where the computation-intensive mining tasks and verified blocks can be offloaded and cached to neighboring nodes. Chai et al. [13] and Sharma et al. [14] suggested replacing fixed terminals with mobile (aerial) vehicles. These proposals represent an evolution in the content delivery network; however, they are still far from adopting the ICNs in WSNs. In other words, the conventional approach places the content servers in the mobile-edge nodes, which is different from the ICN principle of an individual node copying and storing the caching data. Similar to our study, Lei et al. [15] proposed a novel and systematic framework to protect the in-network caching mechanism; it enables fast and efficient content dissemination in mission-critical ad-hoc networks. However, this proposal has a drawback in that it involves an exhaustive verification process, the proposed scheme can improve the burden of verification calculations.

III. Proposed Scheme

In the data life cycle of ICN-WSNs, the atomic data collection, caching, and retrieval processes may suffer from various attacks. The ultimate goal of our study is to develop an anti-tamper caching scheme.

A. System Description

In the proposed scheme, Sensor Nodes (SNs) are massively deployed in the observation field, which is divided into several regions and the segmented area has one coordinator for comprehensive management, as shown in Figure 2. There are four network components, and the entities that logically play roles in content data dissemination are as follows.

- *SNs* periodically generate atomic data that is a data unit of the ICN content.
- *Validators* gather atomic data from SNs and summarize them into a block that is a data unit of the blockchain. Validators are implemented using

movable nodes, such as drones and small vehicles, and blockchains are constructed on them. Validators have less hardware limitations compared with SNs.

- *Coordinators* decide which block to append into the blockchain among verified blocks. Coordinators mediate between regional blockchains and global blockchains to achieve scalable data retrieval.
- *Users* behave as subscribers, i.e., send data retrieval requests, such as interest requests, to validators and obtain data from the original content or the caches in the validators' blockchain network.

In the proposed scheme, blockchains can be functionally systematized as local blockchains and global blockchains. Local blockchains manage not only the atomic data but also the validity keys for atomic data verification. Thus, coordinators exchange the extracted and summarized information of verified blocks between the global blockchain and the local blockchain of the atomic data to share inventory. Namely, they produce knowledge data, which refers to the data summarized from the local blockchain, including the atomic data, signature, meta tag information necessary for the ICN search. By adopting this mechanism, users can obtain content data from the cross-sectional observation areas. Although the implementation cost occurs to introduce a blockchain-based ICN's caching mechanism into WSNs, we believe that it would be a move well worth the cost because blockchain-based ledgers can also use extensive solutions, such as certification key protection, user access control, and resource management.

B. *Verification Procedure*

Before entering into a block certification process, when the SN joins in and connects to the WSN, a secret key should be provided in order to sign an atomic data digitally. As shown in Figures 3 and 4, in the initialization process, the new SN sends a request for its secret key provision to the neighboring validator (①), and then the validator generates a public key, $\mathcal{PK}$, for validation and a secret key, $\mathcal{SK}$, for signature (②). $\mathcal{PK}$ is appended to the validation key's blockchain (③) and $\mathcal{SK}$ is provided to the SN (④).

In the proposed scheme, there are three types of blocks: a candidate block, a verified block, and a chained block. Candidate blocks that have not yet been verified are generated by collecting and summarizing several atomic data (⑤). Besides, candidate blocks include not only the atomic data but also header parts, such as meta-data for ICN retrieval, as well as a sequential number and a unique fingerprint to distinguish one block from another. The reason for using both the sequential number and the unique fingerprint is that the same sequential number cannot be allocated to different candidate blocks.

Candidate blocks are cross-verified based on Proof-of-Consensus (PoC) used in Ripple [16]. In the proposed validation process (⑥), if a candidate block obtained the sufficient consensus of almost all reliable validators, it can be regarded as a correctly verified block. In the event that a number of validators are hijacked and an illegal validation is carried out, the proposed scheme will maintain the robustness

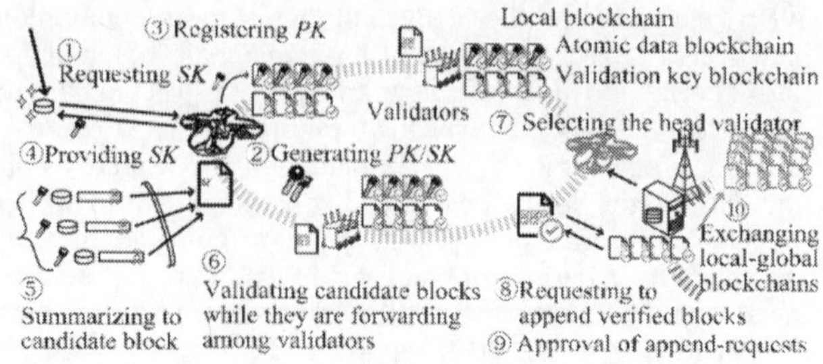

Figure 3. Procedure of the proposed validation process and appending verified blocks into blockchains.

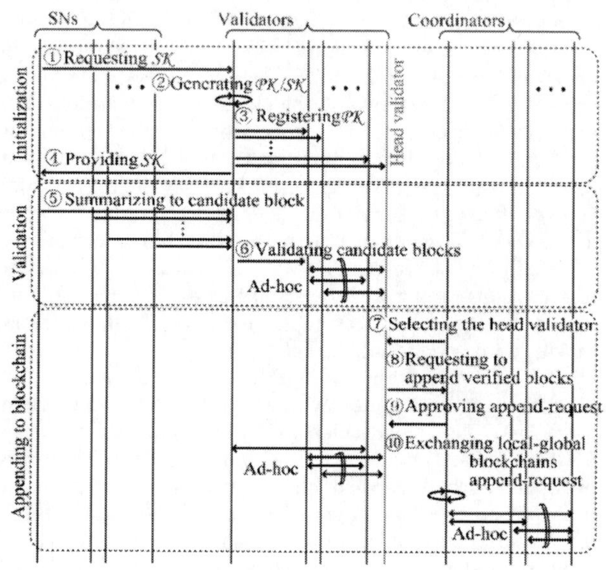

Figure 4. Message and data flow of the proposed scheme.

of the blockchain tanks to the distributed verification feature. The proposed scheme does not require exhaustive mining-based computer calculations for block verification; hence, it is suitable for resource-scarce WSN environments. Candidate blocks are exchanged based on multi-hop wireless transmissions among validators (edge-nodes or fog nodes), i.e., the candidate block can gain the consensus of validity during data forwarding. Note that in the validation process, extra-data transmission with the proposed validation mechanism does not occur. The validator can approve the validity of the atomic data using $\mathcal{PK}$ based on the public key cryptosystem technique (in particular, the digital signature method) to guarantee the integrity and authenticity of the candidate blocks.

The coordinator selects the head (representative) validator (⑦), which will be the nearest validator to the coordinator to avoid complexity in this paper. The head validator selects a new chained block (that might not necessarily be appended to the blockchain) among the verified blocks within its cache memory. Namely, the head validator sends a request of the verified block appending to the coordinator (⑧), and the coordinator approves the request if there are no complications (⑨). In addition, the coordinator calculates a new hash value of the final and fixed chained blocks, instead of a fingerprint in candidate block, consensus information, and the previous block's hash value. In updating the local atomic data's blockchain, the renewal chained block is copied, stored, and cached among validators. Moreover, the coordinator summarizes the inventory of the chained blocks and shares the information with the outside coordinator networks. When the current head validator has no more verified blocks or goes out of the coordinator's coverage, the current head validator swaps with a new one that the coordinator re-selects. Note that the position and the privilege of the head validator are rotated among validators because validators move with time; therefore, we expect that verified blocks are uniformly and fairly appended into the blockchain.

IV. COMPUTER SIMULATION

In this section, we provide fundamental analysis prior to the demonstration in a realistic environment and to compare with other related schemes in our future work. Computer simulator is implemented using C++ language and its program code is run on PC (Windows 10 OS, Intel Core i5-9400 CPU, and 16 Gbyte RAM).

Figure 5 illustrates how many validators are necessary to communicate with all the SNs in the observation area (400 km^2 square) and how many SNs does one validator dominate: 4,000,000 SNs are deployed in an equally-spaced grid pattern, and validators are placed randomly. We assume that the radius of circular-shaped wireless communication coverage between the SN and the validator is set to 1 km, and we ignore the shadowing and the fading depending on the validator's mobility, ground surface, and radio propagation conditions to avoid complexity in the analysis. As a result, 95% of SNs and 98% of SNs can be covered by 400 and 500 validators, respectively. In addition, a scheme for interference reduction should be considered because multiple validators cover almost all SNs. Although the communication range should be small to avoid interference among validators and reduce energy consumption, numerous multi-hops forwarding among validators is necessary for the success of block validations.

Figure 6 shows a relationship between the probability of the validation being completed (and the number of the multi-hops necessary for it) and the communication range. As a result, 95% of blocks can be successfully validated when the communication range is 4 km and the candidate block is forwarding more than four times. In the case when the radius of communication area is large, the number of communications for sufficient consensus becomes small, i.e., the average number of multi-hops also becomes small. On the basis of this scenario, Figure 7 shows the tolerance for caching data pollution, i.e., the number of maliciously taken validators and illegally accepted verified blocks. For example, when the number of maliciously hijacked validators is 1%, 2%, and 3%, the probability of wrongfully verified block is 3.21%, 7.66%, and 12.6%, respectively.

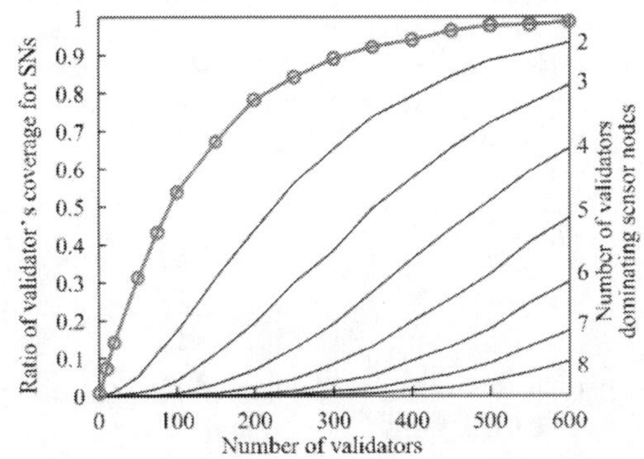

Figure 5. Validators coverage for SNs versus number of validators.

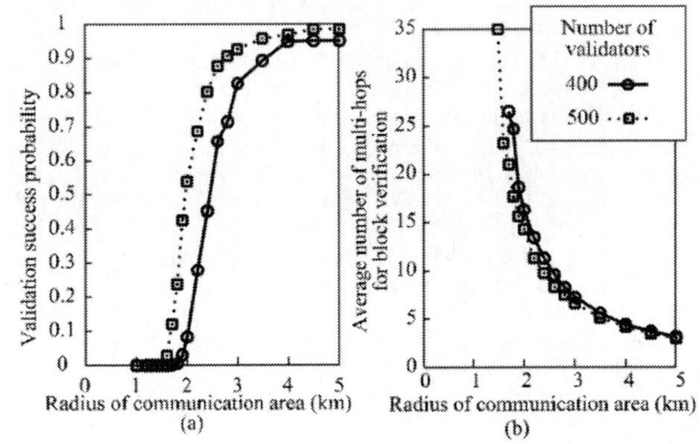

Figure 6. a) Probability of validation being completed and b) average number of multi-hops for block verifying versus radius of communication area between validators.

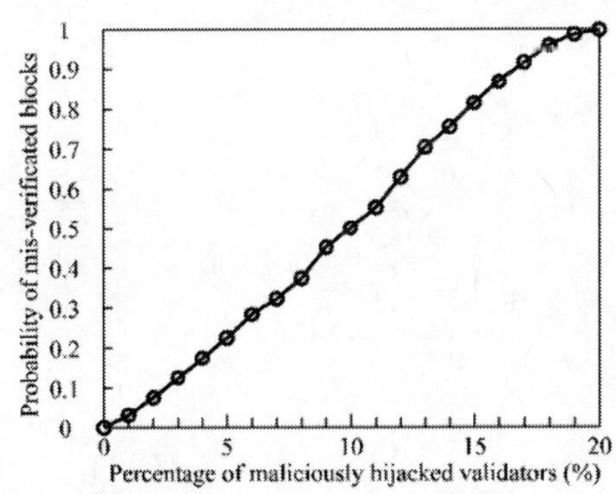

Figure 7. Probability of wrongfully verified blocks versus percentage of maliciously hijacked validators

V. CONCLUSION

In this paper, we adopted the ICN design into WSNs for efficient peer-to-peer data collection, delivery, and publication, and we focused on a secure caching mechanism to privacy and security protections. In order to achieve them, we proposed a novel effective and secure caching scheme using blockchain technology in order to prevent cache pollution attacks. In particular, we proposed a novel light-weight verification mechanism based on proof-of-consensus, and we reveal its fundamental features using computer simulation. As future work, we will consider a data retrieval mechanism based on global blockchain and an incentive mechanism, such as a reward in Bitcoin, and evaluate them using comprehensive simulations.

ACKNOWLEDGMENT

A part of this work was supported by JSPS KAKENHI Grant Number JP19K20261.

REFERENCES

[1] V. Hassija, et al., "A Survey on IoT Security: Application Areas, Security Threats, and Solution Architectures," *IEEE Access*, vol. 7, pp. 82721–82743, 2019.

[2] B. Ahlgren, C. Dannewitz, C. Imbrenda, D. Kutscher, and B. Ohlman, "A Survey of Information-centric Networking," *IEEE Commun. Mag.*, vol. 50, no. 7, pp. 26–36, July 2012.

[3] S. Arshad, M. A. Azam, M. H. Rehmani, and J. Loo, "Recent Advances in Information-Centric Networking-Based Internet of Things (ICN-IoT)," *IEEE Internet of Things Journal*, vol. 6, no. 2, pp. 2128–2158, Apr. 2019.

[4] K. Christidis and M. Devetsikiotis, "Blockchains and Smart Contracts for the Internet of Things," *IEEE Access*, vol. 4, pp. 2292-2303, 2016.

[5] S. Nakamoto, "Bitcoin: A Peer-to-peer Electronic Cash System," *Tech. Rep.*, 2008.

[6] Ethereum, https://www.ethereum.org/ [retrieved: Jan. 2020].

[7] T. Salman, M. Zolanvari, A. Erbad, R. Jain, and M. Samaka, "Security Services Using Blockchains: A State of the Art Survey," *IEEE Commun. Surveys & Tutorials*, vol. 21, no. 1, pp. 858–880, First-quarter 2019.

[8] O. Alphand et al., "IoTChain: A Blockchain Security Architecture for the Internet of Things," *Proc. 2018 IEEE Wireless Commun. and Networking Conf. (WCNC'18)*, Feb. 2018, pp. 1–6, doi: 10.1109/WCNC.2018.8377385.

[9] R. Li and H. Asaeda, "A Blockchain-Based Data Life Cycle Protection Framework for Information-Centric Networks," *IEEE Commun. Mag.*, vol. 57, no. 6, pp. 20–25, June 2019.

[10] J. Guo, et al., "Enabling Blockchain Applications Over Named Data Networking," *Proc. IEEE Int. Conf. Commun.(ICC'19)*, May 2019, pp. 1–6, doi: 10.1109/ICC.2019.8761919.

[11] H. Li, et al., "Trust-Enhanced Content Delivery in Blockchain-Based Information-Centric Networking," *IEEE Network*, 7 pages (in press).

[12] M. Liu, F. R. Yu, Y. Teng, V. C. M. Leung, and M. Song, "Computation Offloading and Content Caching in Wireless Blockchain Networks with Mobile Edge Computing," *IEEE Trans. Vehicular Tech.*, vol. 67, no. 11, pp. 11008–11021, Nov. 2018.

[13] H. Chai, S. Leng, M. Zeng, and H. Liang, "A Hierarchical Blockchain Aided Proactive Caching Scheme for Internet of Vehicles," *Proc. 2019 IEEE Int. Conf. on Commun. (ICC'19)*, May 2019, pp. 1–6, doi: 10.1109/ICC.2019.8761482.

[14] V. Sharma, I. You, D. N. K. Jayakody, D. G. Reina, and K. R. Choo, "Neural-blockchain based Ultra-reliable Caching for Edge-enabled UAV Networks," *IEEE Trans. Industrial Informatics* (in press).

[15] K. Lei, Q. Zhang, J. Lou, B. Bai, and K. Xu, "Securing ICN-Based UAV Ad Hoc Networks with Blockchain," *IEEE Commun. Mag.*, vol. 57, no. 6, pp. 26–32, June 2019.

[16] Ripple, http://ripple.com/ [retrieved: Jan. 2020].

Selective Process Replication for Fault Tolerance in Large-scale, Heterogeneous Environments with Non-Uniform Node Failure Distribution

Longhao Li
Department of Computer Science
University of Pittsburgh
Pittsburgh, USA
Email: lol16@cs.pitt.edu

Taieb Znati
Department of Computer Science
University of Pittsburgh
Pittsburgh, USA
Email: znati@cs.pitt.edu

Rami Melhem
Department of Computer Science
University of Pittsburgh
Pittsburgh, USA
Email: melhem@cs.pitt.edu

***Abstract*—Future systems are scaling to a large number of cores. Consequently, their propensity to failure increases dramatically, making it more challenging to achieve forward progress for compute-intensive applications on a large number of cores. Pure process replication is a widely accepted technique to tolerate fail-stop errors. At extreme-scale, however, it is inadequate to achieve fault tolerance efficiently due to doubled or even tripled computational resources usage. In this paper, we propose a selective process replication model that only assigns replicas to failure-prone processes. It assumes cores fail independently, but non-identically. The simulation results show that, on average, selective replication reduces more than 35 percent of energy consumption and more than 25 percent of the time to completion comparing to full replication with 1 million cores, where 20 percent of them are failure-prone.**

Keywords–fault-tolerance; selective replication; cloud computing; heterogeneous environment.

I. Introduction

Cloud computing has been widely used as a computing platform for resource-intensive applications like *MapReduce*, which require massive data analysis [1]. Meanwhile, computing and information systems have become integral to all aspects of our society, and their significance will inevitably increase in the future. The demand of cloud computing as back-end support of these systems is growing. Exploiting the convenience of on-demand computing power and flexible, low-cost resources is the key to success. With the continuous increase in computational scale, the ability to support massive parallelism is required for the cloud computing platforms of the future.

Massive parallelism is supported by large scale systems that contain millions of computational cores. Such systems are plagued with massive energy consumption and high system failure rate. Even with the expected technology improvement, the rate of system level failures will dramatically increase with the number of computational cores increase. For example, a computing infrastructure with 200,000 cores will experience a Mean Time Between Failure (MTBF) of less than one hour, even when the MTBF of an individual core is as large as 5 years [2], [3], [4], [5].

MapReduce is a popular data processing computational model which is widely used in Cloud computing platforms. Applications based on MapReduce divide large amount of data into subloads and distribute them to small tasks that can execute in parallel and independently. The computational results will merge together after all the subtasks complete execution and produce the final results. Thus, a single failure on any of the sub-tasks may lead to delay time to completion. Also, applications may contain multiple stages of MapReduce computation. Multiple failures on different subtasks may lead to an unacceptable delay in response time. This will likely cause unpleasant experience for customers and lead to revenue reduction.

A Service Level Agreement (SLA) is a contract between a customer and a Cloud Service Provider (CSP). It specifies the response time requirement of the customer. Violations on the agreement would lead to a penalty, which would further result in revenue reduction. Also, longer completion time may cause additional energy consumption of task re-execution and poor utilization of resources. To ensure that the tasks can be accomplished before the agreed deadline, a certain level of reliability is necessary.

In order to maintain system reliability, a resilience strategy is required in such large-scale systems. Process replication fault tolerance strategy relies on redundancy in resources by replicating the entire process. The original and replicated process runs in parallel on different hardware so that if one of the processes failed, other processes would finish the task on time. Comparatively, it is unlikely that the main and replicated processes failed at the same time. Process replication requires additional energy consumption due to the replications of the same process. In large scale, however, the additional energy consumption is significant enough that need to be reduced. Thus, full replication is not suitable for the future large scale systems.

Furthermore, most studies in fault tolerance assume that failures occur independently and identically. However, due to aging and replacement, cores may appear to have different failure rates. New cores may appear to have a comparatively higher failure rate due to manufacturing defects, and old cores also have a high failure rate because the hardware is worn out. Other factors can also lead to difference in failure rates, such as working environment temperature or nodes' usage [6].

In this paper, we propose a selective replication framework for cloud computing that only replicate processes on unreliable cores. In order to minimize the energy consumption, the proposed framework only protect the cores which are prone to failure. The main contributions of this paper are the following:

- A selective replication framework for cloud computing

resilience that select processes on unreliable cores based on the age of the hardware.

- A simulation based experimentation and evaluation which contains sensitivity analysis of different workloads and different ratio of unreliable cores.

The rest of the paper is introduced as follows. We discuss about the related works in Section II and explain the aspects leading to heterogeneous environment in Section III. We introduce the selective replication framework in Section IV. In Section V, we discuss about the simulation setup and the evaluation results. Section VI concludes the paper and discusses about some possible future works.

II. Related Works

The field of fault tolerance in computing systems is well established, and significant advances on how to deal with faults have been achieved by different communities. Rollback and recovery are predominate mechanisms to achieve fault tolerance in current High Performance Computing (HPC) and cloud computing environments [7], [8], [9]. Upon the occurrence of a fault, recovery is achieved by restarting the computation from a safe checkpoint [8]. Both coordinated and uncoordinated checkpointing schemes rollback and recovery schemes have been proposed [7], [8], [9], [10]. The drawback of coordinated checkpointing is a lack of scalability, as it requires global process coordination [5], [11], [12], [13], [14]. Uncoordinated checkpointing has not been widely adopted in HPC environments, due to its dependency on applications [15], [16]. Multi-level checkpointing can benefit from tolerance to failure but may increase failure rates of individual nodes and increase per-node cost [17].

Process and state machine replication has long been used to provide fault tolerance in distributed [18] and mission critical systems [19]. Based on this technique, a process's state and computation are replicated across independent computing nodes. Redundancy has been proposed, to augment existing checkpointing techniques [20], [21], [22].

Study of failure modelling is another direction of research. Eric et al. found that Weibull and Log-normal are the best fitting distributions to model failure in the high performance computing system based on the history data study [23]. Nosayba and Bianca studied the impact of different factors on the reliability of HPC systems such as environmental factors and nodes' usages. Cooling system failure may cause node outages, and high usages can lead to a higher failure rate. They also find that some nodes fail more often than others even when they have the same hardware specification [6].

In general, replication requires doubling the number of cores, with increases power consumption, which might not be efficient enough for future generation exascale infrastructure. Message logging-based approaches have been proposed to harness applications' temporal computation and communication patterns to reduce the cost of checkpointing for hybrid systems. The cost of recovery, however, remains proportional to the system size and not to the degree of failure. Partial redundancy has been analytically studied for HPC environment [24]. In this work, we study a practical selective replication strategy for cloud computing environment.

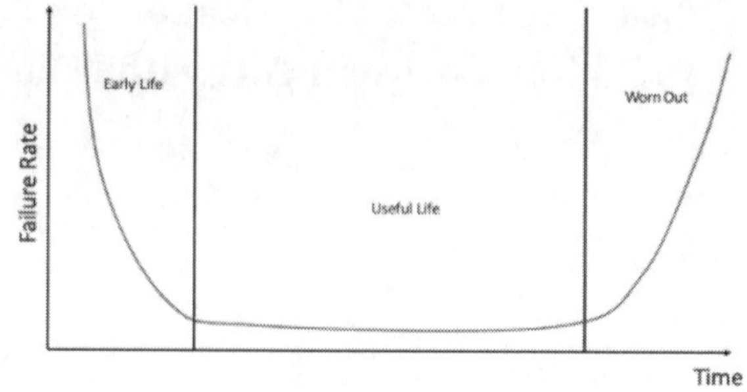

Figure 1. "Bathtub" Curve.

III. Heterogeneous Environment

As the age of computational cores increases, the likelihood of failure changes. It has been well studied and applied that the hardware reliability changes by following a "bathtub curve" as depicted in Figure 1 [25]. The life span of a hardware is divided into three periods: the early life period, the useful life period and the worn out period. The early life period is the beginning of the hardware's life span. It starts with a relatively high failure rate due to possible manufacturing defects. By fixing the defects, the failure rate continually decreases until it reaches the useful life period. The failure rate remains steady during the useful life period, and the useful life period is significantly longer than the other two life periods. When a hardware reaches the end of its life span, it start to wear out and the failure rates gradually increase. However, the increasing of failure rate is more gradual than the early life period.

Considering the hardware replacement and maintenance, systems may contain cores in different life periods and form a heterogeneity. Large-scale systems may encounter considerable amount of replacement of cores. Consequently, influence of unreliable cores in these systems cannot be neglected.

IV. Selective Replication

Process replication is one of the most popular fault-tolerance techniques. Full replication significantly reduces the failure likelihood, but also at least doubles the energy consumption and resource usage. To overcome this disadvantage, we propose a selective process replication model that only replicates processes host on error-prone cores. This is done because when compared to full replication, more cores are utilized for task computation, while processes on unreliable cores are protected. We assume that there are N number of cores assigned to the current job, and each core i has failure rate λ_i. The job has workload W. Assume each process occupies one core and executes in maximum speed. The subload is dependent on the number of main processes, M. In full replication, number of main processes occupies half of the available cores $M_f = \frac{N}{2}$, and the subload $w_f = \frac{W}{M_f}$ for each process. By selectively replicating processes, there are more cores available for main processes compared to that by using full replication, $M_s > M_f$. Therefore, the subload on each main process is reduced and so is the execution time. Consequently, the number of faults encountered may drop during execution and the time to completion may be reduced. Also, because of the reduction in redundancy, the energy

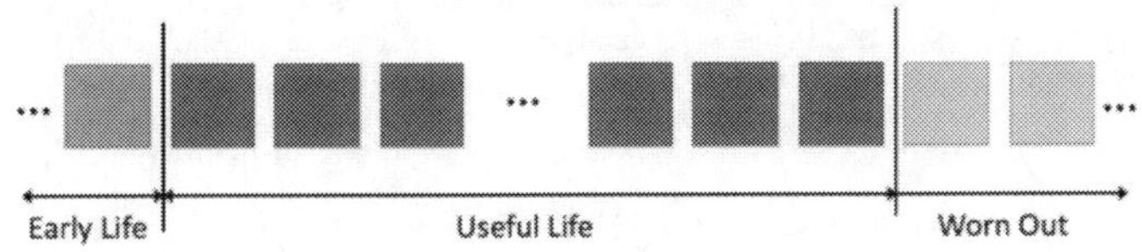

Figure 2. Cores in different life periods.

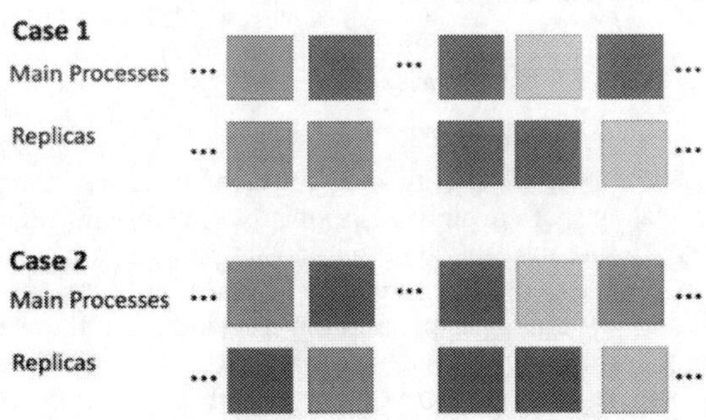

Figure 3. Cases of full replication.

consumption may be reduced. However, there are two major challenges that needs to be addressed for selective replication. The first challenge is to determine which cores need to be protected, and the second challenge is to determine which cores should be used to host replicas.

A. Replication Candidate Selection

Selecting processes that need to be replicated is a hard problem considering there are no absolute standards to determine if a core is reliable. In practice, however, we can estimate the cores' reliability by their history of failure in execution. In this paper, we estimate reliability as the failure rate based on the life span of the cores. Replicating processes on most unreliable cores is an essential guidance for candidate selection. Furthermore, determining the number of cores to replicate is a problem we need to solve. Analytical modeling is one way to determine the optimal ratio. However, it may not be the best solution if the modeling has too many assumptions. Moreover, the optimization may be compute-intensive and may not be able to produce a truly optimal solution. In our model, since cores are divided to three life periods, it may be a good approach to only replicate processes on cores in early life and worn out life period as a practical solution.

B. Replica Assignment

The goal of replica assignment is to determine which core should be used to host replicas to minimize the failure likelihood of any replication pair. It is studied that the best strategy to assign replica is pairing the most unreliable core with the most reliable core for replications [24].

We assume that there are cores in three different life periods, as shown in Figure 2. There is a small portion of cores in early life and worn out period as shown in Figure 2. Figure 3 illustrates the different cases of full replication. The obliviousness of failure rate difference may cause two unreliable cores to be paired for replication. These pairs may

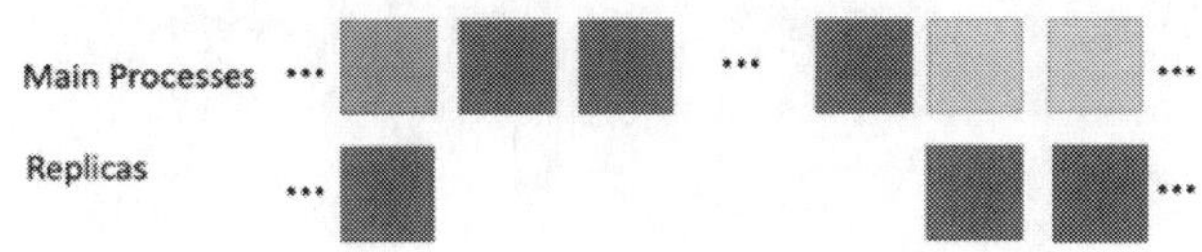

Figure 4. Selective Replication Assignment.

Algorithm 1 Algorithm for Selective Replica Assignment

Input:
$C^e = \{c^e_1, c^e_2, ..., c^e_K\}$
$C^u = \{c^u_1, c^u_2, ..., c^u_L\}$
$C^w = \{c^w_1, c^w_2, ..., c^w_Q\}$
Output: Assignment
Initialization : Assignment = {}
for $i = 1$ to K **do**
  Assignment = Assignment ∪ $\{< c^e_i, c^u_i >\}$
end for
for $i = 1$ to Q **do**
  Assignment = Assignment ∪ $\{< c^w_i, c^u_{L-i-1} >\}$
end for
for $i = K + 1$ to $L - Q$ **do**
  Assignment = Assignment ∪ $\{< c^u_i >\}$
end for
return Assignment

Figure 5. Algorithm for Selective Replica Assignment.

be less reliable than a core in useful life without replication. Additionally, the pairing of two reliable cores will lead to a high probability of energy wastage. Figure 4 depicts the proposed selective replication solution. Processes on cores in early life and worn out period are protected by replicas chosen from cores in the useful life period. The remaining cores in useful life period are utilized to complete the job by themselves. Algorithm 1, as shown in Figure 5, is used for selective replica assignment. C^e, C^u and C^w are sets of cores in early life period, useful life period and worn out period, respectively. The output is a set of tuples where each tuple is an assignment that contains either a pair of cores for replication or a single core for execution by themselves.

C. Discussion

Considering the practicality of the proposed model, it is very easy to apply it to current cloud computing infrastructures. Given the estimation of failure rate changes, which may be estimated by the past data, boundaries of different life periods are easy to determine. Therefore, it is straightforward to categorize the cores into the discussed three life periods. Consequently, the selective replica assignment algorithm is able to execute in linear time. Hence, the replica selection and assignment methods can be easily embedded with current cloud computing job scheduling algorithms for better resource allocation.

V. Experimental Evaluation

To evaluate our model, a comprehensive simulation-based experiment is conducted. To fairly compare selective replica-

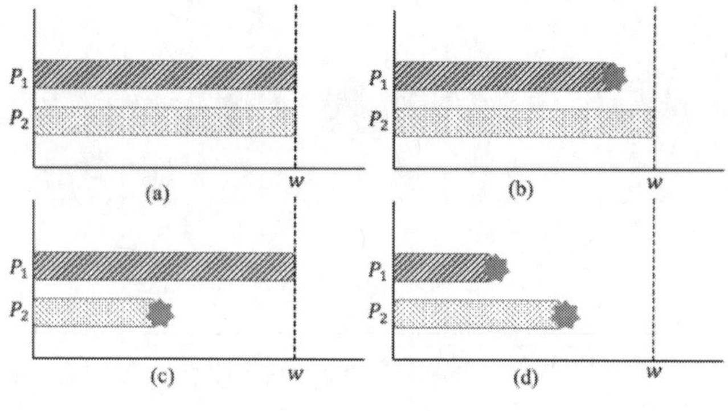

Figure 6. Failure cases on replication group of 2.

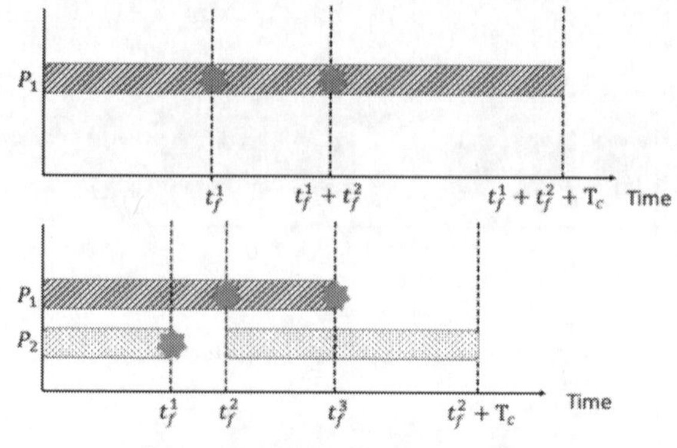

Figure 7. Failure on processes with and without replica.

tion with full replication, we simulate two baseline models – full replication with optimal replica assignment (baseline 1) and full replication with random replica assignment (baseline 2).

A. Simulation Setup

The simulation assumes that there are one million cores available ($N = 1,000,000$) such that each core hosts only one process and executes at maximum speed. To simulate the heterogeneous environment, the experiment assumes that cores are divided into three classes. These three classes represent three life periods: early life, useful life and worn out life period. We assume that the reliability of cores in each class is identical to make the simulation controllable. Furthermore, we assume that failures occur independently, but not identically. With consideration that the computational time is significantly shorter than the life span, we assume that the failure rate does not change during execution. Consequently, we make the assumption that failure follows an exponential distribution with mean set as the MTBF of the core. The MTBF of each core in these classes is 1 year, 10 years and 3 years, respectively. We varied the total workload (W) and ratio of cores in each class to observe how selective replication performed in different scenarios.

We use CSIM19 (C version) to conduct the simulation [26]. To simulate the failure time of a core, a random number is drawn from an exponential distribution with mean set as the core's MTBF. This random number represents the failure time of the core. Failure occurs only if the failure time is earlier than the failure free completion time. If failure occurs and the process has either no replica or a failed replica, the task is re-executed. We assume that the re-execution is on the repaired cores, and maintain the same fault tolerance strategy, with or without replicas. Thus, the re-execution may encounter additional failures on one subload's execution. For processes assigned a replica, there are four possible cases that may occur during the execution, as depicted in Figure 6. Case (a) is the execution of subload w without failure. Cases (b) and (c) represent the execution with one failure on the process or its replica. Case (d) has both the process and its replica failed before the task completion.

We normalize the hourly dynamic energy consumption rate of each core as $R^D = 1$, i.e., for each core, the dynamic energy consumption of executing one-hour job is 1 unit of energy consumption. Other than dynamic energy, static energy is another aspect of energy consumption. It comes from the power leakage of several components (processor, memory, etc.). We define the static energy consumption as a predefined fraction $\rho = 0.5$ of dynamic energy consumption [27]. The calculation of energy consumption is based on the execution time of each process, including execution time before failure and re-execution time. The minimum execution time is the failure free completion time of subload w. There is no maximum execution time for a subload w because it is possible to have failure in every execution and re-execution. For example, a process P_1 without replication encountered two failures during execution as depicted in Figure 7. The execution time before failure for each failed execution is t_f^1 and t_f^2, respectively. The total energy consumption of process P_1 is $E^1 = (1+\rho)R^D(t_f^1 + t_f^2 + T_c)$, where T_c is the failure free execution time of subload w. Since we represent the workload as hours of execution, the failure-free execution time is same as that of the subload, $T_c = w$. For processes with replicas, the computation of energy consumption requires to consider the failure time for both process and its replica when failures occur in both cores. The second example in Figure 7 depicts the case where both the process P_1 and its replica P_2 failed before the completion of task. The re-execution starts from t_f^2, and the replica P_2 finishes the task at $t_f^2 + T_c$. The energy consumption of this process pair is calculated as $E^{1,2} = (1+\rho)R^D t_f^3 + (1+\rho)R^D(t_f^1 + T_c)$. The total energy consumption is the sum of the energy consumption for all the processes. We assume no energy consumption after completion of the execution for each process. The time to completion of the total workload W is the maximum completion time among all the subtasks. For each setup, we simulate the job execution 100 times and report the average result to overcome the bias of randomness.

B. Sensitivity Analysis on total workload

The goal of this analysis is to evaluate the performance of the proposed model with different workloads. Heavier workload indicates longer time to completion. Intuitively, longer time to completion indicates that failures are more likely to occur during execution. We vary the total workload from 10 to 2000 million hours of works. The percentage of cores in each class is 5%, 80%, and 15%, respectively. The results of comparing selective replication with baseline model 1 and 2 are depicted in Figures 8 and 9, respectively. Compared to full replication with and without optimal replica

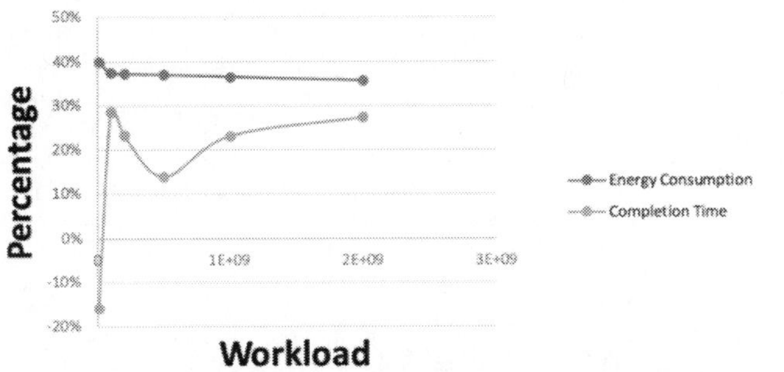

Figure 8. Comparison between selective replication with baseline 1 in different workloads.

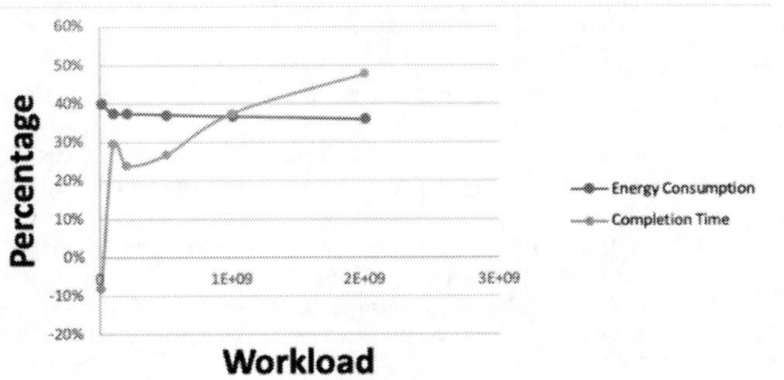

Figure 9. Comparison between selective replication with baseline 2 in different workloads.

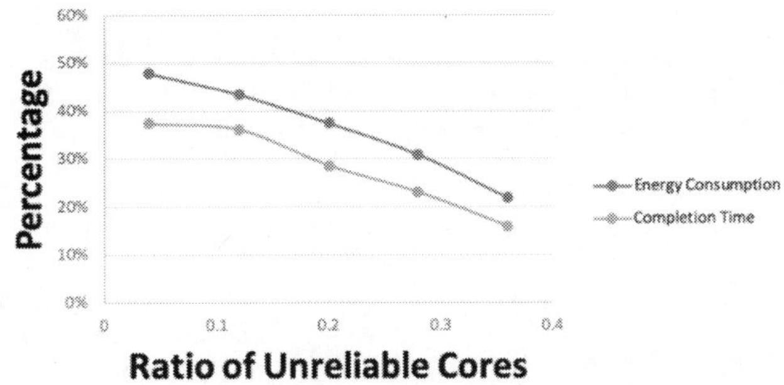

Figure 10. Comparison between selective replication with baseline 1 in different ratios of unreliable cores.

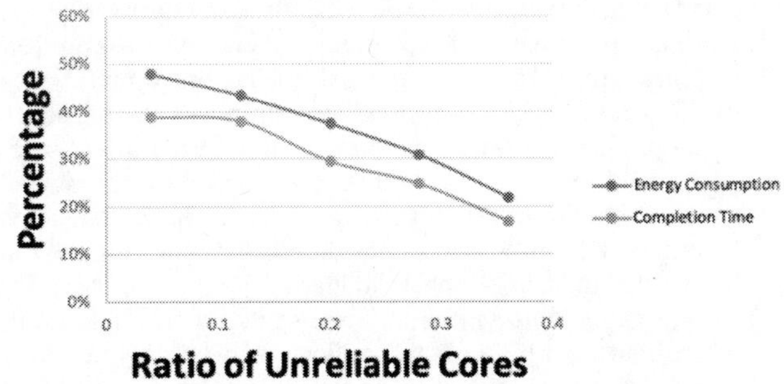

Figure 11. Comparison between selective replication with baseline 2 in different ratios of unreliable cores.

assignment, selective replication can reduce more than 35 % of energy consumption. With 10 million hours of total work, full replication has slightly shorter response time. Selective replication model finishes the job in 23.9 hours. The optimal replica assignment with full replication completes the job in 20.6 hours, while the full replication with random replica assignment completes the job in 22.1 hours. There is about 40 % of energy consumption reduced compared to both baseline models. Due to the fairly light workload, it is very unlikely to have failure on both the process and its replica simultaneously. Therefore, the completion time of full replication is very close to the failure free completion time as $T_c = w = \frac{2W}{N} = 20$ hours. Compared to baseline 2, which is the traditional full replication model, the difference on time to completion is very marginal.

As the total workload increases, the selective replication model has a shorter response time than the baseline models. For 2000 million hours of work, selective replication achieved 48% reduction in time to completion compared to full replication with random replica assignment. It indicates that, with heavier workload, the likelihood of failure on process with replication start to increase and it causes longer total completion time. For selective replication, the total completion time is under double of failure free completion time for full replication when there are no more than 1000 million hours of work. This sensitivity analysis shows that selective replication has advantage on energy consumption with different workloads and advantage on time to completion with heavy workload in cloud computing platform.

C. *Sensitivity Analysis on ratio of cores in each class*

The goal of this analysis is to evaluate the performance of selective replication with different percentage of unreliable cores. The total workload for this analysis is 100 million hours of work. We vary the percentage of cores in early life and worn out period to represent different scenarios. We maintain the ratio of cores in these two classes as 1:3 to ensure that the results are comparable. The results of comparing selective replication with baseline model 1 and 2 are depicted in Figures 10 and 11, respectively. When 36% of cores are unreliable (9% of cores in early life and 27% of cores in worn out period)(a relatively more unreliable scenario of the analysis), selective replication reduces about 22% of energy consumption compared to two baseline models. It also reduces about 16% and 17% of time to completion when compared to full replication with and without optimal replica assignment strategy, respectively. Considering that in our approach, only 28 % of cores are not associated with replicas, the improvements are significant. As the reliability increases, the reduction in energy consumption and time to completion increases. With only 4 % of unreliable cores, selective replication achieves about 48% of reduction in energy consumption and about 39% of reduction in time to completion when compared to the baseline model 2.

Hence, we observe that selective replication has an advantage in all scenarios with different reliabilities, and has more advantage in reliable scenarios. Also, our experiment validated that the optimal replica assignment strategy has advantage on cloud computing platform as the baseline model 1 always has shorter time to completion when compared to baseline model 2.

VI. Conclusion and Future Works

The major contribution of this paper was to address the problem that, when infrastructures grow to large scale, traditional full replication fault tolerance strategy requires high amount of resources. By considering the failure rate difference of computational cores of different ages, we proposed the selective replication model that only replicates processes on unreliable cores to reduce the energy consumption and response time. The results of our experimental evaluations showed that, compared to full replication, selective replication can reduce more than 35 percent of energy consumption and about 30 percent of completion time simultaneously with 100 million hours of workload and 1 million cores.

In this work, we proposed a model categorizing the cores into three different classes. We may gain more reduction in energy consumption if we increase the granularity. Our framework is a practical approach to reduce energy consumption and response time. However, it may not be the optimal solution to this problem. An optimization solution with the necessary assumptions may produce better results. Furthermore, the proposed solution estimated failure rates based on the age of the cores. Other factors such as spatial and temporal dependencies among core failures is not considered. By exploring the emerging online and offline machine learning methods, we may gain better insights into temporally and spatially correlated failures, which can then be used to predict when failures are likely to occur. Therefore, it would be possible to dynamically assign replicas to further reduce energy consumption and execution time.

Acknowledgment

This material is based in part upon work supported by the National Science Foundation under Grants Number CNS-1252306 and CNS-1253218. Any opinions, findings, and conclusions or recommendations expressed in this material are those of the authors and do not necessarily reflect the views of the National Science Foundation.

References

[1] A. W. Services, "Overview of amazon web services," Amazon Whitepapers, 2019.

[2] B. Mills, R. E. Grant, K. B. Ferreira, and R. Riesen, "Evaluating energy saving for checkpoint/restart," in First International Workshop on Energy Efficient Supercomputing (E2SC) in conjunction with SC13: The International Conference for High Performance Computing, Networking, Storage and Analysis, Nov 2013, pp. 1–8.

[3] K. Ferreira et al., "Evaluating the viability of process replication reliability for exascale systems," in Proceedings of 2011 International Conference for High Performance Computing, Networking, Storage and Analysis, ser. SC '11. New York, NY, USA: ACM, 2011, pp. 1–12.

[4] R. Oldfield et al., "Modeling the impact of checkpoints on next-generation systems," in Mass Storage Systems and Technologies, 2007. MSST 2007. 24th IEEE Conference on, sept. 2007, pp. 30 –46.

[5] R. Riesen et al., "Redundant computing for exascale systems," Sandia National Laboratories, no. SAND2010-8709, December 2010.

[6] N. El-Sayed and B. Schroeder, "Reading between the lines of failure logs: Understanding how hpc systems fail," in 2013 43rd annual IEEE/IFIP international conference on dependable systems and networks (DSN). IEEE, 2013, pp. 1–12.

[7] E. N. M. Elnozahy, L. Alvisi, Y.-M. Wang, and D. B. Johnson, "A survey of rollback-recovery protocols in message-passing systems," ACM Comput. Surv., vol. 34, no. 3, Sep. 2002, pp. 375–408.

[8] S. Kalaiselvi and V. Rajaraman, "A survey of checkpointing algorithms for parallel and distributed computers," Sadhana, vol. 25, no. 5, 2000, pp. 489–510.

[9] B. Meroufel and G. Belalem, "Adaptive time-based coordinated checkpointing for cloud computing workfl ows," Scalable Computing: Practice and Experience, vol. 15, no. 2, 2014, pp. 153–168.

[10] J. Daly, "A model for predicting the optimum checkpoint interval for restart dumps," in Int. Conf. on Computation Science, 2003, pp. 3–12.

[11] E. N. Elnozahy and J. S. Plank, "Checkpointing for peta-scale systems: A look into the future of practical rollback-recovery," IEEE Transactions on Dependable and Secure Computing, vol. 1, no. 2, 2004, pp. 97–108.

[12] M. Bougeret, H. Casanova, Y. Robert, F. Vivien, and D. Zaidouni, "Using group replication for resilience on exascale systems," INRIA, Rapport de recherche RR-7876, Feb. 2012.

[13] P. Hargrove and J. Duell, "Berkeley lab checkpoint/restart (blcr) for linux clusters," in J. Phys. Conf. Ser, vol. 46, no. 1, 2006, p. 494.

[14] N. Losada, G. Bosilca, A. Bouteiller, P. González, and M. J. Martín, "Local rollback for resilient mpi applications with application-level checkpointing and message logging," Future Generation Computer Systems, vol. 91, 2019, pp. 450–464.

[15] G. Zheng, L. Shi, and L. V. Kalé, "FTC-Charm++: an in-memory checkpoint-based fault tolerant runtime for Charm++ and MPI," in Cluster Computing, 2004, pp. 93–103.

[16] A. Guermouche, T. Ropars, E. Brunet, M. Snir, and F. Cappello, "Uncoordinated checkpointing without domino effect for send-deterministic mpi applications," in IPDPS, May 2011, pp. 989–1000.

[17] D. Hakkarinen and Z. Chen, "Multilevel diskless checkpointing," Computers, IEEE Transactions on, vol. 62, no. 4, April 2013, pp. 772–783.

[18] F. B. Schneider, "Implementing fault-tolerant services using the state machine approach: A tutorial," ACM Computing Surveys (CSUR), vol. 22, no. 4, 1990, pp. 299–319.

[19] J. F. Bartlett, "A nonstop kernel," in ACM SIGOPS Operating Systems Review, vol. 15, no. 5. ACM, 1981, pp. 22–29.

[20] J. Stearley et al., "Does partial replication pay off?" in IEEE/IFIP International Conference on Dependable Systems and Networks Workshops (DSN 2012). IEEE, 2012, pp. 1–6.

[21] J. Elliott et al., "Combining partial redundancy and checkpointing for hpc," in 2012 IEEE 32nd International Conference on Distributed Computing Systems. IEEE, 2012, pp. 615–626.

[22] H. Casanova, Y. Robert, F. Vivien, and D. Zaidouni, "Combining Process Replication and Checkpointing for Resilience on Exascale Systems," INRIA, Research Report RR-7951, May 2012. [Online]. Available: https://hal.inria.fr/hal-00697180 [retrieved: January, 2020]

[23] E. Heien et al., "Modeling and tolerating heterogeneous failures in large parallel systems," in Proceedings of 2011 International Conference for High Performance Computing, Networking, Storage and Analysis. ACM, 2011, p. 45.

[24] Z. Hussain, T. Znati, and R. Melhem, "Partial redundancy in hpc systems with non-uniform node reliabilities," in SC18: International Conference for High Performance Computing, Networking, Storage and Analysis. IEEE, 2018, pp. 566–576.

[25] W. M. Jones, J. T. Daly, and N. DeBardeleben, "Application monitoring and checkpointing in hpc: looking towards exascale systems," in Proceedings of the 50th Annual Southeast Regional Conference. ACM, 2012, pp. 262–267.

[26] H. Schwetman, "Csim19: a powerful tool for building system models," in Proceeding of the 2001 Winter Simulation Conference (Cat. No. 01CH37304), vol. 1. IEEE, 2001, pp. 250–255.

[27] C. Rusu, R. Melhem, and D. Mossé, "Maximizing rewards for real-time applications with energy constraints," ACM Transactions on Embedded Computing Systems (TECS), vol. 2, no. 4, 2003, pp. 537–559.

Towards a Software Defined Multi-Domain Architecture for the Internet of Things

Leonel Piscalho Junior
Lisboa, Portugal
email: leopiscalho@gmail.com

José Moura
Instituto de Telecomunicações
ISCTE - Instituto Universitário de Lisboa
Lisboa, Portugal
email: jose.moura@iscte-iul.pt

Rui Neto Marinheiro
Instituto de Telecomunicações
ISCTE - Instituto Universitário de Lisboa
Lisboa, Portugal
email: rui.marinheiro@iscte-iul.pt

***Abstract* — The emerging communication networks tend to aggregate heterogeneous networking infrastructures as well as data flows with very distinct requisites. This implies that the complete satisfaction of Quality of Service (QoS) metrics is very difficult to achieve, using the legacy management solutions. Alternatively, the Software Defined Networking (SDN) paradigm offers a logical centralized management of the necessary network resources for data flows, namely the ones originated in sensor devices. Therefore, this work investigates a solution that meets the QoS requirements of traffic from remote Internet of Thing (IoT) devices. To achieve this goal, we have designed a SDN-based solution that manages a network topology formed by several domains. We assume each network domain is controlled by its own SDN controller. In addition, our solution assumes that the several SDN controllers need to be orchestrated among them to maximize the management efficiency of the available end-to-end network resources. This orchestration is done via an SDN transit domain ruled by the ONOS SDN-IP application. We have emulated network topologies with IoT devices to evaluate the proposed solution in terms of its functionality, robustness against network failures, and QoS support. Analyzing the obtained results, our solution can support a cross-controller SDN domain communication. It is also capable of reacting automatically to topology failures. In addition, it can prioritize the traffic within the network infrastructure, providing to the end users strong guarantees on the desired quality for the exchange of data associated to the applications they aim to use.**

Keywords-Multi-domain; SDN; IoT; QoS

I. INTRODUCTION

The exponential data traffic growth and the network heterogeneity are challenging the legacy networks. This occurs due to the high-level of complexity to interconnect several services and smart devices, both related to the emerging paradigm of IoT. They exchange real-time information through the networking infrastructure to be processed by intelligent applications. This implies not only various types of traffic, but also the ability to offer QoS guarantees across the network [1]. With the advent of SDN, it offers new ways to design more flexible networks.

SDN stands out for its flexibility, programmability and centralized logical management, which separates the data layer from the control layer, allowing the passage of logical operations from the data plane devices to a centralized software controller, which operates over those devices [2].

Due to the size, heterogeneity, and complexity of current networks, approaches based on multiple domains are very scalable. This domain multiplicity consists in the network division in different administrative domains, each managing its network subset and optimizing both the domain performance and the fulfilment of QoS requisites.

Previous research [3] tries to improve the IP domain routing management and provide end-to-end QoS paths [4]. Nevertheless, the available work is mostly based on a centralized controller approach that handles routing within a single administrative domain, offering very limited results. In this way, the SDN configuration of inter-domain scenarios is very pertinent. The orchestration among all the SDN controllers is also vital to ensure reliable end-to-end services, such as routing, and QoS deployment.

The interaction between the different SDN domains depends on an inter domain routing protocol, and BGP is a very popular protocol for this. ONOS [5] and ODL [6] are SDN controllers that support distributed scenarios. They are also most commonly used in wide area networks (WANs). Nevertheless, these two SDN controllers have slight performance differences as shown in [10], where ONOS seems to be a better choice for our current WAN scenario.

The authors of [7] suggest a solution designated by Inter Cluster ONOS Network application (ICONA). This solution manages a large networking scenario under the same administrative domain (i.e., GEANT) with geographically distributed controllers. Another contribution [8] proposes a gradual implementation of SDN-based solutions over different administrative domains that interoperates with other non-SDN based domains. They study a peering application among distinct Autonomous Systems (ASs) called SDN-IP, which runs at the top of the ONOS SDN controller.

Due to the low number of literature contributions supporting end-to-end QoS in IoT networks with scarce resources, the SDN-IP application is very important to achieve our goal for ensuring QoS support in distributed systems with multiple SDN controllers. Therefore, the research question that motivated our work is "How to Provide the necessary resources to meet QoS and robustness requirements for traffic from heterogeneous IoT devices in a distributed system with multiple SDN controllers?".

The main contributions of the this paper are the deployment of a SDN solution that manages resources from ASs to meet QoS and robustness requirements for routing heterogeneous traffic across those ASs. The routed traffic is from heterogeneous devices, including IoT ones, located at the network edge.

The remaining part of the current paper is following described. Section II presents the literature review in the related research areas. Section III discusses the design of the proposed solution. Section IV is about the deployment of the proposed contribution. Section V discusses the performed tests and their results. Finally, Section VI presents some general conclusions about the current contribution and some promising future work.

II. LITERATURE REVIEW

This section briefly revises the literature in the next topics: SDN architecture, inter-domain communication, and IoT.

A. SDN Architecture

The SDN is a new emerging network paradigm to simplify networking management, where the data and control layers are separated. In addition, SDN enables the programming of the network operation [2]. This programming can be made with distinct levels of hardware abstraction. In this way, the SDN controller can program the network devices at the data plane but the former needs to know in advance some specifics from the latter ones, such as the number and characteristics of ports at each device. In a distinct way, a networking application at the top-most layer of the SDN architecture, as shown in Fig. 1, can program the network topology without knowing any detail about the network data plane.

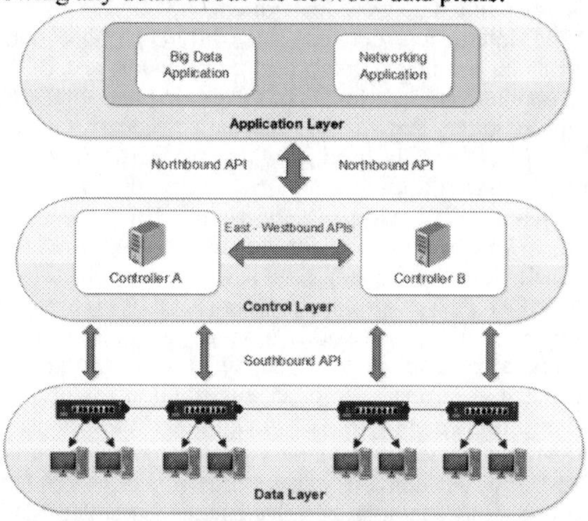

Figure 1. SDN architecture.

Fig. 1 shows an SDN architecture with three layers. The bottom layer is the data layer, which consists of compatible SDN devices, like routers and switches. The intermediate layer is the control layer. It is formed by the controllers that have the global vision of the network. The control layer communicates with the devices at the data layer through a Southbound protocol (e.g., OpenFlow). The application layer is the top-most layer. It communicates with controllers via Northbound APIs (e.g., Restful); this layer has several running applications that deploy many relevant management services.

Separating these layers, there are two vertical communication channels to connect each pair with Northbound/Southbound APIs, as well as East/Westbound APIs to provide horizontal communication between controllers, aiming the federation between domains.

B. Inter-Domain Communication

Initially, SDN was based on a single controller's approach to manage an entire network. Despite its simplicity in terms of both development and operation, it faces some limitations when deployed in large networks, regarding reliability and scalability. An SDN design with a single controller can become unreliable due to the issue of a single point of failure. Moreover, a single SDN controller can become overwhelmed when working with multiple simultaneous requests from the data plane [9]. Alternatively, a multiple controllers approach, provides solutions to mitigate the problems just discussed, such as the single point of failure, and low scalability [2][9]. The authors of [9] discusses some challenges imposed to SDN-based solutions with multiple controllers for managing large networks, such as, complexity, scalability, consistency, reliability and load balancing.

There are several distributed architectures formed by multiple SDN controllers namely horizontal or hierarchical [2]. They also discuss several methods to establish communications among SDN controllers. In [1], a comparative study of the most currently used SDN controllers is presented. From these, we highlight ODL and ONOS. Both support a fully distributed architecture and an SDN implementation across diverse networking domains [2]. Although these two options are similar, there are some differences [10], which justifies ONOS as a more suitable controller than ODL to explore the full potential of SDN in carrier-grade scenarios, as the one of our paper.

A multi-domain SDN architecture refers to a set of different administrative SDN domains or ASs that exchange information regarding network status, configuration, or other relevant network services, such as packet routing to a destination. In addition, Border Gateway Protocol (BGP) [11] is the most commonly used protocol to provide the end-to-end IP routing services over administrative domains. Then, each SDN controller needs to process an external learned BGP route to a destination prefix and translate it to local routing rules, which are only valid within the network domain the controller is responsible for. It is expected that summing up the individual routing contributions from the diverse SDN controllers results in a final aggregated outcome that fulfils the end-to-end BGP route.

C. IoT Overview

An Internet of Things (IoT) domain is a network of physical devices and sensors with embedded technology that interacts with the local environment. The IoT network not only collects data but it also exchanges the data to some servers located at remote clouds or even to some fog servers located at the network periphery. There are many IoT scenarios, such as health, home automation, smart transportation, environmental monitoring, or smart grids.

Recent work [12] has highlighted the relevance of SDN-based systems for controlling network domains formed by IoT devices and surveyed previous related contributions. However, SDN solutions for wireless networks and, more specifically, in wireless sensor (and actuators) networks do not abound [13]. Delivering end-to-end service orchestration chains, across multiple SDN domains, for an IoT infrastructure deployment, including data collection at the cloud, edge processing, and publishing services with quality differentiation is still at its infancy [14].

The present paper provides some novel contributions regarding the line of research discussed in the current section.

III. PROPOSAL DESIGN

As previously mentioned, the main goal of the current paper is to investigate a solution that meets the QoS requirements of data traffic originated at IoT devices in a heterogeneous network with multiple domains ruled by SDN controllers. We next discuss the design of our proposal.

Fig. 2 shows the design of a network topology formed by multiple administrative domains.

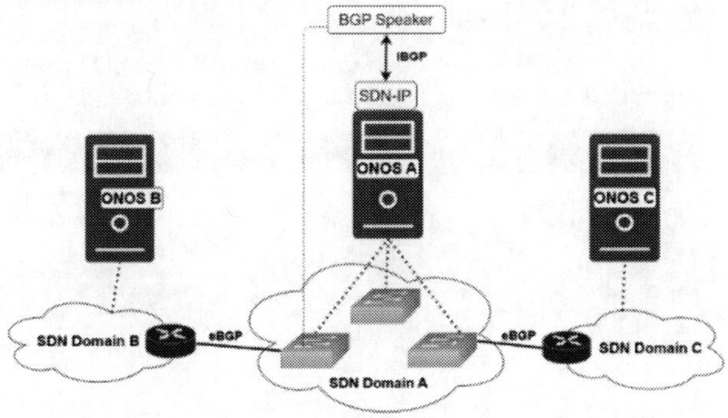

Figure 2. System design.

Each administrative domain is controlled by an SDN controller located at the intermediate level of the proposed architecture. In this way, SDN domain A works as a transit AS, which interconnects different externals SDN domains (B and C) that interface with the domain A, through BGP routers.

The data plane is formed by switches, BGP routers, and end host devices. At the application plane, there are BGP speakers that behave like BGP route reflectors, learning from the BGP routers IP destination prefixes and passing them to the SDN-IP application. Then, this application interacts with the SDN controller. From the previous interaction, the BGP learned paths are mapped to compatible data flow rules, which are transferred via Southbound protocol to the switches.

At the top layer are running applications that define how the network operates. In the transit domain A, the SDN-IP application allows, as already explained, the routing of packets among BGP ASs. The previous routing implies the forwarding of packets among the diverse switches belonging to the SDN Domain A. In addition, some auxiliary applications in the SDN controller of Domain A are also required (e.g., Configs and ProxyARP).

One of the most important QoS concept is that the traffic should not be treated equally, e.g., we need to prioritize the usage of communication link resources. Therefore, in our proposal we also prioritize the traffic in a network that is a mixture of IoT and legacy flows. The traffic prioritization is based on creating distinct virtual output queues offered at the data plane switches. In addition, some flow rules are installed in the data plane switches. These flow rules allow traffic to be served by different queues according to the traffic priority. In our work, we assume that the traffic priority is unrelated with the priority field normally used in OpenFlow flow rules. An interesting future prospect could be to use the OpenFlow priority field for controlling the traffic quality.

IV. PROPOSAL DEPLOYMENT

This section discusses the testbed topology and the deployment of our proposal to manage that topology. It aims to satisfy QoS requirements in the presence of heterogeneous flows, some originated from remote IoT devices. The network infrastructure is formed by several administrative domains.

A. *Multi-Domain Topology*

Table I lists all software and tools used to deploy and validate our proposal.

TABLE I. SOFTWARE USED IN THE DEPLOYMENT

Category	**Software / Technology**
Northbound Application	SDN-IP
SDN Controller	ONOS 1.15.0
Software Switch	OpenvSwitch 2.9.2
Southbound Communication	OpenFlow
Interdomain Protocol	BGP
Network Emulator	Mininet
BGP Software	Quagga
Traffic Analyser	Wireshark, Tcpdump
Virtual Hypervisor	Oracle Virtual Box
VM Operating System	Ubuntu 16.04
Traffic Generator and Measurement	Iperf
Video transmitter Application	VLC

Firstly, the general idea is to deploy a scenario that provides end-to-end communication among diverse SDN domains. A virtual network topology was built to meet these conditions and is presented in Fig. 3. The proposed system consists of three administrative SDN domains, each managed by its own ONOS SDN controller. In the top-most layer of the current architecture the SDN-IP application is running that enables the communication between SDN domains using BGP. At the data path layer there are terminal hosts and software switches (i.e., OpenvSwitch) interacting to the associated SDN controller via Southbound (i.e., OpenFlow).

Therefore, we have configured the entire network topology using the Mininet emulator. The topology has three SDN domains, each managed by its controller. The central domain (A) works as a transit AS, responsible for interconnecting the remaining external networks. Each external network, in this case B, C is considered a different AS, which interfaces with the central domain (A) through routers, running Quagga, a well-known software emulator for routing packets. In the central domain (A), there is an SDN controller with an SDN-IP application running on its top that learns BGP routes to destination prefixes previously announced by the BGP routers of the network topology.

After the learning phase, the SDN controller of domain A translates each learned BGP route to SDN intents. Then, the same SDN controller converts each intent in to several flow rules, which are then transferred from the SDN controller to the data plane switches, using the OpenFlow protocol. These switches are the ones previously selected by the SDN controller to support an AS transit ingress/egress routing intent associated to a previously announced BGP IPv4 prefix.

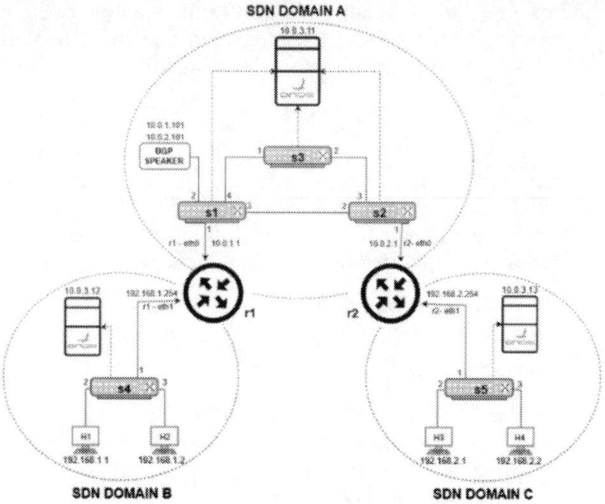

Figure 3. Multi-domain topology.

B. QoS Deployment

This scenario considers a security system monitorization, installed on the public road. This consists of vigilance cameras equipped with motion sensors transmitting RTP video flow by VLC and generic user computers generating UDP traffic. Motion sensor cameras were simulated using network devices. The testbed topology for this is shown in Fig. 4.

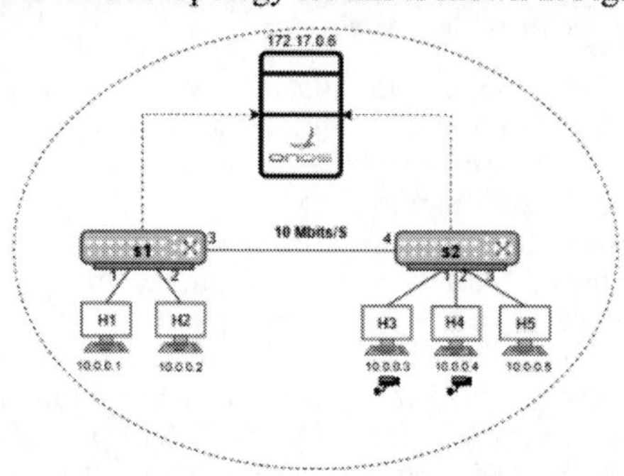

Figure 4. QoS testbed topology.

We deployed in one SDN domain to test quality of service (QoS_topology.py), but the same logic can be extended to larger scenarios implementing multiple domains. We limited all network links to 10 Mbit/s, using the Traffic Control (TC).

Initially all the traffic is going through the same path and if the motion sensor detects movement, the vigilance cameras should have a higher priority than the other non-video traffic. This implies the video traffic is transferred to a new queue and consequently can transmit the video with the highest quality without the competition of another non-video traffic. The queues are configured in OVS switch s1 using *ovs-vsctl* within the Mininet script that builds up the topology used in the current scenario.

As a conclusion of this sub-section, we assume that the traffic exchanged through the testing network should not be treated equally, e.g., we need to prioritize the usage of communication link resources. Therefore, in our proposal we will effectively prioritize the traffic in a network that is used by a mixture of IoT and legacy traffic. The traffic prioritization is based on creating distinct virtual output queues offered at the network switches. In addition, we have used a script that via Northbound API (e.g., HTTP POST request) forces the installation of adequate flow rules on the data plane switches. These flow rules allow traffic to be routed to different queues according to each traffic priority.

V. PROPOSAL EVALUATION

This section evaluates the solution in terms of its main functionality, the automatic reaction to a network failure, and the differentiated support of QoS for concurrent flows.

A. System Validation

The ONOS GUI on Fig. 5 shows the SDN ONOS controlled topology and summary information at the top.

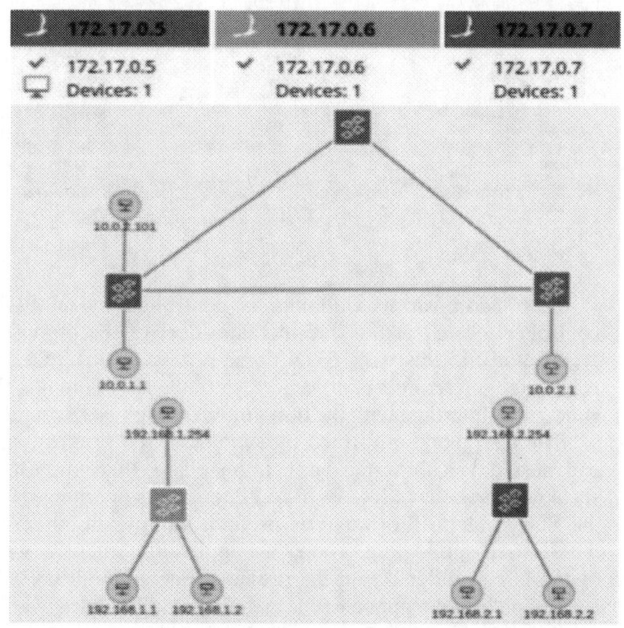

Figure 5. Topology at ONOS web GUI.

There are three SDN controllers, each one represented by a colour to evidence the network devices controlled by that controller. The first SDN controller (172.17.0.5) controls the transit domain, which contains three central switches. The second SDN controller (172.17.0.6), represented by the light blue colour, manages the left domain, which contains a single switch, interconnecting two terminal hosts (for example, h1 with IP address 192.168.1.1/24). The same happen with the SDN domain (172.17.0.7) represented by red colour on the right, which contains a switch with two hosts (h3 and h4). Hence, we have a physically distributed system with multiple controllers, each managing its own domain autonomously, but the central domain is managed by the ONOS SDN-IP Application. We have validated our system using ICMP traffic originated at host h1 (192.168.1.1) with destination at host h3

(192.168.2.1). Analyzing Fig. 6, the first ICMP attempt has a larger Round Trip Time than remaining ones because the SDN controller after deciding about the message routing path of the first attempt (reactive mode), it installs in the switches the path rules for next ping attempts (proactive mode).

```
mininet> h1 ping -c 3 192.168.2.1
PING 192.168.2.1 (192.168.2.1) 56(84) bytes of data.
64 bytes from 192.168.2.1: icmp_seq=1 ttl=61 time=17.0 ms
64 bytes from 192.168.2.1: icmp_seq=2 ttl=61 time=0.441 ms
64 bytes from 192.168.2.1: icmp_seq=3 ttl=61 time=0.129 ms

--- 192.168.2.1 ping statistics ---
3 packets transmitted, 3 received, 0% packet loss, time 2000ms
rtt min/avg/max/mdev = 0.129/5.860/17.010/7.885 ms
```

Fig 6. Successful connectivity test using ping from h1 to h3.

B. Link Failure Test

System failure detection is a very important aspect for ensuring fault tolerance in large scale distributed systems. In our case, if the SDN controller detects a link failure, it should quickly and effectively divert traffic to an alternate path to ensure the continuation of the communication service until the primary link is again operational. The goal is to reduce the time required to detect a failure and mitigate its negative impact on the traffic network routing.

Fig. 7 shows selected messages from several traffic captures made by Tcpdump. At the beginning of the test, the topology was operating without any failure and the used routing path between h1 and h3 was through switches s1 and s2 of the transit Domain A (s1-eth3, s2-eth2). One can also note that the initial ICMP Request TTL is 64 (h1-eth0) and then it is decremented down to 61 (h2-eth0), meaning that message has traversed three routers (i.e., r1, BGP speaker, r2) on its way to the destination node. Through the shortcut "A" in the ONOS GUI, which is shown in the first row of Fig. 7, one can see the traffic path being used and its speed.

Topology

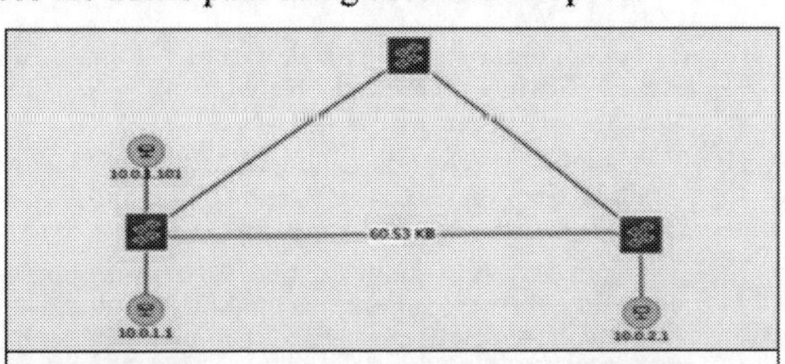

H1-eth0	10:58:36.709985 IP (tos 0x0, ttl 64, id 13117, offset 0, flags [DF], proto ICMP (1), length 84) 192.168.2.1 > 192.168.2.1: ICMP echo request, id 12153, seq 1, length 64
S2-eth2	10:58:36.741345 IP (tos 0x0, ttl 62, id 13117, offset 0, flags [DF], proto ICMP (1), length 84) 192.168.2.1 > 192.168.2.1: ICMP echo replay, id 13117, seq 1, length 64
S3-eth1	
H3-eth0	10:58:36.756439 IP (tos 0x0, ttl 61, id 3307, offset 0, flag [DF], proto ICMP (1), length 84) 192.168.2.1 > 192.168.2.1: ICMP echo replay, id 12153, seq 1, length 64

Figure 7. ICMP request from H1 to H3, S1-eth3 UP

Then, we turned off the link between s1 and s2, forcing that link to fail. This implied an event communication failure associated to a specific ONOS intent. This intent is like a routing path through the transit domain that incorporates the failed link. Consequently, after the failure occurrence, the ONOS analyzes the topology of the transit domain to find out an alternative path, which it should also interconnect the same ingress/egress points of the transit domain that were being used before that failure. In the current experiment, as indicated in Fig. 8, the alternative path through the transit Domain A was as follows s1-eth4, s3-eth1, s3-eth2, and s2-eth3.

We have validated the SDN-IP/BGP integration proposal, using a scenario where a failure in a specific routing path was mitigated by the functional robustness of ONOS intents. For future work, we aim to measure the time required to detect a link failure and to successfully detour traffic from that failure.

Topology

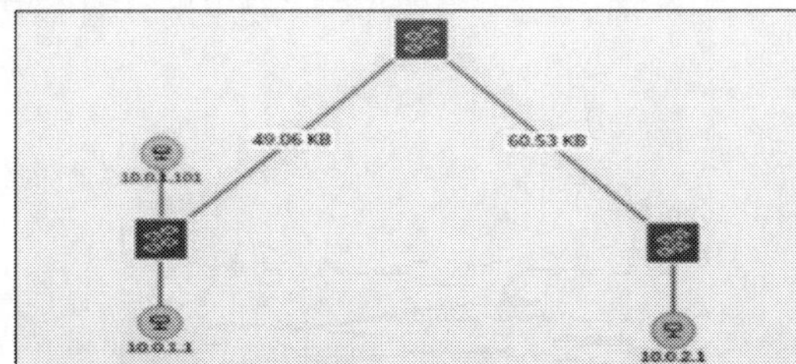

H1-eth0	11:05:34.305256 IP (tos 0x0, ttl 64, id 61729, offset 0, flags [DF], proto ICMP (1), length 84) 192.168.2.1 > 192.168.2.1: ICMP echo request, id 11341, seq 1, length 64
S2-eth2	
S3-eth1	11:05:34.327286 IP (tos 0x0, ttl 62, id 61729, offset 0, flags [DF], proto ICMP (1), length 84) 192.168.2.1 > 192.168.2.1: ICMP echo replay, id 12361, seq 1, length 64
H3-eth0	11:05:34.329246 IP (tos 0x0, ttl 61, id 61729, offset 0, flags [DF], proto ICMP (1), length 84) 192.168.2.1 > 192.168.2.1: ICMP echo request, id 11341, seq 1, length 64

Figure 8. ICMP request from H1 to H2, S1-eth3 DOWN

C. Qos Test Validation

Here, the QoS deployment topology is validated. When the topology is started, three devices will be enabled, two of them are VLC terminals and another is an RTP video server. Each VLC terminal receives a video from a simulated remote vigilance camera. In the device with the video server, the streaming of the video was started, which is consumed by two distinct VLC clients, simulating videos from two remote webcams. As mentioned, one of the videos is on the switch priority queue and the other is on the non-priority queue, sharing the available network resources with other flows.

Fig. 9 shows the rate trend of three flows used in the current test. It shows the system reaction after the video on the non-priority queue suffers the interference from UDP traffic, which tends to starve all the available network resources. Interference may be accessed using quality monitors [15] placed at strategic network point.

The trend of Fig. 9 is basically divided into three time intervals. The first one (between 8s and 24s) is when there is no interference in the video transmission of camera 2, because we still have no interference from UDP traffic over the RTP video traffic that uses the switch non-priority queue. We can see that when the video transmission starts, the blue line (camera 1) is transmitting the video at the same rate (1 Mbps) of the red line (camera 2). In addition, the camera 1 is in the high priority queue and camera 2 is in the low priority queue.

The second interval begins around 24s, when UDP traffic is injected for the purpose to cause interference with the camera 2 video transmission. Therefore, we can see that UDP (black line) traffic uses practically all the link bandwidth (i.e., around 8 Mbps) and the camera 2 rate significantly decreases (temporarily below 80 Kbps), degrading the quality of the received video from that camera (see Fig. 10, right side). This occurs because the UDP traffic is competing with camera 2 traffic at the same output queue. At this moment, we do not yet observe any corrective action from the SDN system to protect the quality of camera 2 video.

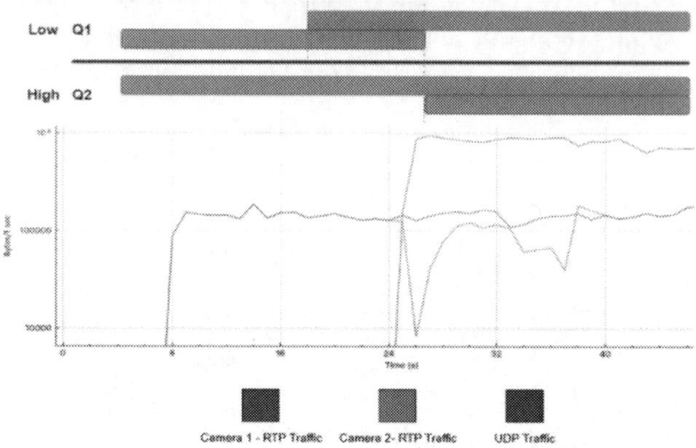

Figure 9. Rate trend of the three flows in our QoS test.

In the last time interval of current test, starting around 26s, the QoS mechanism is applied to improve transmission quality for camera 2. In this way, a flow rule is dynamically set to change the video to the switch high priority queue. In this way, we can see that the video transmission of camera 2 return to its normal rate and consequently enhance the perceived quality at the receiver. We can conclude that at that moment the UDP traffic is no longer interfering with the transmission quality from camera 2.

Figure 10. Remote vigilance videos with UDP traffic competition.

VI. CONCLUSIONS AND FUTURE WORK

The current work main goal was to understand how to deploy and manage a network infrastructure formed by several administrative domains, with multiple SDN controllers, satisfying QoS and robustness requirements of heterogeneous flows, some originated from IoT devices.

Our experimental results have shown that the proposed SDN-based solution can ensure communication between physically distributed SDN domains via the BGP protocol through a transit SDN system with the SDN-IP application running on the ONOS controller. We also demonstrate that our contribution is sensitive to link failures by redirecting traffic directly to another available path and ensuring the normal network operation.

Referring to quality of service, we have also validated within a network domain ruled by an SDN controller that traffic prioritization can be deployed. For that, some OpenFlow rules were installed in the data plane switches, which have output queues differentiated by the level of quality of service they aim to serve. In this way, we have shown that video from remote surveillance cameras, despite the presence of UDP traffic that normally starves all the available resources, can be transmitted with an optimum quality, thus meeting pertinent safety concerns in public environments. Further work is envisioned for testing the QoS scenario with IoT IPv6-compatible devices across ASs.

REFERENCES

[1] F. X. A. Wibowo, M. A. Gregory, K. Ahmed, and K. M. Gomez, "Multi-domain Software Defined Networking: Research status and challenges," *J. Netw. Comput. Appl.*, vol. 87, pp. 32–45, Jun. 2017.

[2] Y. Zhang, L. Cui, W. Wang, and Y. Zhang, "A survey on software defined networking with multiple controllers," *J. Netw. Comput. Appl.*, vol. 103, pp. 101–118, Feb. 2018.

[3] A. Gupta *et al.*, "SDX: A software defined internet exchange," *Comput. Commun. Rev.*, vol. 44, no. 4, pp. 551–562, 2015.

[4] V. Kotronis, X. Dimitropoulos, R. Kloti, B. Ager, P. Georgopoulos, and S. Schmid, "Control Exchange Points: Providing QoS-enabled End-to-End Services via SDN-based Inter-domain Routing Orchestration," pp. 3–4, 2016.

[5] P. Berde *et al.*, "ONOS : Towards an Open , Distributed SDN OS," pp. 1–6.

[6] S. Badotra, "Open Daylight as a Controller for Software Defined Networking," no. May 2017, 2018.

[7] M. Gerola *et al.*, "ICONA: Inter Cluster ONOS Network Application," 2015.

[8] D. Gupta and R. Jahan, "Inter-SDN Controller Communication: Using Border Gateway Protocol," no. April, pp. 1–16, 2014.

[9] T. Hu, Z. Guo, P. Yi, T. Baker, and J. Lan, "Multi-controller Based Software-Defined Networking: A Survey," *IEEE Access*, vol. 6, pp. 15980–15996, 2018.

[10] F. Bannour, S. Souihi, and A. Mellouk, "Distributed SDN Control: Survey, Taxonomy, and Challenges," *IEEE Commun. Surv. Tutorials*, vol. 20, no. 1, pp. 333–354, 2018.

[11] V. Kotronis, A. Gämperli, and X. Dimitropoulos, "Routing centralization across domains via SDN: A model and emulation framework for BGP evolution," *Comput. Networks*, vol. 92, pp. 227–239, 2015.

[12] M. Ndiaye, G. P. Hancke, and A. M. Abu-mahfouz, "Software Defined Networking for Improved Wireless Sensor Network Management : A Survey," pp. 1–32, 2017.

[13] A. C. Anadiotis, L. Galluccio, S. Milardo, G. Morabito, and S. Palazzo, "SD-WISE: A Software-Defined WIreless SEnsor network," *Comput. Networks*, vol. 159, pp. 84–95, 2019.

[14] W. Cerroni *et al.*, "Intent-based management and orchestration of heterogeneous openflow/IoT SDN domains," *2017 IEEE Conf. Netw. Softwarization Softwarization Sustain. a Hyper-Connected World en Route to 5G, NetSoft 2017*, 2017.

[15] J. R. S. Soares, L. A. Da Silva Cruz, P. Assuncao, and R. Marinheiro, "No-reference lightweight estimation of 3D video objective quality," in *2014 IEEE International Conference on Image Processing, ICIP 2014*, 2014, pp. 763–767.

RSSI-Based Access Points and Channel Selection Method Using Markov Approximation

Masato Kagaya*, Tomotaka Kimura†, Kouji Hirata‡, and Masahiro Muraguchi*
* Faculty of Engineering, Tokyo University of Science, Tokyo 125-8585, Japan
Email: murag@ee.kagu.tus.ac.jp
† Faculty of Science and Engineering, Doshisha University, Kyoto 610-0321, Japan
Email: tomkimur@mail.doshisha.ac.jp
‡ Faculty of Engineering, Kansai University, Osaka 564-8680, Japan
Email: hirata@kansai-u.ac.jp

***Abstract*—In recent years, a large number of Access Points (APs) have been deployed in public facilities such as stations and airports. These allow users with wireless devices to select their APs from several APs. In general, the communication quality depends on the selected APs, and thus the AP selection is an important technical issue. In this paper, we propose an access-point and channel selection method based on Received Signal Strength Indication (RSSI) value using Markov approximation. In Markov approximation, the system is optimized by individual behavior of users forming a time-reversible continuous-time Markov chain. In the proposed method, to suppress frequent and useless state transitions, users do not select APs with small RSSI values. This reduces the number of state transitions, and thus the time-average objective function value can be increased rapidly. Through simulation experiments, we demonstrate the effectiveness of the proposed method.**

Keywords–Access point selection; channel selection; Markov approximation; RSSI.

I. Introduction

In recent years, wireless LANs have become increasingly common, and Access Points (APs) have been deployed with very high density [1][2]. In particular, the number of APs deployed in public facilities, such as stations and airports, has increased rapidly. This allows users with wireless devices to select the APs that they can connect from several APs. In general, the communication quality depends on AP selection, and thus the AP selection is an important technical issue.

In the existing AP selection method [1][3], the AP with the highest Received Signal Strength Indicator (RSSI), which is an indicator of the received signal power strength, is selected from the APs within the communication range of each user's device. Because each user selects an AP independently, the user selections are concentrated to the AP with the highest RSSI even when there are other APs nearby. As the load on the AP increases, the throughput decreases, and thus the existing AP selection method does not work well.

In order to solve this problem, other AP selection methods have been considered [4][5][6]. The authors in [6] proposed an AP selection method using Markov approximation. Markov approximation is a recently developed decentralized optimization framework [7]. In Markov approximation, an approximate solution to the optimization problem can be obtained by designing the system to follow a time-reversible continuous-time Markov chain [8][9][10]. Specifically, the time spent in each state in the Markov chain depends on the objective function value, and the aim is to maximize the objective function value in terms of the time-average. The system is designed so that when the system state has the high objective function value, the system stays in this state for a long time. In contrast, when the system stays at the state with the low objective function value, the system quickly transitions from these states. This causes the system to remain in a state with a high objective function values. It was shown in [6] that throughput fairness can be achieved by using Markov approximation to minimize user throughput as an objective function. However, this existing method has the problem that the increases in the objective function value are suppressed because the transitions to states with low objective function values occur frequently.

In this paper, we propose a new AP and channel selection method using Markov approximation based on RSSI values. In our proposed method, each user changes their connections to APs with a high RSSI compared with the current RSSI, and does not change the connection to an AP with a low RSSI value. This makes it possible to suppress the transition to states where the objective function value is low, and to increase the time average value. Through simulation experiments, we demonstrate the effectiveness of the proposed method.

The rest of this paper is organized as follows. In Section II, we explain the system model of this paper. Section III discusses our proposed method. In Section IV, the performance of the proposed method is examined using the results of the simulation experiments. Finally, we conclude the paper in Section V.

II. System Model

We consider a situation with multiple users and multiple APs, as shown in Figure 1. Let $\mathcal{K}$ be the set of users and $\mathcal{A}$ be the set of deployed APs, respectively. Further, let $\mathcal{C}$ be the set of channels that can be used by each AP. In this case, each AP $a \in \mathcal{A}$ selects one channel from $|\mathcal{C}|$ channels, and each user $k \in \mathcal{K}$ selects one AP from the set $\mathcal{A}$ of APs.

The system state is represented by the combination of the channels selected by each AP and the APs selected by each user. Here, let the $1 \times |\mathcal{A}|$ vector $\boldsymbol{x}$ and $1 \times |\mathcal{K}|$ vector $\boldsymbol{y}$ denote the channels selected by the APs and the APs selected by the users, respectively, where the ith element $x_i \in \{1, 2, \ldots, |C|\}$ of $\boldsymbol{x}$ is the channel selected by AP i and the jth element $y_j \in \{1, 2, \ldots, |\mathcal{A}|\}$ of $\boldsymbol{y}$ is the AP selected by user j. The system state is represented as $(\boldsymbol{x}, \boldsymbol{y})$, and the set $\mathcal{Z}(t)$ of feasible

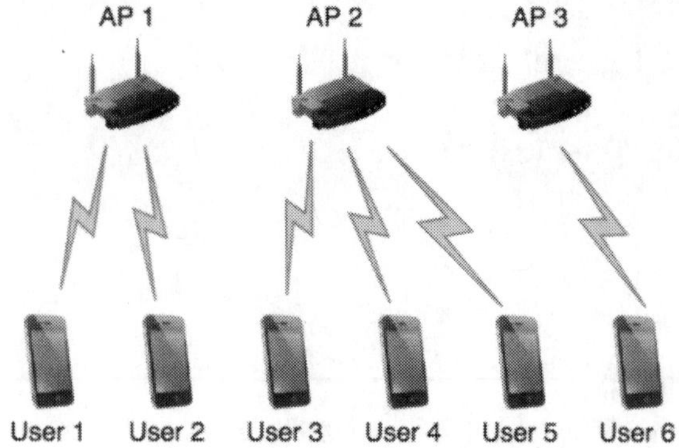

Figure 1. System model ($|\mathcal{K}| = 6, |\mathcal{A}| = 3$).

system states at time t can be represented as follows:

$$\mathcal{Z}(t) = \{(\boldsymbol{x}, \boldsymbol{y}) \mid x_i \in [1, |\mathcal{C}|],\ y_j \in [1, |\mathcal{A}|] \\ i = 1, 2, \ldots, |\mathcal{A}|,\ j = 1, 2, \ldots, |\mathcal{K}|\}. \quad (1)$$

In the following, we call a feasible state $z \in \mathcal{Z}(t)$ a *strategy*.

When multiple users select the same AP, it is assumed that frequency resources can be used evenly by time division multiplexing. Therefore, when strategy z is adopted, the throughput $u_k(z)$ for each user k is defined as

$$u_k(z) = m_{k,a}/N_c(z), \quad (2)$$

where $m_{k,a}$ is the throughput that can be achieved when only user k is connected to AP a, and $N_c(z)$ is the total number of users connected to the same channel $c \in \mathcal{C}$ used as user k. Note that this multiplexing assumption is simple, and thus we will tackle to the more realistic situation.

In order to achieve the throughput fairness, we consider the problem of maximizing the *utility* $\min_{k \in \mathcal{K}} u_k(z)$, which is the minimum throughput among all users in $\mathcal{K}$. The problem of maximizing the utility at time t can be formulated as

$$\max_{z \in \mathcal{Z}(t)} \{\min_{k \in \mathcal{K}} u_k(z)\}. \quad (3)$$

III. RSSI-BASED AP AND CHANNEL SELECTION METHOD USING MARKOV APPROXIMATION

We first explain about the Markov approximation, and then describe the details of our proposed method.

A. Markov approximation

This section assumes a static situation where there is no increase or decrease in the number of users. In such a static situation with $\Phi_z = \min_{k \in \mathcal{K}} u_k(z)$ as an objective function, an approximate solution can be obtained by solving the following problem [7].

$$\max_{\boldsymbol{p}(t) \leq 0} \quad \sum_{z \in \mathcal{Z}(t)} p_z \Phi_z - \frac{1}{\beta} \sum_{z \in \mathcal{Z}(t)} p_z \log p_z, \quad (4)$$

$$\text{subject to} \quad \sum_{z \in \mathcal{Z}(t)} p_z = 1, \quad (5)$$

where p_z is the time ratio at which the strategy $z \in \mathcal{Z}(t)$ is adopted, and $\boldsymbol{p}(t)$ is a $1 \times |\mathcal{Z}(t)|$ vector $(p_1, p_2, \cdots, p_{|\mathcal{Z}(t)|})$. Furthermore, β is a parameter for controlling the accuracy of the approximation, which improves as β increases. Because this problem is a nonlinear programming problem, the optimal solution p_z^* can be obtained by solving the following problem based on the KKT (Karush-Kuhn-Tucker) condition.

$$\Phi_z - \frac{1}{\beta} \log p_z^* - \frac{1}{\beta} + \eta = 0, \quad \forall z \in \mathcal{Z}(t) \quad (6)$$

$$\sum_{z \in \mathcal{Z}(t)} p_z^* = 1, \quad (7)$$

$$\eta \geq 0, \quad (8)$$

where η is a Lagrange multiplier.

The solution p_z^* ($z \in \mathcal{Z}(t)$) to the above problem is given by

$$p_z^* = \frac{\exp(\beta \Phi_z)}{\sum_{z' \in \mathcal{Z}(t)} \exp(\beta \Phi_{z'})}. \quad (9)$$

Note that this solution p_z^* also represents the steady-state probability of a time-reversible continuous-time Markov chain on $\mathcal{Z}(t)$ [7]. Therefore, if the APs and the users follow the Markov chain in which the steady-state probability is p_z^*, we obtain an approximate solution to the original problem.

It is known that a continuous-time Markov chain is time-reversible when the following local equilibrium equations for all strategies z, z' in $\mathcal{Z}(t)$ are satisfied:

$$p_z^* q_{z,z'} = p_{z'}^* q_{z',z}, \quad (10)$$

where $q_{z,z'}$ is the transition rate from strategy z to strategy z'. Substituting (1) into the above equation yields the following equation:

$$\exp(\beta \Phi_z) q_{z,z'} = \exp(\beta \Phi_{z'}) q_{z',z} \quad (11)$$

To achieve a time-reversible Markov chain, the transition rate $q_{z,z'}$ is set to be $q_{z,z'} = \alpha(t)/\exp(\beta \Phi_z)$, where $\alpha(t)$ is a parameter that controls the transition rate. In [6], we evaluated the performance in a static situation, and showed that an accurate solution with high accuracy can be obtained by fixing $\alpha(t)$ to be an appropriate value.

B. Details of our proposed method

In our proposed method, each AP and each user select a channel and an AP according to the Markov chain on $\mathcal{Z}(t)$, respectively. Figure 2 presents a flowchart of our proposed method. Each AP $a \in \mathcal{A}$ chooses a random number r according to the exponential distribution with parameter $\lambda(t) = \alpha(t)(|\mathcal{C}| - 1)/\exp(\beta \Phi_z)$. On the other hand, each user $k \in \mathcal{K}$ chooses a random number r according to the exponential distribution of $\lambda(t) = \alpha(t)(|\mathcal{A}_k| - 1)/\exp(\beta \Phi_z)$, where $\mathcal{A}_k$ represents the set of APs with the high RSSI values for user $k \in \mathcal{K}$. After choosing the random number r, all APs and users start counting down.

When the count for either an AP or a user falls below 0, the strategy is changed according to the following procedure. If the count for AP $a \in \mathcal{A}$ is less than 0, then one channel is randomly selected from the channels in $\mathcal{C} \setminus \{c\}$, and AP a switches to the selected channel. On the other hand, if the count for a user $k \in \mathcal{K}$ is less than 0, then one AP a is randomly selected from the set $\mathcal{A}_k$ of APs with the high RSSI values, and then switches to AP a. When switching is completed, the APs and users are notified of the new utility value. Specifically, if the strategy is changed to z_{new} by switching, then the utility is

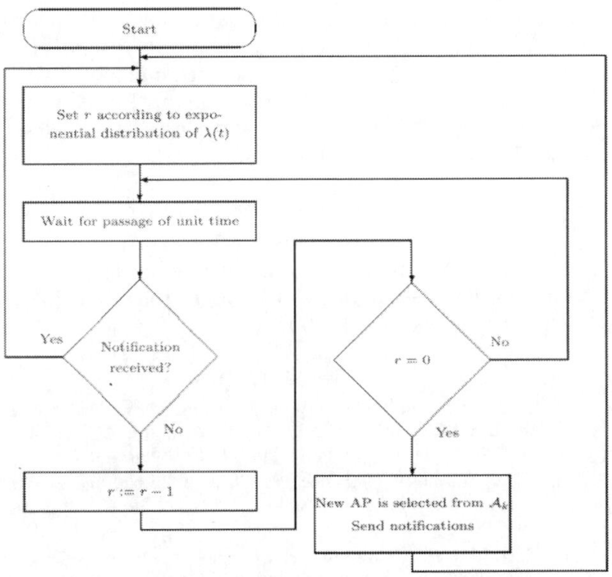

Figure 2. Flowchart of AP k in our proposed method.

updated to $\Phi_{z_{\text{new}}}$. After that, the APs and users that received the notification of a strategy change cancel their countdown and reset the random number r.

In our proposed method, $\alpha(t)$ is set as follows:

$$\alpha(t) = \frac{\gamma \cdot \exp(\beta M(t))}{|\mathcal{A}|(|\mathcal{C}|-1) + \sum_{k \in \mathcal{K}}(|\mathcal{A}_k|-1)}, \tag{12}$$

where $\gamma > 0$, and $M(t)$ is the maximum utility from time 0 to time t. Therefore, if $\Phi_z > M(t)$, $M(t)$ is updated to $M(t) := \Phi_z$.

IV. Performance Evaluation

We first describe the simulation model, and then present the simulation results and discuss the effectiveness of our proposed method.

A. Simulation model

The number of users is $|\mathcal{K}| = 50$, the number of APs is $|\mathcal{A}| = 20$, and the number of channels is $|\mathcal{C}| = 10$. The maximum throughput $m_{k,a}$ is chosen randomly from $\{40, 45, 50\}$. In addition, the parameter γ controlling the transition rate is set to be 0.01. Unless otherwise specified, the set of APs with the high RSSI values for user k is represented by $\mathcal{A}_k = \{a \mid m_{k,a} = 50, a \in \mathcal{A}\}$. Unless otherwise stated, we set β the moderate value, i.e., $\beta = 3$, because for large β, the accuracy of the approximation improves but the number of state transitions is very large.

We compare the performance of our proposed method with that of the existing AP selection method using Markov approximation in [6]. In the existing AP selection method, the connected AP is selected from $\mathcal{A} \setminus \{a\}$ regardless of the RSSI value. When $\mathcal{A}_k = \mathcal{A}$ in the proposed method, the behavior of the proposed method is equivalent to that of the existing method.

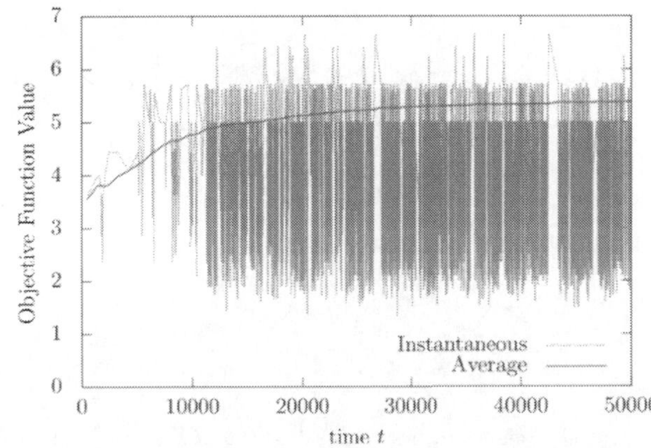

(a) Our proposed method.

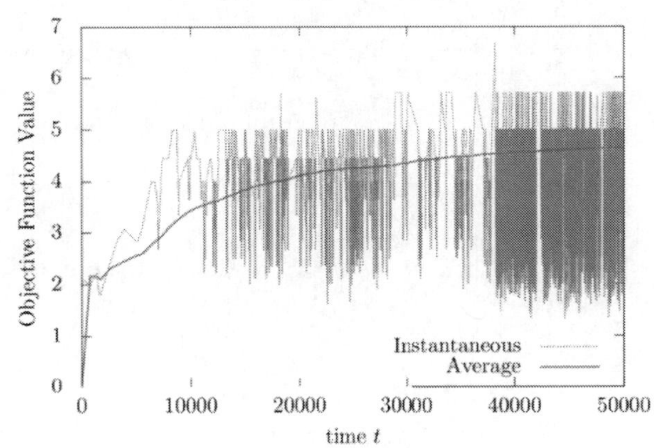

(b) Existing method.

Figure 3. Objective function value as a function of the elapsed time t.

B. Results

Figures 3(a) and 3(b) show the objective function value of our proposed method and the existing method as a function of the elapsed time t, respectively. The instantaneous value in Figure 3 represents the value of the objective function $\Phi(t)$ at time t, and the average value represents the time average value of the objective function value $\bar{\Phi}(t)$, which is defined by the following equation.

$$\bar{\Phi}(t) = \frac{1}{t}\int_0^t \Phi(t)dt. \tag{13}$$

From Figure 3(b), because the existing method does not consider the RSSI value, the system state transitions to states with small objective function values and stays in those states for a long time. Therefore, the time-average $\bar{\Phi}(t)$ of the objective function value increases slowly. On the other hand, as we can see from Figure 3(a), the time-average $\bar{\Phi}(t)$ of the objective function increases more rapidly compared with that of the existing method. This result indicates that considering the RSSI values suppress transitions to states with low objective function values.

Next, we examine the effects of differences in the set of APs $\mathcal{A}_k$ with high RSSI values. Figure 4 shows the time-average objective function values $\bar{\Phi}(t)$ for $\mathcal{A}_k = \{a \mid m_{k,a} =$

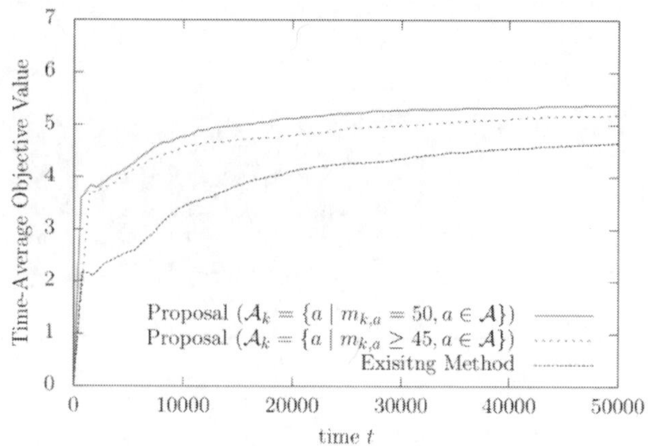

Figure 4. Time-average objective function value as a function of the elapsed time t.

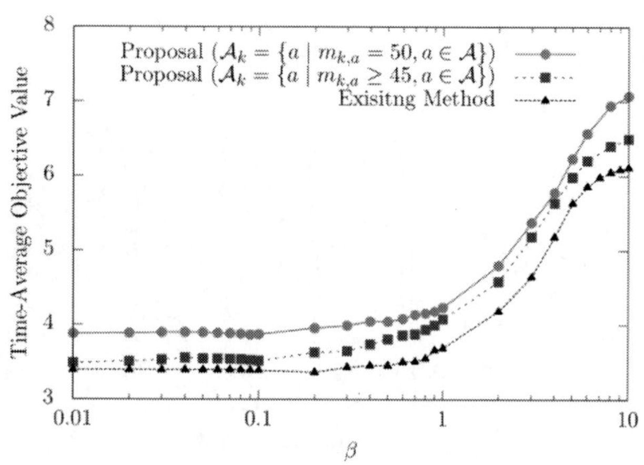

Figure 5. Time-average objective function value as a function of the parameter β.

$50, a \in \mathcal{A}\}$ and $\mathcal{A}_k = \{a \mid m_{k,a} \leq 45, a \in \mathcal{A}\}$. From this figure, it can be seen that by not selecting the AP with the lowest RSSI value ($m_{k,a} = 40$), the objective function value increases rapidly.

Figure 5 shows the time-average objective function value $\bar{\Phi}(t)$ as a function of the parameter β that controls the approximation accuracy. Note that each point represents the value $\bar{\Phi}(50,000)$, i.e., the time-average value when 50,000 time units have passed. From Figure 5, the value of the objective function value increases monotonically as the parameter β increases. This is because increasing parameter β also increases the accuracy of the approximation increases, so that the objective function value also increases. In addition, the objective function value for the proposed method is larger than that for the existing method for all β, and thus confirming the effectiveness of considering the RSSI value.

V. Conclusion

In this paper, we have proposed an AP selection method using Markov approximation by considering RSSI values. The performance of the proposed method was compared with that of the existing method using simulation experiments, and it was shown that the rate of increase of the objective function value could be improved. In this paper, we have considered a static environment with a fixed number of users. In reality, AP selection occurs in a dynamic environment where the number of users changes. Therefore, a topic for future research is evaluating the performance of the proposed method in a dynamic environment.

Acknowledgment

This work was supported in part by the Ministry of Internal Affairs and Communications Japan through the Strategic Information and Communications R&D Promotion Programme (SCOPE) under Grant 195007002.

References

[1] Y. Bejerano, S. Han, and L. Li, "Fairness and load balancing in wireless LANs using association control," *IEEE/ACM Transactions on Networking*, vol. 15, no. 3, pp. 560–573, June 2007.

[2] A. Nicholson, Y. Chawathe, M. Chen, B. Noble, and D. Wetherall, "Improved access point selection," *Proc. of MobiSys' 06*, pp. 233–245, June 2006.

[3] S. Vasudevan, D. Papagiannaki, C. Diot, J. Kurose, and D. Towsley, "Facilitating access point selection in IEEE 802.11 wireless networks," *Proc. of IMC ' 05*, pp. 293–298, Oct. 2005.

[4] Y. Fukuda, T. Abe, and Y. Oie " Decentralized access point selection architecture for wireless LANs," *Proc. of WTS ' 04*, pp. 137–145, May 2004.

[5] V. A. Siris and D. Evaggelatou, " Access point selection for improving throughput fairness in wireless LANs," *Proc. of 10th IFIP/IEEE IM ' 07*, pp. 469–477, May 2007.

[6] T. Kimura, K. Hirata, and M. Masahiro, "Adaptive access-point and channel selection method using Markov approximation, " *International Journal of Distributed Sensor Networks*, vol. 14, no. 2, pp. 1–11, Jan. 2018.

[7] M. Chen, S. C. Liew, Z. Shao, and C. Kai, " Markov approximation for combinatorial network optimization," *IEEE Trans. on Information Theory*, vol. 59, no. 10, pp. 6301–6327, June 2013.

[8] B. Alinia, M. H. Hajiesmaili, A. Khonsari, and N. Crespi, "Maximum-quality tree construction for deadline-constrained aggregation in WSNs, " *IEEE Sensors Journal*, vol. 17, no. 12, pp. 3930–3943, June 2017.

[9] T. Z. Oo et al., "Offloading in HetNet: A coordination of interference mitigation, user association and resource allocation," *IEEE Transactions on Mobile Computing*, vol. 16, no. 8 pp. 2276–2291, Sep. 2016.

[10] J. Jiang, T. Lan, S. Ha, M. Chen, and M. Chiang, "Joint VM placement and routing for data center traffic engineering, " *Proc. of IEEE INFOCOM ' 12*, pp. 2876–2880, Mar. 2012.

Spectral Handoff in Cooperative Cognitive Radio Networks

Cesar Hernandez, Diego Giral
Technological Faculty
Universidad Distrital Francisco José de Caldas
Bogotá, Colombia
email: cahernandezs@udistrital.edu.co, dagiralr@correo.udistrital.edu.co

Abstract - **Depending on the targeted wireless application, a collaborative spectrum allocation strategy may offer additional advantages over a non-collaborative strategy. The challenge lies in combining the information received from users organized in a collaborative manner. The purpose of the present article is to propose a collaborative spectrum allocation model for a decentralized cognitive radio network. In this sense, the cognitive radio user shares his information with other neighboring network users. The shared information is characterized through five levels of collaboration (10%, 20%, 50%, 80% and 100%) where each one represents the percentage of information that is to be shared for training and subsequent model validation. The comparative assessment is carried out with the decision-making multi-criteria algorithms SAW and TOPSIS. The results reveal that the SAW algorithm outperforms the alternatives under different scenarios and collaboration levels in terms of the handoff metric.**

Keywords - Cognitive Radio Networks; Cooperative; GSM; Handoff; SAW; TOPSIS.

I. INTRODUCTION

The increasing use of wireless applications poses new challenges in the future of communication systems. Cisco states that the traffic from mobile data has grown 18 times over the past 5 years and it is expected that the total traffic of mobile data reaches 49 exabytes per month in 2021 [1]–[6]. This particular scenario and given that current allocation policies are fixed and regulated by the state [7], have led to overall scarcity in the radio-electric spectrum. However, the results show that certain bands between 50 and 700 MHz, are being underused since their duty cycles are practically non-existent. In these bands, spectral usage times remain below 10% [8], in contrast with other bands which are normally saturated and allocated to cellphone networks.

Cognitive Radio (CR) is defined by the International Telecommunications Union (ITU) as "a radio or system that is aware and detects its surroundings and that can be adjusted dynamically and autonomously according to its radio operation parameters". Its solution consists on Dynamic Spectrum Access (DSA), achieving an opportunistic and intelligent use of the frequency spectrum. Hence, an unlicensed cognitive radio user (Secondary User – SU) can take over an available licensed band, yet he must release said channel and seek another one whenever: 1. a primary user (PU) needs to occupy the same channel, 2. when the quality of the channel is downgraded by the SU or 3. when the mobility of the SU leaves him outside of the coverage area. Seeking a new channel or spectral opportunity (often called white space or spectral hole) in order to proceed with transmission is known as spectral handoff (SH) [9]–[13]. This gives CR the capacity to provide large bandwidth (BW) share to the SU, through heterogeneous wireless architectures.

Centralized networks are architectures with an infrastructure controlled by a central coordinator. The information visualized by each SU feeds the central base, so it can make decisions to maximize communication parameters. However, this may not be the best option for large scale systems and public safety network applications. The increase in measuring costs, the complexity of the system, as well as the unbalance and potential chaos derived from possible failures (vulnerability) in the base station, turn this architecture into an unfeasible option for all CRN structures [14]. The problem can be solved by distributing the responsibility of the information among different control points, which are a crucial criterion in decentralized cognitive radio networks (DCRN).

The focus of this research consists on establishing the decision-making process for a DCRN, by giving the nodes the capacity to learn from the environment and propose new strategies that enable SU to exchange information in a collaborative manner. The above is achieved from the analysis of the history of the spectral occupation data and the behavior of decision criteria such as the probability of availability, the average time of availability, the signal to noise ratio and the bandwidth of each frequency channel.

Collaborative strategies have delivered new models to support the efficient use of radio resources and the decision-making process in CRN. In collaborative decision-making, users communicate between each other by exchanging availability and interference measurements, among other information retrieved locally. Seeking to harness spatial diversity, unlicensed users share their information with neighboring users [15]. The information shared is characterized with the definition of five collaboration levels (10%, 20%, 50%, 80% y 100%), where each one represents the percentage of information that is to be shared for training and subsequent model validation. The collaborative approach offers additional advantages over its non-collaborative counterpart. One of the challenges in spectrum allocation relates to how to combine the information from users organized in a collaborative manner while maintaining transmission [16].

This article presents a comparative assessment of Simple Additive Weighting (SAW) and Technique for Order of Preference by Similarity to Ideal Solution (TOPSIS) which are two multi-criteria decision-making algorithms most used in a Global System for Mobile communications (GSM) DCRN [17]–[22]. Both algorithms are assessed and compared in terms of the average number of handoffs generated during a 9-minute of data transmission using the same amount of data. The comparison is carried out in four different scenarios, depending on the type of service (real time and better effort) and the traffic level (low and high): real time (RT) with high traffic (HT), better effort (BE) with low traffic (LT), RT with LT and BE with HT. The main contribution of the present work is to include different collaboration levels (10%, 20%, 50%, 80% and 100%) between secondary users who share space-time data regarding the spectral occupation that ultimately feeds the database of the decision-making algorithms.

The rest of the document is structured as follows. Section II shows a description of the simulation environment.. Section III presents the results obtained in the comparative analysis of the performance evaluation for the proposed algorithms. Finally, conclusions are drawn in Section V.

II. METHODOLOGY

For the comparative assessment of multi-criteria decision-making strategies, a simulator was developed based on information retrieved from 551 channels. The test-validation technique is used for training and validation with an 83% - 17% proportion, which corresponds to 10800 training data and 1800 validation data, equivalent to 1 hour for training and 10 minutes for assessment. The information corresponds to real data captured in a metering campaign in the GSM frequency band.

The spectral occupancy data corresponds to a week of observation captured at Bogota City in Colombia. The energy detection technique was used to determine the occupation or availability of the analyzed GSM band, with a decision threshold for the power of 5 dBm above the noise power. To determine whether a frequency channel is busy or not, the proposed decision threshold is based on the average noise floor for the frequency band used. Thus, the average noise floor is -113 dBm and the decision threshold is set to -113 + 5 = -108 dBm.

Figure 1 presents the general structure of the implemented model. The simulator is comprised of four processing blocks. The first block is called the "collaborative block" which segments the power matrix into five collaboration levels and distributes it among SU. The second block known as "MCDM" includes all the mathematical models needed in the decision-making process for SAW and TOPSIS algorithms. The third block is the "Search Algorithm" which is a structure in charge of simulating and quantifying throughput characteristics. The block "Figure" builds the respective charts.

A. *Functions of the collaborative block*

For the specific description of the collaborative algorithm, the three functions must be analyzed that can segment the matrix. Figure 2 presents the specific block diagram of the collaborative model. The blocks where the input and output signals converge correspond to the functions of the algorithm. The first function is called "User Division" and is in charge of dividing the matrix according to the adjustments of the number of users (Number of user and User Full). The second block is comprised of two functions: User Zone Continuous and User Zone Random. These functions are in charge of selecting the block of users. The selection method is parameterized by the "Segmentation" variable. If the continuous selection method is chosen, the function "User Zone Continuous" will be in charge of the selection. If the random method is chosen, then the "User Zone Random" function performs the selection. The following sections describe the characteristics and adjustments of each input and output variable of the implemented collaborative model.

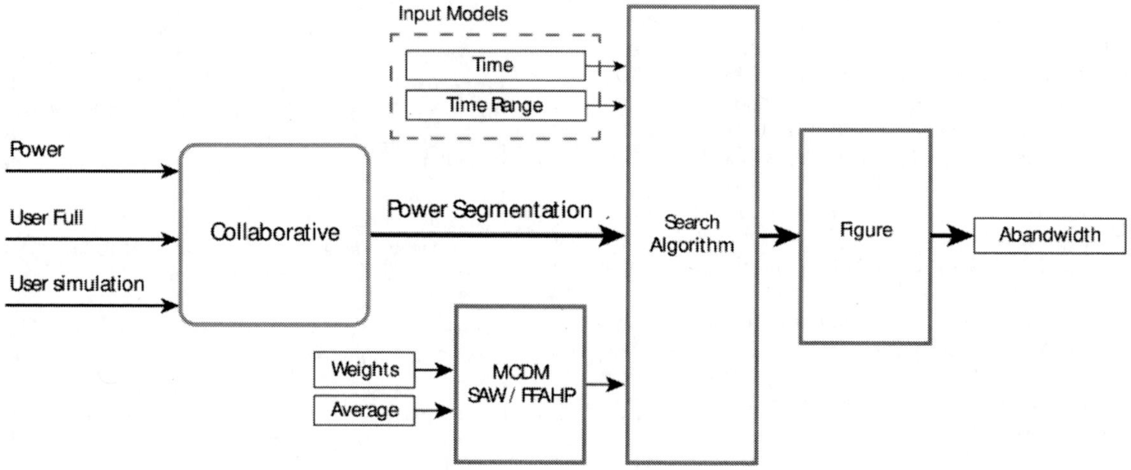

Figure 1. General structure of the model

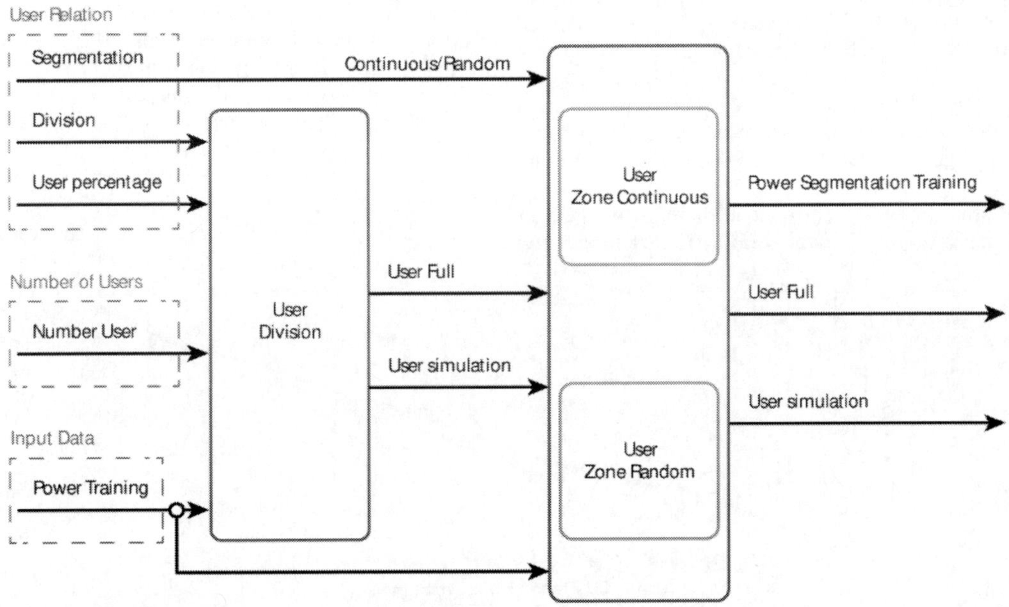

Figure 2. Functions of the collaborative block.

B. TOPSIS

This algorithm is based on two parts: the solution which cannot be accepted under any situation and the ideal solution of the system. The decision matrix X is initially built and normalized using the square root method discussed in (1) [17][23][24].

$$\tilde{X} = \begin{pmatrix} \tilde{\chi}_{11} & \cdots & \tilde{\chi}_{1M} \\ \vdots & \ddots & \vdots \\ \tilde{\chi}_{N1} & \cdots & \tilde{\chi}_{NM} \end{pmatrix} = \begin{pmatrix} \omega_1 \tilde{\chi}_{11} & \cdots & \omega_M \tilde{\chi}_{1M} \\ \vdots & \ddots & \vdots \\ \omega_1 \tilde{\chi}_{N1} & \cdots & \omega_M \tilde{\chi}_{NM} \end{pmatrix} \quad (1)$$

where ωi is the weight allocated to criterion i, and the sum of all weights must be equal to 1.

Afterwards, the ideal solution and the worst solution are defined as described in (2) and (3).

$$A^+ = \{(\max \tilde{\chi}_{ij} | j \in X^+), (\min \tilde{\chi}_{ij} | j \in X^-)\} = \{\tilde{\chi}_1^+, \ldots, \tilde{\chi}_M^+ \quad (2)$$

$$A^- = \{(\min \tilde{\chi}_{ij} | j \in X^+), (\max \tilde{\chi}_{ij} | j \in X^-)\} = \{\tilde{\chi}_1^-, \ldots, \tilde{\chi}_M^- \quad (3)$$

where i = 1…M, y X+ y X- are the set of benefits and costs, respectively.

Then, the Euclidian distance D is computed for each alternative as seen in (4) and (5).

$$D_i^+ = \sqrt{\sum_{j=1}^{M} \left(\tilde{\chi}_{ij} - \tilde{\chi}_j^+\right)^2} \qquad i = 1, \ldots, N \qquad (4)$$

$$D_i^- = \sqrt{\sum_{j=1}^{M} \left(\tilde{\chi}_{ij} - \tilde{\chi}_j^-\right)^2} \qquad i = 1, \ldots, N \qquad (5)$$

Finally, the alternatives are organized in descending order based on the preference index given by (6).

$$C_i^+ = \frac{D_i^-}{D_i^+ + D_i^-}, \quad i = 1, \ldots, N. \qquad (6)$$

C. SAW

This algorithm builds a decision matrix comprised of criteria and alternatives. The algorithm assigns a weight to each intersection of the matrix based on the criterion set by the designer. This establishes a score for each assessed spectral opportunity (SO) and determines a ranking that includes all alternatives. The SO with the highest score is ultimately chosen [17][23][24]. In (7), $r_{i,j}$ belongs to the matrix and the sum of weights is equal to 1.

$$u_i = \sum_{j=1}^{M} \omega_i r_{i,j} \quad \forall i \in 1, \ldots, N \qquad (7)$$

The steps used to develop this algorithm were: (1) identifying the objectives and alternatives; (2) assess the alternatives; (3) determine the weights of each combination; (4) add the aggregated values based on preferences; and (5) analyze sensitivity [17].

III. Results

Two applications were considered during performance assessment: Real Time (RT) and Better Effort (BE) as well as two traffic levels: High Traffic (HT) and Low Traffic (LT), to create four types of scenarios: GSM RT HT, GSM RT LT, GMS BE HT and GSM BE LT. They were analyzed in terms of the average accumulative handoff (AAH) both for the SAW (Figure 3) and the TOPSIS algorithms (Figure 4).

Figure 3 and Figure 4 show that there is a stronger variation of handoffs in LT than in HT. Another interesting finding is that the number of handoffs is fairly similar between BE and RT for the same traffic level, which undermines the importance of this variable within a spectral allocation model. It could also lead to redefining the operation of the chosen algorithm.

In the case of the SAW algorithm, the collaboration level of 100% reaches a reduction of 4.5% for RT-HT, 9.5% for RT-LT, 2.3% for BE-HT, and 16.3% for BE-LT.

In the case of the TOPSIS algorithm, the collaboration level of 100% reaches a reduction of 2.1% for RT-HT, 3.9% for RT-LT, 6.4% for BE-HT, and 15.4% for BE-LT.

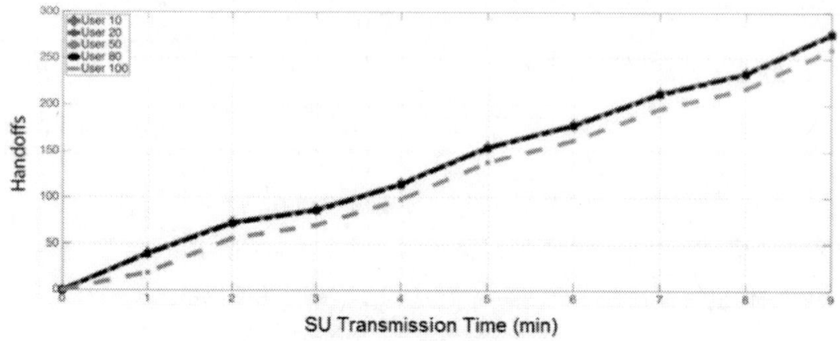

a. GSM RT HT

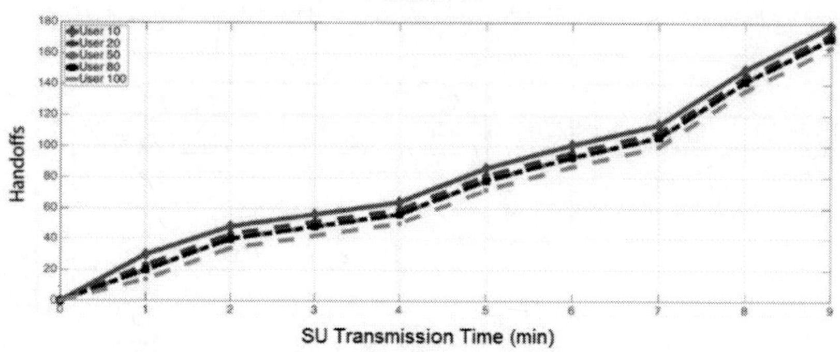

b. GSM RT LT

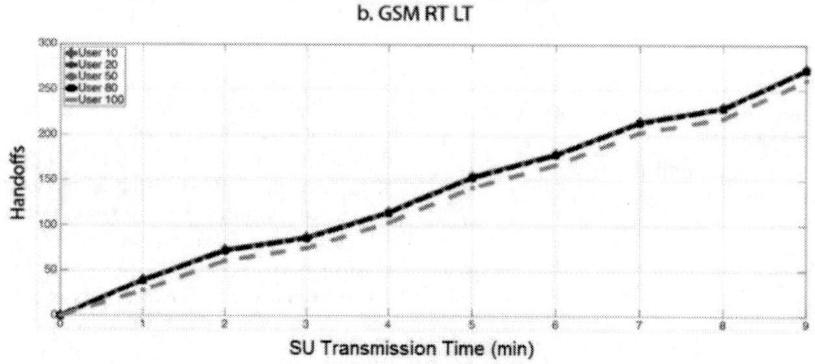

c. GSM BE HT

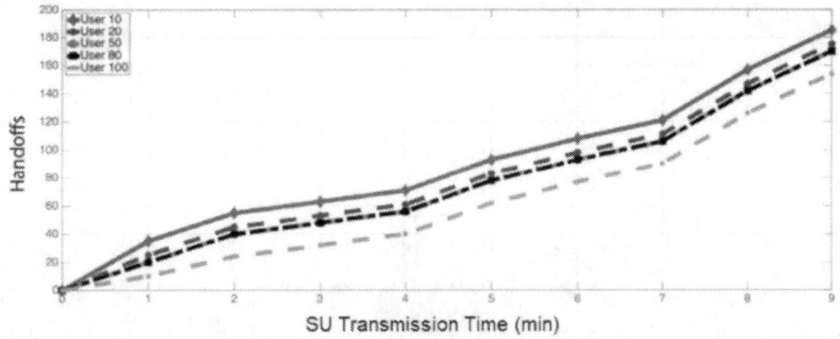

d. GSM BE LT

Figure 3. AAH in GSM for SAW algorithm

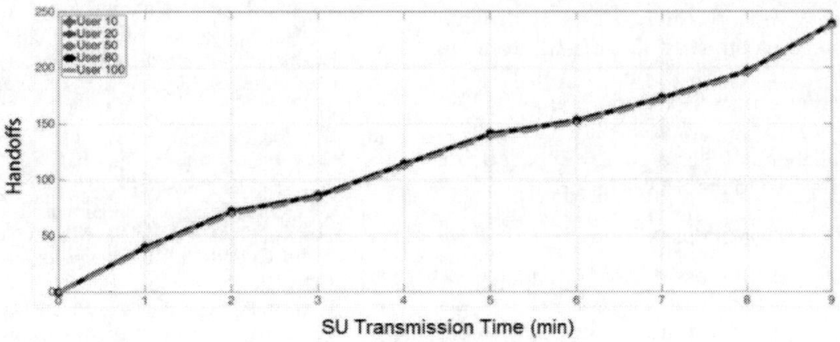

a. GSM RT HT

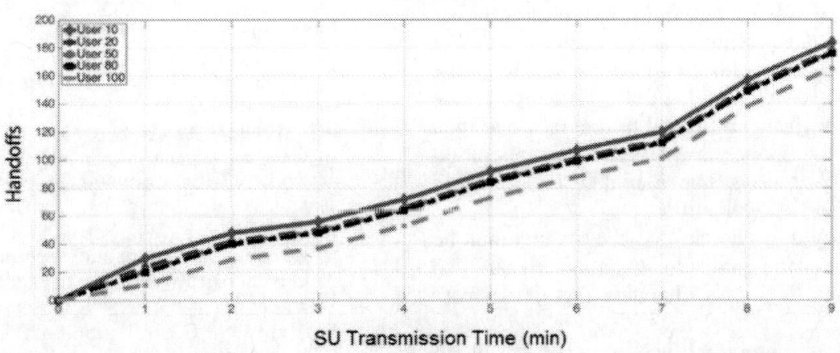

b. GSM RT LT

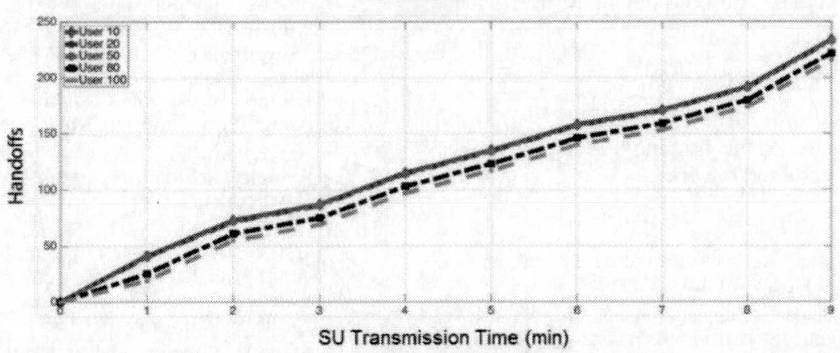

c. GSM BE HT

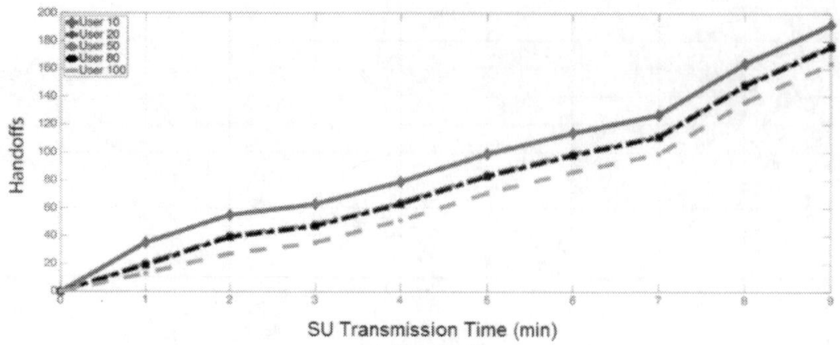

d. GSM BE LT

Figure 4. AAH in GSM for TOPSIS algorithm

The behavior of the handoffs and the failed handoffs are similar in the corresponding evaluation scenarios, with RT-HT presenting the least variation of handoffs at different levels of collaboration, in contrast to the BE-LT scenario, which experiences the greater variation. In general, low traffic scenarios experience a high variation, around 20%, compared to high traffic, whose variation is low, around 7%. It is also noted that collaboration has a greater impact on the TOPSIS algorithm compared to the SAW algorithm.

IV. Conclusions

A collaborative spectral assignment model was developed through the exchange of information between secondary users for two multi-criteria decision-making algorithms, SAW and TOPSIS. The comparative evaluation of these two techniques was carried out through the number of handoffs made during a 9-minute transmission.

The spectral decision-making algorithm affects the results obtained in terms of handoff. However, the differences are not significant compared to the ones obtained with the variation of the cooperation level. The cooperation level between secondary users has a higher incidence in better effort and low traffic applications.

When the secondary user chooses to access a channel, he should not only consider the quality of the channel, but also factor in the decisions to access channels incoming from other users.

As future work we propose the implementation of machine learning techniques and consider multi-user access to the spectrum.

Acknowledgment

The authors wish to thank Universidad Distrital Francisco José de Caldas for the funding and support given during the course of this research work.

References

[1] CISCO, "Cisco Visual Networking Index: Global Mobile Data Traffic Forecast Update," CISCO, 2017. .

[2] M. Tahir, M. Hadi Habaebi, and M. R. Islam, "Novel distributed algorithm for coalition formation for enhanced spectrum sensing in cognitive radio networks," AEU - Int. J. Electron. Commun., vol. 77, no. Supplement C, pp. 139–148, 2017.

[3] K. Kumar, A. Prakash, and R. Tripathi, "Spectrum handoff in cognitive radio networks: A classification and comprehensive survey," J. Netw. Comput. Appl., vol. 61, pp. 161–188, 2016.

[4] C. Hernandez, H. Marquez, and D. Giral, "Comparative Evaluation of Prediction Models for Forecasting Spectral Opportunities," Int. J. Eng. Technol., vol. 9, no. 5, pp. 3775–3782, 2017.

[5] B. Wang and K. J. R. Liu, "Advances in cognitive radio networks: A survey," IEEE J. Sel. Top. Signal Process., vol. 5, no. 1, pp. 5–23, 2011.

[6] C. Hernández, L. F. Pedraza, I. Páez, and E. Rodriguez-Colina, "Análisis de la Movilidad Espectral en Redes de Radio Cognitiva," Inf. tecnológica, vol. 26, no. 6, pp. 169–186, 2015.

[7] S. Cruz-Pol, L. Van Zee, N. Kassim, W. Blackwell, D. Le Vine, and A. Scott, "Spectrum Management and the Impact of RFI on Science Sensors," in Specialist Meeting on Microwave Radiometry and Remote Sensing of the Environment (MicroRad), 2018, pp. 1–5.

[8] F. Forero, "Detección de códigos de usuarios primarios para redes de radio cognitiva en un canal de acceso DCMA," Colombia, 2012.

[9] I. F. Akyildiz, W.-Y. Lee, M. C. Vuran, and S. Mohanty, "A survey on spectrum management in cognitive radio networks," IEEE Commun. Mag., vol. 46, no. 4, pp. 40–48, 2008.

[10] I. F. Akyildiz, L. Won-Yeol, M. C. Vuran, and S. Mohanty, "NeXt generation/dynamic spectrum access/cognitive radio wireless networks: A survey," Comput. Networks, vol. 50, no. 13, pp. 2127–2159, 2006.

[11] E. Ahmed, A. Gani, S. Abolfazli, L. J. Yao, and S. U. Khan, "Channel Assignment Algorithms in Cognitive Radio Networks: Taxonomy, Open Issues, and Challenges," IEEE Commun. Surv. Tutorials, vol. 18, no. 1, pp. 795–823, 2016.

[12] G. Tsiropoulos, O. Dobre, M. Ahmed, and K. Baddour, "Radio Resource Allocation Techniques for Efficient Spectrum Access in Cognitive Radio Networks," IEEE Commun. Surv. Tutorials, vol. 18, no. 1, pp. 824–847, 2016.

[13] M. Ozger and O. B. Akan, "On the utilization of spectrum opportunity in cognitive radio networks," IEEE Commun. Lett., vol. 20, no. 1, pp. 157–160, 2016.

[14] D. A. Pankratev, A. A. Samsonov, and A. D. Stotckaia, "Wireless Data Transfer Technologies in a Decentralized System," in 2019 IEEE Conference of Russian Young Researchers in Electrical and Electronic Engineering (EIConRus), 2019, pp. 620–623.

[15] C. Salgado, S. Mora, and D. Giral, "Collaborative algorithm for the spectrum allocation in distributed cognitive networks," Int. J. Eng. Technol., vol. 8, no. 5, pp. 2288–2299, 2016.

[16] P. Thakur, A. Kumar, S. Pandit, G. Singh, and S. N. Satashia, "Spectrum mobility in cognitive radio network using spectrum prediction and monitoring techniques," Phys. Commun., vol. 24, pp. 1–8, 2017.

[17] C. Hernández, D. Giral, and I. Páez, "Benchmarking of the Performance of Spectrum Mobility Models in Cognitive Radio Networks," Int. J. Appl. Eng. Res., vol. 10, no. 21, 2015.

[18] C. Hernández, L. F. Pedraza, and E. Rodriguez-Colina, "Fuzzy Feedback Algorithm for the Spectral Handoff in Cognitive Radio Networks," Rev. Fac. Ing. la Univ. Antioquia, 2016.

[19] C. Hernández, I. Páez, and D. Giral, Modelo adaptativo multivariable de handoff espectral para incrementar el desempeño en redes móviles de radio cognitiva, Primera Ed. Bogotá: Editorial UD, 2017.

[20] S. Tripathi, A. Upadhyay, S. Kotyan, and S. Yadav, "Analysis and Comparison of Different Fuzzy Inference Systems Used in Decision Making for Secondary Users in Cognitive Radio Network," Wirel. Pers. Commun., vol. 104, no. 3, pp. 1175–1208, 2019.

[21] Y. Rizk, M. Awad, and E. W. Tunstel, "Decision Making in Multiagent Systems: A Survey," IEEE Trans. Cogn. Dev. Syst., vol. 10, no. 3, pp. 514–529, 2018.

[22] L. R. M. Pinto and L. H. A. Correia, "Analysis of Machine Learning Algorithms for Spectrum Decision in Cognitive Radios," in 2018 15th International Symposium on Wireless Communication Systems (ISWCS), 2018, pp. 1–6.

[23] C. Ramírez Pérez and V. M. Ramos Ramos, "Handover vertical: un problema de toma de decisión múltiple," in Congreso Internacional sobre Innovación y Desarrollo Tecnológico, 2010.

[24] C. Ramirez-Perez and V. Ramos-R, "On the Effectiveness of Multi-criteria Decision Mechanisms for Vertical Handoff," in International Conference on Advanced Information Networking and Applications, 2013, pp. 1157–1164.

Development of Secure IoT System based on Secret Sharing

Hiroyuki Dekihara

The Faculty of Economic Sciences
Hiroshima Shudo University
Hiroshima, Japan 731–3195
Email: hdekihar@shudo-u.ac.jp

Abstract—**In Cyber Physical Systems based on sensor networks, one of the important requirements is that the data in the system are protected from a variety of incidents. In this study, a secure IoT system is proposed for Cyber Physical Systems using sensor networks, and a prototype was developed on the input side. The novel concept of the proposed method is to apply encryption at the physical layer into the IoT system from input processing to output processing. The system is based on Shamir Secret Sharing, which is a type of encryption using distributed processing. The encrypted data in the system would maintain confidentiality even when a part of the data is browsed by a third party by unauthorized access of a malicious third person or by human operator error. In addition, it is possible for a user to control accessibility by holding key information of the encryption. The prototype system on the input side was created by an Arduino, a Sakura LTE module, and the Sakura IoT Platform.**

Keywords–Internet of Things; Network security; Wireless sensor networks; Encryption; Shamir Secret Sharing.

I. Introduction

In the Fourth Industrial Revolution [1], it is expected that Cyber Physical Systems (CPSs) connecting the real world and virtual world will serve as one advanced system. Usually, the CPS gathers information from the real world using wireless sensor networks. Of course, the CPS must protect the gathered data from a variety of incidents, such as an attack by a malicious third person, a leak due to human error, etc [2], [3]. The objective of this research is to develop a new secure IoT system for the CPS, and the final goal is to proposal the encrypted processes from input to output in CPS, in other words from user side to operator side. The system is based on secret sharing [4], [5], which is a type of encryption using distributed processing. The encryption has been applied at the physical layer into the IoT system from input processing to output processing. The encrypted data by secret sharing can be decrypted when there are more data than the threshold number. Therefore, the encrypted data in the system would be kept confidential even when a part of the data smaller than the threshold number is browsed by a third party by unauthorized access of a malicious third person or by human operator error. In addition, it is possible for a user to control accessibility by holding key information of the encryption. In this paper, the prototype system on the input side was created using an Arduino [6], a Sakura LTE module, and the Sakura IoT Platform [7]. From the prototype, it was verified that the algorithm of Secret Sharing was performed on Arduino, the two paths were connected by Sakura LTE modules, and Sakura LTE modules and a SD card module were performed on a single Arduino together.

In Section 2, the schemes of the proposed system and the prototype system of the input side are explained. Finally, a brief conclusion is presented in Section 3.

II. Proposed System

In this study, a secure IoT system was developed and is proposed for CPSs using wireless sensor networks. In this section, the scheme and prototype of the proposed system are described.

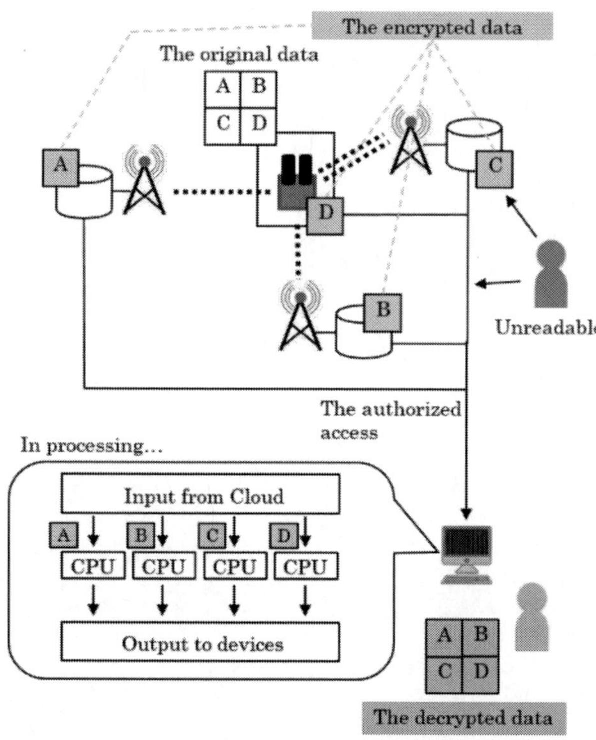

Figure 1. The scheme of the proposed system.

A. Scheme

The scheme of the proposed system is shown in Figure 1. The IoT devices in the CPS receive a signal or stimulus (i.e., heat, light, pressure, motion, etc.). The received data are encrypted and divided by the secret sharing algorithm. Figure 2 illustrates an example graph in Shamir (k, n) secret sharing. Let $k = 3$ and $n = 5$ in this case. The secret is the original data, and it is encrypted and divided into five shares. A share is a set of coordinates (x, y). The secret data can be decrypted from three shares out of five. The divided data are transmitted to cloud computing via multiple routes. The key data for the decryption may be held by the IoT device (or the user side). For example, the original data received by a sensor are divided into four data points (A, B, C, and D) in Figure 1. Then the four data points are sent to cloud computing devices and stored there. In authorized access, the original data are decrypted from the four data points on each cloud computing device. The proposed system would maintain data division, even in the computing and output components, by parallel processing using multiple processors and computer vision using mixed reality.

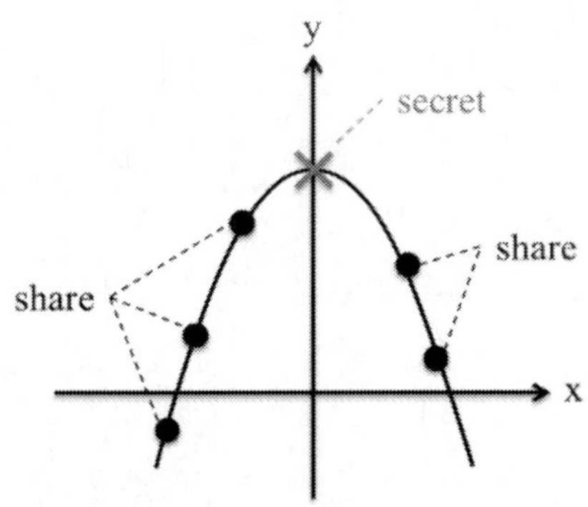

Figure 2. An example of (k, n) secret sharing.

B. Prototype System of the input side

The prototype system of the input side was created by an Arduino, a Sakura LTE module, and the Sakura IoT Platform. The Sakura IoT Platform which has been supplied by SAKURA internet Inc. is a service that has integrated the communications environment for IoT and data storage and processing systems. Figure 3 illustrates the prototype component corresponding to the dashed-line area of Figure 1. The Arduino was connected to a sensor on a breadboard by jumper wires, and had several shields mounted, such as the Sakura LTE modules and the SD card shield (shown in Figure 4). The Arduino communicated with the Sakura IoT Platform by LTE to upload data from connected sensors that were encrypted by secret sharing. The Sakura IoT Platform stored the uploaded data from the Arduino. In this step, it is possible for a user to hold key information about the encryption and to control accessibility. In the case of the prototype system, (3, 3) secret sharing was used for encryption, and the original data were divided into three shares. In other words, the original data were decryptable when all three shares were present. One share is stored on the IoT device on the user side. The Arduino connects to the Sakura IoT Platform on the Internet with a dual communication path using LTE and sends three other shares to the Sakura IoT Platform to store. The original data can be decrypted from one share on the user side and two shares on the Sakura IoT Platform. The user side was able to reject unauthorized accesses from a malicious third party. The numbers of data communication media from sensor to cloud are depend on hardware. In the case of the prototype system, it was depended on Sakura LTE modules (max 2). Moreover, SD card module could be added to the Arduino that had attached to the two Sakura LTE modules by solving duplication of used pin numbers among modules. Therefore, it is necessary to notice the duplication of Arduino's pins when the number of physical media storing or sending data of Secret Sharing will be increased.

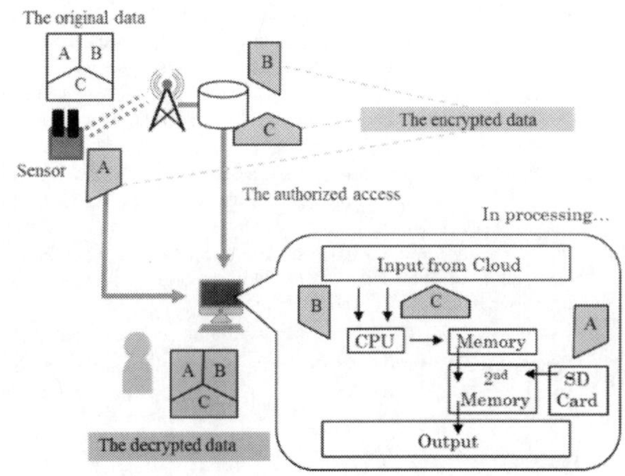

Figure 3. The prototype system of the input component.

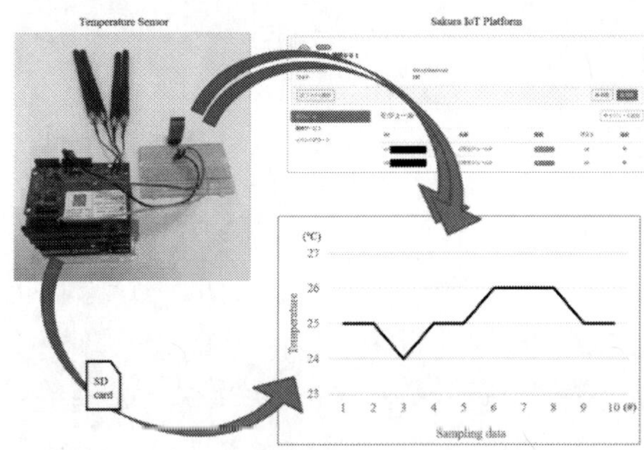

Figure 4. A result of storing data from sensor.

III. CONCLUSION

In this study, a secure IoT system was proposed for the CPS using wireless sensor networks, and the prototype system of the input component was created using an Arduino, a Sakura LTE module, and the Sakura IoT Platform. The system is based on secret sharing for encryption, and has been applied to encryption at the physical layer into the IoT system from input processing to output processing. It was confirmed that the original data could be decrypted from the divided shares on the IoT device and the Sakura IoT Platform. In addition, it was confirmed that the original data could not be decrypted in the case of a lacking, necessary share.

In the future, the data computing and output components will be developed. Moreover, the developed prototype system will be extended for multi-IoT platforms, adapting to the visualization and calculation of secret sharing, etc., and the data structure will be developed for the proposed system.

REFERENCES

[1] R. Kenett, R. Swarz, and A. Zonnenshain, Systems Engineering in the Fourth Industrial Revolution: Big Data, Novel Technologies, and Modern Systems Engineering. Wiley, 2019.

[2] R. Gurunath, M. Agarwal, A. Nandi, and D. Samanta, "An overview: Security issue in iot network," in 2018 2nd International Conference on I-SMAC (IoT in Social, Mobile, Analytics and Cloud) (I-SMAC)I-SMAC (IoT in Social, Mobile, Analytics and Cloud) (I-SMAC), 2018 2nd International Conference on, Aug 2018, pp. 104–107.

[3] A. Assiri and H. Almagwashi, "Iot security and privacy issues," in 2018 1st International Conference on Computer Applications Information Security (ICCAIS), April 2018, pp. 1–5.

[4] G. Blakley, "Safeguarding cryptographic keys," in Proceedings of the 1979 AFIPS National Computer Conference. Monval, NJ, USA: AFIPS Press, 1979, pp. 313–317.

[5] A. Shamir, "How to share a secret," Commun. ACM, vol. 22, no. 11, Nov. 1979, pp. 612–613. [Online]. Available: http://doi.acm.org/10.1145/359168.359176

[6] "Arduino", 2019, URL: https://www.arduino.cc/ [accessed: 2019-07-27].

[7] "Sakura IoT Platform", 2019, URL: https://sakura.io/ [accessed: 2019-07-27].

Design and Implementation of Passwordless Single Sign On Authentication Mechanism

Fatima Hussain*, Rasheed Hussain†, Damir Samatov†, Andrey Bogatyrev† and Salah Sharieh*,
†Innopolis University, Innopolis, Russia, Email: r.hussain@innopolis.ru
*Royal Bank of Canada, Toronto, Canada, Email: fatima.hussain@rbc.com

***Abstract*—Single Sign-On (SSO) is an access control mechanism that enables a user to get authenticated only once through an authenticated server, and get access to all other available services (related to authentication server) without providing credential again. Passwords are considered as the most popular method for user authentication. However, password selection and management is a challenging task. In this paper, we design and implement a *password less* authentication mechanism and also present the SSO implementation with magic-links technique. In essence, we design two password less SSO scenarios. In the first scenario of the proposed SSO technique, we create global and local sessions based on JSON Web Token (JWT) tokens and then grant access to services (based on JavaScript). In the second scenario, the open-source identity server framework is modified in a way to create a session key (token) distributed among the connected services and users can be authorized by using protocols, such as OAuth with OpenID Connect. The proposed mechanism addresses the problem of limitations with the passwords and further scales the SSO techniques across different services.**

Index Terms*—*SSO(Single Sign-On), Passwordless, Keycloack, OAuth, OpenID Connect, Identity Server, Magic-Link, Authentication, Authorization.

I. Introduction

In the wake of increased security risks and sophisticated cyber attacks, mutual authentication among clients, as well as servers, is of utmost importance for validating legitimate users and services. Modern authentication and authorization are usually based on a *username* and *password*. Since passwords are the easily manageable option for authentication, most of the users prefer using the same password for different Internet services. If a critical service requires the users to change their passwords frequently or has a restrictive password policy, users usually change the password(s) to obvious and guessable words and often repeat the same passwords. As a result, even if an unrelated application gets hacked or the application data is compromised, it puts users' account at risk because of the frequent use of same and related passwords. This way, the dictionary attacks on passwords are feasible and cheaper means of hacking passwords. In order to overcome these challenges, password less approaches are considered as revolutionary approaches to improve the existing username and password mechanisms. As an alternative, the users can just provide their usernames, and the system generates a one time code, and delivers it to the users via email, dedicated application or an SMS. Afterwards, users provide this code back to the system and the system verifies the credibility of the code (code is issued by the system). Benign users are authenticated if the verification process is successful.

Similarly, Single Sign-On (SSO) approach enables the consolidation of user identity and management. In our daily lives, we use plethora of different applications every day, such as email, issue tracker, file hosting, Customer Relationship Management (CRM) software, and so on. If unique set of credentials are required for each of these applications, it leads to a very fragmented identity system. To date, various software solutions are available for SSO integration [1]; however, the existing solutions are expensive and complex.

In this regard, it is important to decide whether a Software-as-a-Service (SaaS) subscription should be purchased that provides a ready-to-use SSO solutions that can be integrated into our products or is it better to build our own solutions. To answer these questions and put light on the existing SSO solutions, in this paper, we discuss different approaches of SSO implementation, and then design our own home-grown implementation of a password less SSO with a discussion on selecting the best of both approaches, i.e., SSO and passwordless authentication to one system. The rest of the paper is organized as follows. In Section II, we discuss the existing work on SSO and then outline our research goals and methodology in Section III. Passwordless SSO is discussed in Section IV and our proposed SSO model along with its implementation is discussed in Section V. In Section VI, we conclude the paper.

II. Related Work

SSO authentication allows users to get an access to different domains without the requirement to enter their credentials repeatedly. This allows users to maintain only one account instead of many. Some of the benefits of SSO include, but not limited to, boost to the user experience, improved security, and reduced cost in terms of creation and storage of passwords for different services. However, it also introduces various challenges to the authentication systems, such as difficult implementation, password security, dictionary attacks on the passwords, password management, and above all, the smooth integration into traditional password-based login systems. Furthermore, some of the most pressing issues are listed below:

- Reduced security as users create weak passwords and hackers usually use smart tools. Also, if access to the identity provider is compromised, all the connected services are also compromised.

- Degraded Quality of Service (QoS) experience for customers, employees, and users already forced to create and manage many passwords. According to the existing researches, the users do not like passwords and do not manage the passwords efficiently [2].

There are several password alternatives:

- Email-based authentication (also called *magic-link*). It is a unique link sent to the email with permission to authenticate only once. It becomes invalid automatically when the user is logged into account. It eliminates the password requirement entirely and makes use of the email address to validate an identity. It is worth mentioning that email is one way to send the magic-link. We could use another means such as messaging application and so on. Nevertheless, the security of the magic link is dependent on the secure use of the email. If the attackers can compromise the email service, then the authentication will be jeopardized as well.
- Social media sign-on or oAuth: A third-party application requests access to the identity provider (Google, Facebook, GitHub etc.) to gain information about the requested profile.
- Certificate-based: Users get a secure access to a server by exchanging a digital certificate. It is suitable in most cases and used only for the internal authentication in a company.
- Biometric technologies: The idea is "You are your key". This includes fingerprint, facial, eye, speech recognition and so on.

To date, there are commercially available solutions, frameworks, and protocols that allow us to provide SSO-based authentication as given below.

- OAuth 2.0 protocol is used for authorization and OpenID Connect on top of it, is used to verify the identity of the end-user.
- Keycloak is another open-source solution to allow SSO with identity and access management.
- IdentityServer4 framework is built on ASP.NET Core and it implements OAuth and OpenID protocols.

Furthermore, in [3], the authors proposed Loxin universal security framework for passwordless login. It supports two-factor and multifactor-authentication and consists of modular architecture. The architecture includes application, server, Certificate Authority and Push Message Service (PMS) that can resist the main security attacks, such as Man-In-The-Middle (MITM) and replay attacks. However, Loxin does not provide a wide list of authentication mechanisms and single sign-on abilities. Moreover, in [4], the authors describes a way of using CAPTCHA on the mobile phones when the server performs verification of the user's response according to the sender's IMEI code. In another work [5], the authors performed extensive experiments on FIDO-based passwordless authentication along with Shibboleth single sign-on technique.

Despite all afore-mentioned work, there is lack of research and implementations of combining benefits of password less approaches with SSO that will not only improve the efficiency, but also increase the security. This research intends to combine the SSO and passwordless techniques to improve security and user experience as well as increase efficiency and ease-of-use.

III. RESEARCH GOALS AND METHODOLOGY

In this section, we explain the goals of this research work. Furthermore, we also devise the methodology for our proposed SSO mechanisms. The research goals are summarized below.

A. *Goals*

- Build an authentication mechanism in which users are authenticated to multiple services without passwords. In other words, devise a passwordless SSO mechanism.
- Investigate the existing SSO techniques that (after necessary tweaking and modification) can be used for our proposed authentication system. Afterwards, we aim at implementing the SSO framework to provide access to various services through a single entry point.
- Combining SSO with the already developed or outsourced passwordless authentication is a daunting challenge since the existing SSO still needs password. Our goals is to integrate SSO with passwordless authentication.

B. *Methodology*

We divide the methodology into the following four stages.

- The first stage is mainly focused on preparation and field research. We thoroughly studied and analyzed the existing works related to SSO and authentication methods. Furthermore, we considered most popular methods for SSO implementation (and built from scratch, Keycloak, oAuth-based, OpenID Connect).
- In the second stage, the most suitable techniques for password less authentication are determined based on exploring the existing solutions.
- The third stage is focused on combining SSO and password less authentication approaches and develop the integrated system.
- In the fourth stage, we conduct the experiments to verify the proof-of-concept.

IV. PASSWORDLESS SSO

In this section, we discuss the passwordless SSO techniques.

A. *OAuth 2.0 and OpenID Connect*

OAuth 2.0 is a protocol that allows a user to provide limited access to their resources on one application, to another application without having to expose their credentials. The typical work-flow of the protocol is shown in Figure 1. To get access to the protected resources, OAuth 2.0 uses access tokens. An `access token` represents the granted permissions. Typically, access tokens are in JSON Web Token (JWT) format. JWTs contain three parts: a metadata about the type of token and the algorithms used to encrypt its contents, a set of statements about the permissions that should be allowed, and a signature to validate that the token can be trusted. The permissions represented by the access token are known as `scopes`. The application specifies the scopes it wants when authenticates. If scopes are authorized by the end-user, then the access token will involve these authorized scopes.

The following roles are allowed in OAuth:

- Client: it is the application that requests access to a protected resource on behalf of the Resource Owner.
- Resource Owner is the end-user who has the credentials.
- Resource Server is the resource or API server. The resource server handles authenticated requests after the application has obtained an access token.
- Authorization Server: the server that authenticates the resource owner, and generates access tokens after getting proper authorization.

The OAuth 2.0 protocol specification defines different flows in which access token can be accessed. These flows are called grant types. Grant types are decided on the basis of individual cases, i.e., type of the application. Following are the common grant types.

- Authorization Code: is used by web applications with back-end server. This also can be used by mobile apps, using the proof key for code exchange technique.
- Implicit: is used by Single Page Applications executing only in browser without any back-end. There is no extra step of exchanging authorization code to access token.
- Resource Owner Password Credentials: In this grant type, the username and password are exchanged directly for an access token.
- Client Credentials: is mostly used for machine to machine communication.

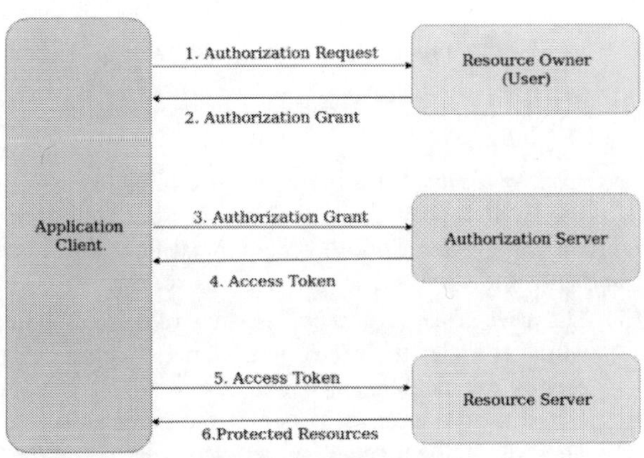

Figure 1: Protocol flow

OAuth and OpenID Connect are used together and compliment each other. OAuth 2.0 is used for resource access and sharing, while OpenID Connect is used for the user authentication. It is applied on top of OAuth protocol as an extra layer. It uses simple JSON Web Tokens (JWT), which are obtained using flows conforming to the OAuth 2.0 specifications. OpenID Connect provide one login for multiple sites, and whenever a user log into a website using OIDC, he is redirected to OpenID site for authentication and taken back to the original website.

OpenID Connect allows applications to verify the identity of the user based on the authentication performed by an authorization server, as well as to get basic profile information about the user by requesting an ID token. Various tokens and terminology used with OpenID Connect is explained as under.

- Access Tokens: are credentials used by an application to access any API. Access Tokens can be an opaque string, JWT, or non-JWT token. Access token informs the API that the owner of this token has been granted delegated access to the API and is in position to request specific actions.
- Identity Token: is a JSON Web Token (JWT) that contains identity data. Application use this to get user information such as , name, email etc. (typically used for UI display). ID Tokens contain three parts: a header, a body and a signature.
- Claims: JWT Tokens contain claims, which are statements (such as name or email address) about an entity or an user and some additional metadata. Set of standard claims are obtained through OpenID Connect specification, which include name, email, gender, birth date, etc. Custom claims can also be created and is added to token, if the information needed about a specific user isn't in a standard claim.

Now we explain basic functionality of OpenID Connect by using use case of, logging into using OAuth and OpenID Connect (by employing Google account.

1) When a client sign into OAuth using his Google account, OAuth sends an Authorization Request to Google.
2) Google authenticates client credentials and asks client to login if he is not already signed in. It also ask for authorization (lists all the permissions that OAuth wants, for example read permissions for email address, and asks client if he is ok with that).
3) Once client authenticate and authorize the sign in, Google sends an Access Token, and (if requested) an ID Token, back to OAuth.
4) OAuth0 can retrieve client information from the ID Token or use the Access Token to invoke a Google API.

V. Proposed SSO Model

We propose and develop SSO solution customized according to our specifications and requirements. This will not only reduce the cost and dependencies on the external vendors, but also give us a complete control over all of the data (storage, processing etc.). However, specific expertise and experience is required for developing solutions for identity management.

A. *Keycloak SSO*

Since Keycloak is the most popular Open Source Identity and Access Management application [6], we choose it as main tool for SSO implementation. To work with Keycloack, we performed following steps to enable SSO. We succinctly enumerate the steps that will enable the SSO feature of Keycloack.

1) Login to Keycloak on localhost:8080 with default credentials admin:admin.
2) Create new realm.
3) Create new client applications (as many as we want), in the menu Configure − > Clients. Choose `Client Protocol` as `openid-connect` and `Access Type` as `confidential`, also put `Implicit Flow Enabled` in `ON` position.
4) Create a new user, which will be our test client, in the menu Manage − > Users
5) Copy client application credentials. And then go through the following path: Configure − > Clients − > `Your app name` − > Installation. Choose `Format Option` as `Keycloak OIDC JSON` and copy all provided configurations.
6) Download and launch the test NodeJS app from repository [7], which will use authentication methods provided by the Keycloak.

After performing these steps, if we are able to login in first launch, we will automatically login to second as well.

B. Identity Server 4 Passwordless SSO

Identity Server4 is an OpenID Connect and OAuth 2.0 framework for ASP.NET Core platform [8]. It enables the feature of Single Sign-on and Sign-out for our applications.

Identity Server is used as an authorization service in our case. In order to configure it for our needs, we developed the architecture as shown in Figure 2.

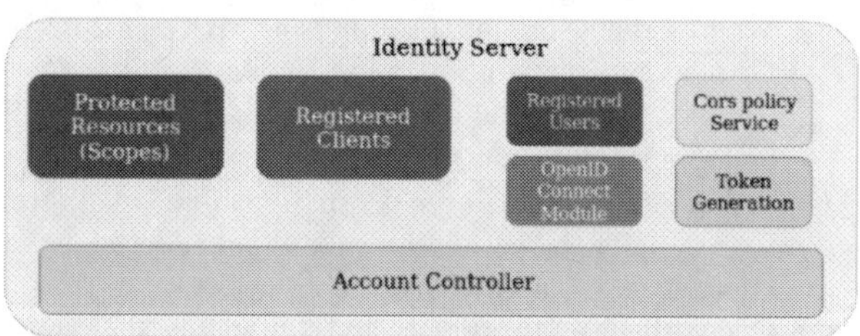

Figure 2: Identity Server Architecture

Client is an application or software that requests tokens from the Identity Server - either for authenticating a user or for accessing a resource. An application must be registered with Identity Server before it can request the tokens. We want to protect the resources, such as APIs, identity data for our users. Each resource has a distinctive name, and applications use these name to specify to which resources it need to induce access to. A user is a person that uses a registered client to access certain resources. We add CORS service to avoid problems with this policy. Moreover, we add support for OpenID Connect Identity Scopes. This is in contrast to OAuth, scopes in OpenID Connect do not represent resources, but represent identity data of user, such as ID, name or email address. At the end, we configure `AccountController`. We also created a method to check if the user's email exist or not, and if it does, we will generate a token for this user. Then we create a link which should be sent to the user's email with the generated token attached. By following this link, the user is then redirected back to the authorization server and it checks if the attached token is valid or not. If it successfully passes this checking the consent screen which requests the access to user's data for the application is generated. Users choose which kind of scopes they want to give to the application and then redirected back to the service itself. Developed solution can be found in the repository [9].

C. Magic link implementation

In traditional authentication scenario, a user is required to provide a username and password, while in passwordless authentication, users only provide their username. With this username, the system issues a one-time passcode and delivers it to the user via email. The user then provides this code back to the system and the system verifies that the provided code is legitimate (correct, not expired and never used). If the code is legitimate, the user is authenticated. Basic authentication flow of magic links implemented on NodeJS is described in Figure 3.

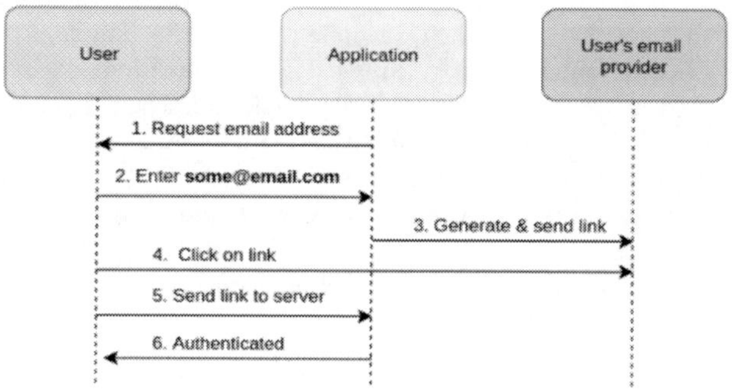

Figure 3: Magic link flow

D. SSO implementation

As proof of concept, we perform basic implementation and we create an SSO provider and clients on NodeJS as shown in Figure 4. Details description of the logical flow and sequence of authentication process is described as follows.

1) The user tries to access resource of system domain1 which is under the protection. domain1 detects that the user is not authenticated and jumps to the sso-server, using its own address as one of the parameters.
2) The SSO authentication server also detects that the user is not logged in and redirects the user to the generated login page.
3) User enters credentials and the SSO authentication server then verifies information that the user provided.
4) The session between the user and the SSO authentication server is established. This is called a global session. Then the server sends authentication token to "domain1". And the session cookies are stored in the browser cookie storage.

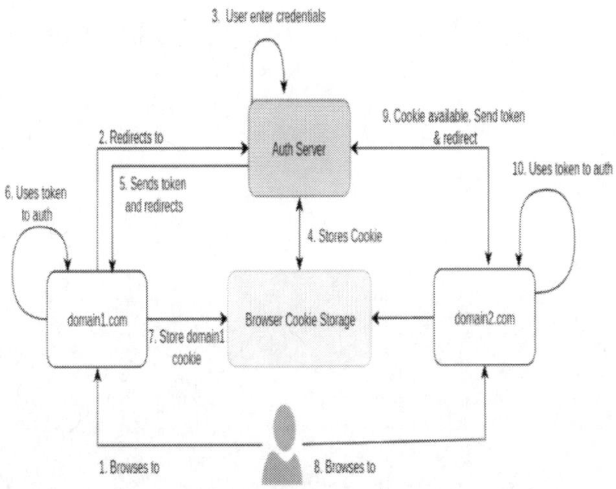

Figure 4: SSO workflow

5) The SSO authentication server takes the authorization token and jumps to the initial request address (system domain1).
6) The domain1 uses this token to create and establish a connection with the user. In our case we will return a signed JWT with user profile information if validation was successful.
7) Application under "domain1" then creates local session based on JSON Web Tokens payload. Furthermore, domain1 cookie is also stored in the browser.
8) Now the user can reach any other websites connected as consumers without entering any credential because there are the global session stored by the SSO authentication server that will redirect the user to "domain2" already with user profile info.

E. Testing environment

After implementation of our proposed SSO model, we tested it in practical environment. Therefore, after launching the server and clients, we use web-browser to validate the implementation of our SSO mechanism. When a client application is opened in the browser, it is automatically redirected to SSO server and it also provides a prompt for a valid email address. An authentication link is sent to the email provided and the user has to click on the link sent to the email. The link serves as an authentication token and after clicking the link, the user is authenticated with the SSO-provider. After authentication, the user can request any client sites and the access is granted without providing the user credentials again.

VI. Conclusion and Future Work

In this work, we provide some alternative password techniques for protecting user credentials and identity for improving user experience and security. We presented methods of creating SSO based open-source solutions followed by their successful implementation and testing. Also, we implemented authentication system by combining SSO and passwordless approaches.

For future work, we aim to design and implement new passwordless techniques. It will also enable flexible adjusting of the users authentication flow. The development of the mobile application related to the SSO authentication server can be one of the possible solutions to grant access to the resources by confirming the request for authentication. Moreover, the ways of communication between the browser and physical device, such as USB stick can be developed to get the stored keys or certificates which will authenticate the user without prompt to enter a password.

References

[1] N. Heijmink, "Secure single sign-on a comparison of protocols." 2015. [Online]. Available: https://www.coursehero.com/file/21561672/z-researchpaper-sso-final-nick-heijmink-s4250559/
[2] S. Wise, "Is memorizing passwords the easiest way to manage them?" 2015. [Online]. Available: https://www.passwordboss.com/password-habits-survey-part-1/
[3] B. Zhu, X. Fan, and G. Gong, "Loxin. a solution to password-less universal login," 2014. [Online]. Available: https://ieeexplore.ieee.org/abstract/document/6849280
[4] M. S. Shahreza and S. S. Shahreza, "Passwordless login system for mobile phones using captcha," 2007. [Online]. Available: https://ieeexplore.ieee.org/document/4418840
[5] M. Morii, H. Tanioka, and K. Ohira, "Research on integrated authentication using passwordless authentication method," 2017. [Online]. Available: https://ieeexplore.ieee.org/document/8029677
[6] T. Darimont, "Awesome keycloak." [Online]. Available: https://github.com/thomasdarimont/awesome-keycloak
[7] A. Bogatyrev and D. Samatov., "So-server & consumer implementation, keycloak test client." 2017. [Online]. Available: https://bitbucket.org/bogatyr285/sso/src
[8] S. Brady, "Getting started with identityserver 4," 2016. [Online]. Available: https://www.scottbrady91.com/Identity-Server/Getting-Started-with-IdentityServer-4
[9] A. Bogatyrev and D. Samatov., "Identity server with client and apis." 2019. [Online]. Available: https://bitbucket.org/demmy_art/passwordless-sso

International Academy, Research,
and Industry Association (IARIA)
412 Derby Way
Wilmington, DE 19810

ISBN 978-1-7138-1207-4

CURRAN ASSOCIATES INC.
proceedings.com

International Journal on Advances in Security

2016 Volume 9 Number 1&2

ISSN: 1942-2636

IARIA